Soldiers,
Scholars,
Scientists
& Citizens

by

James Wright

Proctor Publications, LLC • Ann Arbor • Michigan • USA

Copyright © 1997 by James Wright

Library of Congress Card Number: 97–67280

Publisher's Cataloging in Publication
(Prepared by Quality Books, Inc.)

Wright, James R.
    Soldiers, scholars, scientists & citizens / by James Wright. -- p.cm.
    ISBN: 1–882792–44–0

    1. Civilization, Western--History.   I. Title

    CB245.W75 1997   909'.09812
                               QBI97–40794

Second Edition, 1997, Proctor Publications, LLC
First Edition, 1992, Gregory Publishing Co.

Printed in the United States of America

Table of Contents

The Rebel

The Stuart Dynasty and English History

When Queen Elizabeth died without issue, the throne of England passed to the House of Stuart, the Kings of Scotland. King James VI of Scotland became King James I of England. It is fair to say, despite the contemporary doctrine of the divine right of kings, the match was not made in heaven. The Stuarts longed to rule in the manner of Louis XIV, but were checked by Parliament which demanded a say in how tax money was spent. Puritan zealots hoped the Presbyterian Stuarts would purify the Church of England, that is, purge it of any remaining elements of the Roman Church. They were disappointed. Conflict between King and Parliament culminated in the Civil War (1642-47), the beheading of King Charles I and the military dictatorship of Oliver Cromwell. Nobility and gentry feared the needy multitude which might be transformed into a senseless and furious beast with many heads, elements of which were present in Cromwell's New Model Army. Levellers among his regiments argued that only those with fixed estates had any rights in the kingdom and sought the destruction of established church and monarchy. Diggers opposed private property and sought to set the land free. Cromwell's England closed the churches on Christmas and kept the shops open, but suppressed extreme radicals as well. The Rule of the Saints closed alehouses and theaters, banned race-meetings, cockfights and duels, censored and punished severely those who took the Lord's name in vain. It made England a republic, finding monarchy unnecessary, burdensome and dangerous, and abolished both the episcopacy and the House of Lords.

At the death of Cromwell, the English, not finding sainthood to their taste, invited Charles II to return from exile in France (1660) and be king. Charles II, probably the most intelligent man ever to be

1

king of England, enjoyed the prerogatives of monarchy and avoided conflict with Parliament. Great political and social issues remained: what position would the established Church of England take toward the other religious denominations, and how would the king rule through parliament? Charles did exert himself to secure the throne for his brother James, Duke of York, an avowed Catholic, by dissolving the Commons after the House passed an exclusion bill which, consequently, never became law. King James II was as stupid (perhaps even more so) than his brother was intelligent. James appointed his co-religionists to positions in the army, the universities and local government. His declaration of indulgence, granting religious freedom to all, was opposed by the Church of England. Seven bishops were sent to the Tower. Meanwhile, the fifty-five year old James' marriage to the sixteen year old Mary of Moderna produced a male and catholic heir to the throne. This was the final straw, and the throne of England was offered, by the influential men of the Kingdom, to James' Protestant daughter Mary, and her husband Prince William of Orange. This bloodless coup d'etat is known as the Glorious Revolution.

In **The Rebel**, *we learn of Sir John Fisher who, like his father, has been in attendance at the Stuart Court, and regards himself as a King's man. "I have eaten the King's bread and served him and will not do so base a thing as to forsake him," stated another contemporary, Sir Edward Verney. Despite his Tory politics, however, Fisher is well aware of James' personal and political deficiencies, and disdainful of his Catholic religion. William and Mary were Protestant and invited to become King and Queen by Parliament. Who can be sure, however, that a revolution can be controlled and will not result in another Cromwell? Fisher contemplates these issues while he escorts Mary of Moderna, James' wife, to safety.*

"We make for Portsmouth; the coach will be unmarked. The Lady will travel with but one servant, and take little luggage, only what is needed for the babe, and trust the rest will be sent on. Bring pistols and your sword and as little else as you can. We must make haste."

"Portsmouth? I thought William's fleet was sighted moving toward the south coast. Harwich is the logical choice."

"The choice has been made my Lord Suffox. Either you ride with us or stay, as usual, on your useless arse." Lord Gunfleet sneered as he spoke the words.

Suffox grasped the handle of his rapier and drew the weapon from its sheath. The blade gleamed, razor sharp. His lordship stepped forward and announced to Gunfleet, "Even in this time of danger and haste there is yet opportunity for us to settle our differences."

"Willingly," Gunfleet retorted. "While these others make their preparations, let us find a place to transact our business."

"For the love of God, gentlemen, will you so foolishly squander your blood and time in the hour of their Majesties' peril? Go, go to your business. Make haste!" The spokesman wore the garb of a bishop of the Church.

Sir John Fisher watched, fascinated. He did not pay much attention to the apparent conflict between Gunfleet and Suffox, their sparring like the argument of Jesuits always led nowhere. They ceaselessly blustered and threatened but never actually crossed swords, though if their honor were violated, they would fight. There was no doubt about that. John underestimated neither man. Both led troops in the civil war and acquitted themselves well. Gunfleet wore signs of the experience about his face. The scars which crisscrossed in mounds over his eyes and on his cheeks from saber slashes were livid like raw liver. A saber cut to the corner of his mouth had never properly healed, and when he smiled, his lips opened as far back as his molars. "Keep yer mouth shut in battle is the best advice I can give," he would joke and smile his grim smile. Such a one was now turned on John. "Get yourself ready, Lad. Plain hat, cloak, warm clothes, you'll be a long time in the saddle in rain and fog." Gunfleet smacked him vigorously on the back, encouragingly.

"Is the King right to send the child to France? Does not the act play into the hands of his enemies?"

"Not my place to question the King, Lad, nor yours. The King is the King. He commands; we obey. Quick now. Meet me in the courtyard before the Watch changes."

Sir John had no difficulty reaching his inn. The cold had emptied the streets, sending the residents of London to fires and beds for warmth. As he did not wish to raise all in residence, he knocked with as much restraint as possible until the landlord appeared, candle in hand.

"I must away. Have my horse brought at once. Keep the room for me. I shall return at week's end. Here is sufficient coin." The perpetual shortage of rooms in the capital prompted some surliness and presumption in the tone of innkeepers, especially when disturbed in the middle of the night. John had no wish to quarrel and so turned his back and skipped up the stairs. His haste was further increased by a lust for action. There was no glory to be won for a generation on this island; sons, raised by widows and nourished by tales of the glorious deeds of their fathers, would at last be able to prove themselves men. He opened the door to his room and looked about. On the bed were his saddle bags which contained his six pistols. He retrieved them and selected an older, somewhat worn cloak. He glanced around the room, wondering whether he would see it again, and went down to the yard.

"Handsome animal, Squire, though he's not happy 'bout being out this night."

Fisher took the reins from the stable man, who smelled of horse dung, and mounted without replying.

"Night, Squire." He tipped his hat. Fisher nodded and flipped the man a coin and spurred his horse toward the palace. He was surprised to find he could ride through its gates unchallenged. There ought to have been troops about. He surveyed the grounds from the saddle while waiting for a footman to take charge of his horse. At the top of the stairs Lord Gunfleet, his great black cloak blowing about him like giant bat's wings, signaled that Fisher should enter the palace. The foyer, like the courtyard, was empty and in apparent disorder. Chairs and drapes were missing.

"Where are the guards?" he demanded.

"They've deserted, Lad, either gone over to the enemy or simply run off to care for themselves. The King has summoned troops from outside London. And, Lad, there's none but me and thee come to escort the carriage. I don't expect more." Gunfleet watched the blood drain from Fisher's face. He was convinced the boy was no coward, but Fisher was without experience and confronted now by the prospect of action. The report of the hooves of the carriage's horses on the cobblestones thundered like a gun discharged in a closed room. Gunfleet put a steadying hand on the shoulder of his young protege. "This is it, Lad. The Queen and the babe will come down, and we'll be off. Anything you want to say or ask?"

Fisher shrugged his shoulders.

"Have you been shot at or fought a duel, John? Have you seen a man killed in action?"

"I was with the troops who suppressed Monmouth's rebellion."

"Did you acquit yourself well?"

"I was sick – puked my guts before the battle." Fisher stared at nothing to avoid Gunfleet's watchful eye. "I did not run away. Though unlike yourself, I did not enjoy it."

"Are you acquainted with the history of Sir Thomas Wentworth?"

"The Earl of Stratford, you mean, main prop of the martyred King Charles."

"The same. He was as brave a man and soldier as Joshua or Samson. Like me, Fisher, he valued his life little. I can't explain it properly. It's not my religious conviction certainly." Gunfleet smiled his crooked smile. "When death takes me, I expect to be dead. I've seen a lot of men depart this world but none return. But Lad, life is dull for a soldier when he's not actively engaged in combat. The price you pay for the pleasure of battle is the risk of death. Ah, but the taste of battle is sweet. The blood courses through your veins, you move swift without effort, and see beyond the power of your eyes. You're alive, totally alive."

Gunfleet dropped to his knee. Fisher thought him physically struck down until he heard the footsteps.

"Your Majesty," Gunfleet said.

The King's appearance did not inspire confidence. He wore his sword but had forgotten his wig, and the bald spots and graying bristles on his chin were startling in a man overly concerned with his person. Disconcerted, without the pomp of kingship, James looked like the limited, even stupid man he was. Bishop Burner described him as having no true judgment, and Gunfleet realized long ago this was so. Nevertheless he was the King, and the King was God's anointed. Gunfleet was a Tory, and his party stridently proclaimed their support for throne and altar. The Church preached for a generation from every sanctuary in the land the doctrine of submission to authority, and the King was the supreme authority. His Lordship's presence at the palace and his determination to serve his master, whatever personal feelings about James Stuart, were completely consistent with his principles and his personality. As a consequence of his general contempt for humanity, Gunfleet did not contemplate the whereabouts of others who professed the same loyalties.

Sir John experienced confusion as his primary emotion. The ardor for action declined as the likelihood of it became more certain. Fisher's loyalties owing in part to his youth were not set, and his ability to determine where they ought to reside was confused by his nurture and education. His mother was an enthusiastic Puritan, his father a Cavalier. His beloved tutor, Anthony Tuft, was one of King Charles' famous wits. To counter the influence of "that evil man Tuft," his mother engaged a chaplain, Dean Stokes, a thorough going Puritan. Into young John's ears, for he was a diligent student, were vehemently poured contradictory lessons by educators convinced of the absolute rightness of their ideas.

The King reached out to both men and raised them to their feet. "I shall remember you, my Lords, when these difficult times are passed."

"Your Majesty," the two responded.

A woman dressed in black with a veil partially covering her face, carrying a heavily wrapped child, descended the steps. The King bowed but made no other gestures; the woman acknowledged the bow but continued down the steps. A second woman, heavily burdened, staggered down the steps. The King ascended and relieved her of some packages. Gunfleet was taken back by this humane gesture on the part of the King. The four descended to the carriage. The driver held the door until the nurse and her burden were settled, then climbed to his seat. The Queen's escorts mounted and received a salute from the King, who wheeled and strode back into the palace. Gunfleet signaled the driver, and the carriage surged forward. He slapped Fisher on the shoulder and said, "Just like the old days, me and your father. You should have seen us, Lad, worth a regiment the two of us. You look like 'im." Gunfleet shook his head as if to bring himself back to the present. "There'll be nothing for us to do until we pass deeply into the countryside. Highwaymen we need beware – not rebels. We shant see any of them. I'll ride on ahead to keep the clowns out of our way."

They clattered through the empty streets of the capital. There were few abroad, the Watch, drunks, and the various people who lived in the streets, sleeping where buildings had overhanging roofs, or under bridges, or in the vestibules of such churches as were left open. In another two hours, the streets would be filled with wagons bringing produce and goods. Fisher mused about what Gunfleet told him. Why should there not be rebels on the road to Portsmouth? The King was not popular in the provinces; Monmouth's rebellion had demonstrated that. Most Englishmen were fearful of James Stuart's Papism. The King foolishly appointed Papists, Hales and Stuckland, Governor of the Tower, and Lord High Admiral of the fleet. He permitted a Jesuit school to be founded and received a papal nuncio at Court. Jeffery's "Bloody Assizes" reminded Englishmen of "Bloody Mary Tudor," another Papist. King James filled his army with Catholics recruited in Ireland. Few Englishmen knew the extent of the slaughter of the Irish by Cromwell. Fisher did. His father took refuge there before he was able to flee and join Charles II on the continent. Even without such knowledge, the English feared sol-

6

diers from that hostile, barbarous land. Sir John himself did not like having such men as allies and feared the consequences of insufficiently disciplined Irish troops or worse yet, Irish troops to whom the King was beholden for the throne. It might truthfully be said of James II, "he never did a wise thing." Such thinking posed the obvious question, why did he ride with Gunfleet and the Queen? Ought he not to be among those on the road to welcome William of Orange? Fisher's presence was a tribute to his tutor, Anthony Tuft, who filled his brain with so many stories about the court of Charles II that it was difficult for Fisher to separate kingship and the Stuarts.

"Open the gates you turd!" Gunfleet roared with characteristic diplomacy. The guards, half awake, bored, might turn upon them, Fisher realized. Gunfleet was a foolish, reckless man. Perhaps only such men were left to serve the King. The officer on duty approached the carriage. "I must search within. Open the door and step out that I may know none but honest and loyal citizens are abroad."

"You shall know what it is to be ridden down and trampled by your betters." Gunfleet caused his mount to rear and brought him down close to the officer. Startled by this conduct, the young lieutenant retreated but signaled his men to level their weapons. Fisher hesitated no longer. He dismounted and ran to the lieutenant.

"Disregard the braying of this ass," he said, "who belongs to a time when manners were unknown and soldiers, ruffians, not to be trusted. Look inside with me and discover nothing but a lady whose reputation will be thrown in the dust should it become known she has given birth."

"Who is the woman?"

Fisher shook his head but winked conspiratorially, "That I may not say but she is well-known at court."

The lieutenant smiled. "I have heard King James acts as if his mistresses are given him by his priests for penance. Even his whores are stuffy."

Fisher winced hoping the Queen did not hear the remark, though he admitted its truth. He opened the door and permitted the lieutenant to see the occupants of the coach. John glanced at Gunfleet and saw the man was purple with rage. Fisher hoped he would do nothing stupid although he admitted it was possible. Luck was with him this time. The lieutenant withdrew his head, smiled at Fisher, and gestured for his men to open the gate. Gunfleet pounded through though not without making an obscene gesture. Fisher caught his bridle and swung into the saddle.

"I do not envy you traveling with that," the lieutenant pointed in Gunfleet's direction. "You best find some way to dismiss him. Cool heads are necessary in these times. Rumors fly about a landing on the coast, and the patrols are anxious."

"Thank you," said Fisher. "I intend to do something about him. You have just had the nonpareil honor of meeting Gunfleet."

"The old grand old soldier," responded the lieutenant, "and of course, the Queen. Do you think her flight to Portsmouth is a secret?"

"Are there any secrets that are secrets?"

"We are curious to know what action is planned by the King. Will he send Churchill to fight?"

"About that the King keeps his council."

"Or has not yet received instructions from his Papist advisers." The lieutenant spat in disgust. "How is it that you ride with them?"

Fisher shrugged his shoulders. "My father rode with his father. Fare you well."

The lieutenant responded, "And you." Sir John's crop came down upon the rump and he hurried to catch his companions. He thought about his father. Lord Willcox loved not Charles I, but he feared the Puritans and other radicals in Parliament and was convinced their intrusion into his country domain would be greater than the monarch's. The King was limited by law; Parliament would first unmake the law and then remake it to suit itself. Willcox applauded the executions of Wentworth and Laud for they antagonized the country but wished the assault upon the King would cease. He kept no house in London; he loved not the metropolis. He distrusted the merchants who dominated there, whose store of money grew grotesquely and whose manners declined as their quantity of coin increased. They no longer knew their place. Worse, they took their goods into the country altering with their fashion and their dirty money the manner in which life was lived. Parliament merely aroused his suspicion; the Puritans he passionately loathed. They put forward such nonsense as "the humblest thoughts which rise from a poor man's cottage are as sweet unto the Lord as the deep contemplations of the prince's palace." Such sentiments were enough to make a man puke. The rabble, the poor, had to be kept down lest they rise up and ruin their betters.

"Fisher! Fisher! Are you there man?"

John knew he must speak before Gunfleet made civility impossible. "I hope your Lordship will forgive my interference at the gate. I feared your Lordship was about to be ignobly attacked by a man-at-arms who would never dare risk honorable combat. A man with your Lordship's responsibilities, especially now," John gestured at the carriage, "ought not to take risks, even small ones. Their Majesties rely on you."

Gunfleet visibly relaxed. "Did you ever meet Royal Charles, Lad? What a man! What a King! An astrologer was brought to court – the most profound in the realm it was said. Charles, who believed the doctrine nonsense, took the man to the track and bade him pick winners. Ha!" And he added, as an afterthought, "Would that the present king were like him."

There was nothing Fisher dare say.

Gunfleet prattled on. "Have you ever seen the southeast coastal towns?"

Fisher indicated he had not.

"You will this night."

"But surely you mean southwest?"

"No, John. First, we go east, then south. We cannot risk a direct route to Portsmouth since we do not know where the Duke of Orange will land, or how much of the country will be in arms for him."

"But southeast? To, to?"

"Dover, then Romney, through Winchelsea and Chichester."

"That will take extra days."

"We shall drive the horses hard along the beaches. Ha! It will be fun!"

From London, they progressed to Greenwich and then to Charleton. The roads remained relatively empty as they distanced themselves from the metropolis. Few moved goods early in the countryside. They rolled through Woolwich where the Navy maintained great facilities for building and repair, and ordinance stores. They passed Gravesend with its marshes and unhealthy low grounds and Gad's Hill where seamen were robbed after receiving their pay at Chatham. Sir John's clothes became heavy and uncomfortable, though not yet soaked through. The driving wind and the speed of the horses magnified the cold and pushed the increasingly damp material closer to his flesh. High adventure in the warm Spanish Main, Fisher thought, would be more to his liking. He was surprised that the normally gregarious Gunfleet remained silent. This thought had the apparent effect of stimulating the latter who said, "Do you know about Charleton?"

Fisher shook his head; he knew nothing about the town other than it now lay behind them.

"Horn-Fair is held there. They collect mad people and loose women and put them on display. All manner of indecency and immodesty can be observed there without reproach, during Horn-Fair, that is. Ha!"

"You jest."

"You have much to learn of the world, Lad. There are people who cut hands off their babes, or poke out their eyes, or twist their legs so the newly made cripples can beg for a living to support their parents."

"I have heard so," Fisher nodded.

The coach slowed and turned hard right leaving the road for Cantebury and Dover. Gunfleet saw Fisher's look of surprise and told him, "We're for Maidstone, next."

"That's almost straight south of Rochester."

"Aye, and thence to Hastings; then we'll hug the coast."

Fisher felt a flood of warmth in his face as his anger grew. He had been deceived about the route. He was risking his life for the Queen and the Prince but was not thought sufficiently trustworthy to be properly informed. His secret mind observed that even now he was evaluating his loyalty to the King, but he silenced its reason with indignation. The temperature continued to drop. The horses' breaths and his own were visible. The rain changed to flakes and drifted rather than drizzled upon them. They passed mile upon mile of bare limbed trees in the mist and snow, looking like the agonized souls in hell, casting arms wildly about in the smoking pit. Fisher snorted to himself at the ironies. Their trip would be hellish because the roadway would freeze and become treacherous for the horses. Yet the coach did not slacken its pace. The driver was determined to get as far as he could before conditions worsened. John was not certain whether the accumulating snow or the first tentative rays of the dawn were responsible for the growing amount of light. Before he could consider the question, Gunfleet leaned close and shouted, "We'll be to Hastings soon where there will be fresh horses."

At no time during his life did Sir John remember being so miserable. His clothes were now soaked and his body numb with cold. This was a dimension of heroism the singers of old had neglected. It was impossible to imagine Odysseus hanging his clothes before the fire after a hard day's fight in a downpour. He regarded their destination as some colossal joke being played upon them by God. Hastings! The very place where a successful invasion force once landed was going to be their way station. And that conqueror was another William, worse and worse! Gunfleet signaled that he should draw close enough to receive instructions.

"We must get ahead of the coach and inspect the grounds. There may be spies or troops afoot. Come on." Gunfleet spurred his mount, and Fisher followed him around the vehicle. Sir John held his breath when his mount stumbled momentarily in the loose mud slowly being made rock hard by the cold and heaved a tremendous sigh in as his horse steadied and caught stride. Gunfleet drew even with the coach and half-shouted, half-signed his intention. The driver pulled on the reins, and the horsemen took the lead. Gunfleet whipped and spurred his mount as did Sir John, who hoped the animal could see better than himself. The thick waves of flakes melted against his eyes, obscuring his vision. They intersected another road where Gunfleet turned, west Fisher concluded, and closed upon a sprawling inn. They slowed to a walk. "Circle and reconnoiter, Lad. Look for enough horses for a troop, or evidence of a sentry. Sharp now! If soldiers are about, we should be able to spot them." Fisher did as he was bidden but saw nothing out of the ordinary. There were four horses in the yard awaiting their coach, he guessed. Sir John waved to Lord Gunfleet who rose in the saddle and waved both arms vigorously. The coach appeared and made for the inn.

Coach and riders clattered into the courtyard and Gunfleet bellowed over the din, "Horses!" His intention was to change the team and continue the journey. He was surprised when the carriage door opened and the occupants stepped down. The Queen, carrying the Prince, marched resolutely toward the inn while the nurse conversed with the driver. Then she turned to their escorts and said, "Go in by the fire and dry yourselves, rest and eat. The Queen is determined to stay until the babe has slept for several hours."

"There is no time for," Gunfleet sputtered and received a sympathetic look from the driver, who retorted, "You and I know what we know but have been overruled. I accept my defeat. Besides, warmth and food have their attractions."

Gunfleet shrugged and smiled. "Aye they do. Let's find a lackey to care for the horses and remove the carriage to the stable." He turned to Fisher and directed the youth to go inside where he was greeted by a vast mountain of fat, who turned out to be the proprietress.

"I have bread, cheese, tea, and cold bacon. Nothing special. Take it or no." Fisher marveled. Her cheeks were so distended he could not actually see her lips; the voice appeared to come from a circular opening under her nose, above her chins.

John cared little about food. He went to the fire and presented his hands to the blaze. "Have you a room with a fire burning now that was occupied last night?"

"Several rooms were taken last night, and the fire burned the whole or has already been lighted."

"And the beds still warm?"

She had but to sway a fraction and her body leaned heavily against his. "If it ain't warm now, it can be made so quickly." And she winked.

John had a sudden vision of sleeping with an elephant. "Just the room," he said. "I want to get these clothes hung out to dry."

11

Gunfleet who came through the door observed, "They'll only get wet again."

"Come with me, Dearie," the Leviathian told Fisher. "I'll get you undressed and to bed and see that food is sent up."

Gunfleet's face bisected in a smile as Fisher blushed and was led away, then he thrust other customers aside and demanded food and drink.

Gunfleet's knock, Fisher decided, was louder than the crack which would announce the last judgment. "Step lively, Fisher. We're off at last." A glance through the window did not reveal the hour. It was dark, but the darkness may have bespoken more inclement weather than the o'clock. Fisher dressed rapidly, delighting in the dry clothes and entered the hallway just as a heavily veiled woman emerged from the next room. Fisher thought he saw appreciation, perhaps even affection, in her eyes. He would like to see her mouth he thought as he descended the stairs. The coach stood before the door, and behind it Gunfleet waited holding the bridles of their horses.

"Another long night and day to Portsmouth and we may return to London and the King's favor at our leisure."

"Assuming we will find the King still in London when we return," Fisher said.

Gunfleet signaled his displeasure at such a flippant remark by putting an unusually large pinch of snuff in his nose and sneezing loudly. He mounted without effort then waited for Fisher. "Villages along this coast have smugglers and highwaymen, and the villains are often organized and led by the local squire. We must watch for them and for dragoons on regular patrols." The driver cracked his whip over the horses, and they were again on the open road. John watched Gunfleet. The older man did not seem frightened, but he was particularly wary. His head spun about owl-like, so far did it traverse in fits and starts. His body displayed no nervous energy at all, only his head and eyes, glancing, staring, penetrating, as if he were determined to miss nothing that could be seen. The miles passed, not so quickly as before given the precarious footing for the horses, without incident. Finally they entered the first town since Hastings with some streets and substantial structures. Fisher saw or imagined he saw the hairs at the back of Gunfleet's neck rise, though he saw nothing alarming. There were people at the side of or crossing the road, but the coach continued at a moderate pace. John turned again to Gunfleet who was clearly expecting trouble. He thumped about his body feeling the pistols and slid his sword a few inches from its sheath to make certain it did not bind. Fisher glanced about the road and was almost thrown from his horse when the beast stopped to avoid colliding with the coach. Gunfleet did not hesitate but hurried to investigate the matter and found the coach immobilized and surrounded. Fisher quickly joined him, and the two stared down the barrels of pistols and muskets. Gunfleet, to Fisher's relief, understood the gravity of the situation and did nothing. No one spoke. Sir John saw Gunfleet's head tick in calculating their firepower. "Move!" the old man ordered. "Make way! Make way I say or by the heavens . . ."

"'E'll move us hisself. He's a bleeding strong man he is." The mob roared its approval.

"He looks more like a clown with that red face and nose!"

The rabble drew more tightly about them. Fisher knew they would soon reach for his person and considered whether it would be better to submit to the abuse or arouse them further by fight. He had never actually seen the lower orders inflamed. He had witnessed riots in London, but this was different. He could smell their hatred as he could smell their unwashed bodies. The unwritten rules upon which his class depended for safety were shattered by revolution and invasion. The deadlock, almost a tableau, continued as neither side could steal itself to strike first. Fisher knew it would not last. A voice from outside the surrounding circle screamed, "The Spanish Slut! The Spanish Slut!" Hands were placed upon the coach and began to rock it with great violence.

Gunfleet growled, "They know we're from the court; draw Fisher," and produced his rapier, but they were dragged down by the mob and beaten. Fisher put his hands over his head and face to ward off the blows. He saw nothing and felt nothing for the beating and kicking stunned him. He heard Gunfleet's roar above it all. Then it stopped. The mob parted and a man wearing the cloth of an Anglican divine bent over them. "Rise quickly," he said, "You must away. My authority rests upon my being a local man, not a churchman. They shall begin again soon."

Fisher rose and went to Gunfleet who was unable to move. "My Lord?" Fisher knelt and looked into the old man's face. There was determination but agony as well. "I must help you to your feet, My Lord." Fisher put his arm around his compatriot and lifted, staggering with the load.

"Get him in the coach," advised the cleric.

"I cannot. The Queen and Prince are inside."

"This is not the time to be ceremonious."

"Sir John," said an imperious voice, "place my Lord Gunfleet here on the seat next to my nurse. And pray, make haste." Fisher and the clergyman struggled with Gunfleet's bulk but succeeded at last in depositing him on the seat. Meanwhile, the voices outside had grown loud and restive again.

"Chambers is the name, Archibald Chambers, vicar of Saint Norbert's." The vicar looked at neither Fisher nor the Queen; he examined Gunfleet's trunk and limbs. "Nothing broken but there is sufficient hurt to keep a man his age on his back for some time. You, Mr. Fisher, had best be on your horse, now, and lead the coach." Chambers stepped from the carriage and addressed the crowd. "Be on your way, all of you. You have done harm enough to these gentlemen and ladies." Fisher slipped to the rear and took the reins from unresisting hands. He secured Gunfleet's horse to the rear of the coach and mounted.

"Out of the way yourself, your worship," Chambers was ordered. "We have not done with the Papist bitch!" Many shouted their approval.

"There's a wounded man and a baby in that coach," the Vicar said, "do you make war upon them?"

"They may depart. But let the Spanish Slut walk to Portsmouth!" This well-spoken voice did not come from the rabble but from a nearby dwelling.

"The Spanish Slut must walk to Portsmouth!" thundered the mob. It was better than a cry for blood, though not far short of that in tone. Fisher prepared to ride into them, hoping the diversion might enable the coach to break free.

Before he could act, a command came from the coach. "Make way for your Queen." Mary stood on the step and glared at them without fear, without anger, defiantly. She had removed her hat and veil and looked magnificent, Fisher thought, standing at bay. She stepped forward and like the Red Sea before Moses, they parted. "I shall walk to Portsmouth as my good people desire. Release the coach and permit it to drive on."

Fisher dismounted and tied his horse to the coach. He ordered the driver, "Go as the Queen commands; I shall accompany her."

"No, my Lord."

"I must insist, your Majesty. You may not travel alone."

"Away and do not halt until you have delivered the Prince to the Lord High Admiral at Portmouth," she ordered firmly. The driver raised his whip, and the mob moved away from the horses. Mary watched the retreating vehicle until it was lost in the distance. "And now I must inform you, my people, that my lineage is even more illustrious than Spanish – I am Italian in a direct line of descent from Roman Emperors." The Queen bowed to the rabble and followed the coach; Fisher followed the Queen. He intended to remain between Her Majesty and the ruffians who had not determined what to do next.

"Let us hold her for ransom. The King will pay to have her back."

"Let us hold her for my Lord of Orange."

"Let us show her how we feel about Papists," said another picking up horse dung. Voices gave approval to one or all of the propositions. Fisher tensed, but, battered and without weapons, there was little he could do to prevent them working their will against the Queen. Just as all seemed lost, a fine figure of a man armed with pistol and sword aboard a sturdy mount appeared riding toward the Queen. He ignored her and halted when he confronted the crowd. "What is the meaning of this unseemly gathering? These are hours for supper and prayer! Get to your homes."

"The late Queen of this Kingdom has paid us a visit, your Honor, and we all came out to welcome her," explained one bolder than the rest. The others laughed.

"The Papist Queen is here?" They pointed to the solitary figure who had reached the outskirts of town. "She shan't get through our hands so easily. We have suffered under her damned husband!" He spurred his horse.

Fisher launched himself at the legs of the onrushing horse. As he hoped, though didn't expect, it lurched to a stop, throwing the rider over its head. John got to his feet as quickly as the pain permitted, caught the bridle and pulled the horse over to the prone body. He removed sword and pistol, and fired the weapon at the fast closing mob. Fisher put foot in the stirrup, mounted, and rode after the Queen. As he drew beside her, he leaned over the saddle and swept her into his arms. "Your pardon, Majesty," he said and dug his heels into his mount. The horse surged past the last buildings and down the road which was empty as far as one could see.

Fisher anticipated the crack of small arms and muskets but there was none; he knew there must be pursuit. The roads, first rutted by wheels pulled through the melting snow, were now frozen, and the weight of two riders made him loathe to whip his mount. Trying to outdistance pursuers would be futile; they must leave the road and seek shelter. "We have no hope, your Majesty, if we stay on this highway; they shall soon overtake us. We must go into the forest and make our way as best we can."

The Queen smiled, gestured at her position between Fisher's bulky arms and observed, "It would appear I am completely in your hands. I shall not," she continued, "distract you with speech, but do not mistake my silence for disapproval. You have acted as a true gentleman."

It would be difficult to track them in the accumulating snow, especially if he found a stream to follow north or south (or east or west for all he knew at

15

this moment) for some distance. Fisher needed inspiration; surely there was a Muse for heroes in flight? Luck was with him. He heard rather than saw a stream and, without much thought, plunged into its waters. Fortunately the water was not above the horse's belly. To protect her legs, the Queen moved backward tightly against Sir John. Their mount half walked, half swam, against the current. To Fisher's relief the stream became more shallow, and the horse easily walked.

Besides their immediate predicament, Fisher's mind grappled with two other related problems – what to do with the Queen should they escape capture and what position he should take toward the monarchy. Unfamiliar with this part of the country, he knew not in which direction to turn for an inn, village, or even isolated dwelling. He would simply have to ride and to trust his luck. His attitude toward the King and Queen was an even more difficult problem. He did not know their Majesties intimately, or even distantly for that matter. King James lacked the attributes which made Charles a successful king and lacked others which might compensate. Before this day, he had seen Mary Beatrice only from a distance. She was beautiful; there was no doubt of that. A good, solid Protestant, Lord Peterbrough described the Queen's eyes as possessing sovereign power to kill, or to save. The Queen was fluent in four languages, cultivated her natural musical ability, read prolifically, and was an excellent wife and mother. The only charge against her as woman or queen was her firm Papist belief. Mary was named for Saint Beatrice who came down from heaven and knocked on the door of the ducal palace to announce the death of members of her family. Forgetting himself, Fisher spat in disgust at such a story and felt the Queen's back stiffen against his chest. "Your Pardon for my oafish behavior, Majesty. I was lost in thought." The Queen slid backward against him again, jarring Fisher back to his immediate problem. It was becoming colder, and the snow persisted. It did not fall directly upon them, protected as they were by the trees, but it meant her Majesty would soon be wet through the cloak and might catch the fatal chill. Fisher recognized he must risk capture by forsaking the stream to search directly for a roof and walls. Sir John felt desperation close upon him, like the fatal water around a drowning man. He drew upon the reins to guide the horse to the bank and waited patiently for the animal to find solid footing. He permitted his mount to pick the way through the trees choosing to be safe albeit slow moving. Shelter and food were his greatest concerns, or so Fisher thought, until he heard the wolves close by. The horse reared. Almost unseated, Fisher grabbed for the mane and hung on even as the back of the Queen's head smashed against his nose. Blood ran over his lips into his mouth. Fisher shook his head to clear it and saw in the midst of the woods what appeared to be a hut! He turned away and looked again, and the building remained. John pulled with all his strength on the mane and dug into the horse's belly with his knees. The great animal turned, recognized a structure and trotted toward it.

Fisher dismounted and drew his rapier and pistol. "Hello! Hello in there!" He tried the door. The inside was dark. He entered and found nothing but a hearth, wood, and hay. He returned to the Queen who nodded her approval and placed his hands on her waist to help her dismount. He bowed and ushered her inside, then led their horse inside as well. Immediately he went to the hearth, found flint and tinder, and carefully nursed a spark into a small flame, and then a good fire. "Here, your Majesty, if you please." The Queen moved directly in front of the flame. Fisher took one of the small pieces of burning wood to use as a torch to examine the rest of their abode. Near the hearth there were bundles of hay which served, he guessed, as beds and would feed the horse as well. There was no ceiling between the room they occupied and the thatched roof. Warm they might be tonight, but the pangs of hunger would be sharp. At least I ought to check the corners thought Fisher, and as he stepped, his toe sunk into the ground, and he fell heavily, landing on his face. The familiar trickle of blood began anew. Luckily the torch landed on the bare earth and not in the dry hay.

"Sir John, are you all right?"

"Right enough, your Majesty," he replied, scrambling to his feet, "but dreadfully clumsy."

"I never heard of a cavalier dying as a consequence of nose bleed though you seem well-established in that direction." The Queen smiled at him, and Fisher felt a warmth surround him and smiled in return. He picked up his torch and searched for the object on which he stumbled. With his rapier, he prodded a depression in the earthen floor which did not seem as solidly packed as the rest. The blade penetrated some inches and stopped. He put more pressure upon the hilt but the point refused to go further. Fisher dropped to his knees and began to dig.

"My Lord?"

"There is something hidden here, your Majesty. Perhaps a strong box or some yokel's idea of treasure. Wait, there are bottles of," he drew one out to examine, wine! And, he thrust his arm deeper and withdrew a stained bag which contained slabs of some pliable material. Fisher pulled open the bag and another inside it and announced to the Queen, "Salted meat! We shall feast this night!"

The Queen clapped her hands. "So God does not permit the great to fall without some compensation after all. Give me a bottle, Sir John. We shall not wait upon ceremonies." Fisher brought the bag of meat and the bottles of wine to the fire. He handed a bottle, several pieces of the meat, and his dagger to her. She cut and delicately chewed while he pulled his meat apart with his teeth. She paused to glance at him and then took her kerchief, moistened the tip with wine, and wiped around his nose and lips.

"Your Majesty, please, you embarrass me."

"Who shall know but we? You have risked your life for me. Surely I may perform some small service in return."

"In the first place, Madame, I have already taken the liberty of sitting in your presence. In the second, it is both my duty and an honor to be of service to my Queen."

"I cannot remember the last time I sat upon the ground, certainly not since I came to England," Mary smiled. "Your attendance at Court is of recent origin, Sir John."

"Indeed, your Highness. My mother was loath to permit me to come at all; she disapproved of my father's behavior at Court."

"Your father?"

"Was dead before your Majesty came to England. It was at the court of Royal Charles that he won my mother's disapproval."

"He was unfaithful?"

John smiled. "He was faithful always to my mother after his fashion, but his behavior was hateful to her. She is a Puritan."

"And you, my Lord?"

"I, your Majesty, am," Fisher paused dramatically for some length, "not a Puritan and the servant of my Queen."

Mary blushed. "You may look forward to a career in the diplomatic service." The Queen resumed her supper. "Sir John," her tone changed completely and Fisher watched closely to see what this meant, "you will think me mad."

"Your Highness?"

"You will think me mad, Sir John, when I make a request."

"Your Highness?"

"I wish you to escort me outside."

"What? My apologies, Majesty, but you wish me to do what?"

"I want to go for a walk in the snow. I have never had the opportunity to walk in the forest at night in the snow."

"But your Majesty, there are wolves and other beasts, and we may be lost, and besides you will become cold again."

"I do not wish to command you, Sir John."

"Your Majesty, it is most ill-advised."

"Very well, I shall go by myself."

Fisher, exasperated, sighed with sufficient force to propel a ship across the Channel. Where does your Highness wish to go exactly?"

"Only for a walk, my Lord. It will be fun."

Only for a walk, Sir John, he mouthed to himself; it will be fun. The Queen rose and went to the door. Fisher followed, drew his great cloak from his shoulders and placed it around the Queen. "It will keep you dry and warm, Madame." Mary accepted the gesture as one appropriate between their ranks, as well as between a gentleman and a lady. "We must walk in a straight line so that we may come directly back. We cannot risk moving left or right lest we confuse the track and become lost. With shelter, fire, and the hay for a bed, the night will be cold but tolerable; without them, we might not see the morrow.

"How somber you are, Sir John, and yet I've heard your father was a great wit."

"My father never had the honor of being the lone guardian of his Queen in a nest of her enemies, almost without resources, in winter." The Queen without warning rushed into the night. Fisher caught off guard followed, his lips forming a command. As the order formed in his throat, her Majesty's snow ball caught him squarely in the mouth. He choked on snow and water. Fisher gasped and blushed in rage and surprise but could not move until he caught his breath. The Queen laughed and tossed another ball, then another. Sir John, his vision blurry from another hit and tears from his coughing, rushed his Queen and with a glancing blow knocked her into a drift. It was his turn to laugh as she struggled to regain her feet, looking as a turtle turned upon its shell waving its legs vigorously but futilely. She grasped his extended hand and was drawn to her feet.

"Shall you not beg my pardon?" she demanded imperiously.

"Your pardon for what, Madame?" Fisher asked.

The Queen laughed prettily, he thought.

"You are no gentleman; you are a brute."

"Let us walk now, your Highness; we dare not stay out too long." They walked about the forest, the Queen chattering happily while Fisher kept his hand on the butt of his pistol, watched, and listened. For the Queen, the landscape was magic, powdered sugar or cotton, or feather pillows. For Fisher, the prospect was sterile, the snow a shroud. With another woman, one for whom he was permitted to have feelings, this night would be high romance indeed. "Perhaps a moon," he said aloud.

"That would be perfection indeed," the Queen said. "Do you find me pretty, Sir John?"

"I beg your pardon, Majesty?"

"Again? You need beg my pardon only if your reply will displease me. I said, do you find me attractive?"

"Her Majesty's beauty is legendary. Helen the Trojan and Cleopatra would be jealous of my Queen."

"Yes, yes," she said, "but in truth."

Fisher took her hand and surveyed the Queen as thoroughly as a new monarch will scrutinize a kingdom and nodded vigorously.

"Then you will not find sleeping next to me repulsive?"

"To be in the same room with her Majesty is to experience the outer heavens; to be near Her Majesty is to taste the bliss of paradise."

"You are your father's son," she said, laughing and blushing. "Let us go back now." Mary of Moderna continued to discharge her mind while they walked. She told Fisher how unhappy she was, surrounded by those who hated her for the manner in which she worshiped God. She compared the damp, cold climate of her new home to the warm and sunny place of her birth. "I do love the snow!" She thought the imprisonment of royalty made her position in England seem worse than it was. "I knew the people of Moderna."

"Our English people love their rulers, Majesty. In more propitious times, you would be worshiped." She did not reflect upon that old, dull, limited man she was compelled to marry, though John fervently wished she would. He did not believe she could love him or be happy with him, though he did not doubt she would honor her vows. There were several inches of new snow before the door when they returned. The fire greeted them with warmth and light. Fisher arranged the hay and bid the Queen lie closest to the fire. He fed the horse and, while it ate, removed the saddle. He tied the reins to the saddle which he placed upon the floor. Fisher trusted that habit and the light weight would keep the animal still. Finally he dropped the heavy bar in place to secure the door and lay down next to the Queen. "Good night, John," she whispered, and he shivered with joy and pleasure, and wished he was her lord indeed. Perhaps he only dreamed having such a foolish wish.

Sir John was suddenly awake. It was not the sun which awakened him he realized, since the hovel had no windows. If it was a wolf, it had gone to hunt somewhere else, Fisher thought. He strained, but hearing nothing, permitted his other sense to command his attention. He watched his Queen sleep and felt her sleep as well; she was so close to him that with each breath her breasts touched him. How can appendages which perform so mundane a task be such an inspiration to literary men, Fisher mused, while framing his own verses to celebrate her bosom. Her breath, even as she slept, was sweet. Mary, he mused, such a dull name in English – two syllables of uninspired consonants. Maria, how much more beautiful her name was in her native language. Fisher twirled a long strand of her hair around and around in sensuous pleasure. Maria, Mary, mother of God for the Papists, he recalled, but like his father John thought like a pagan. This Mary of Moderna among the Greeks and Romans would be deemed a consort of, not a mother for, the gods.

"You in there! Come out!"

John started so vigorously it woke the Queen. "Sir John?"

"Hush, Majesty." Fisher rose to search the walls and door for any cracks he might use as a spy hole but found none. He must face their adversaries without knowledge of their number or weapons.

"Come forth quickly, or we shall be obliged to shoot."

Sir John opened the door enough to slip through, holding his rapier in his right hand, visible, the pistol in his left tight to his side. "What do you want?"

"First to know, my good fellow, what you are doing in my house?"

The mounted man who spoke was accompanied by three hulking ruffians. He had pleasant features, his person and his clothing were clean, and his voice bespoke education. A gentleman fallen upon hard times turned highwayman, thought Fisher. "I became lost in the storm and was in danger of death when I came upon this hut. It was not occupied and did not appear to have been occupied for some time."

"So you helped yourself to another man's roof and wood."

"I shall be happy to pay for what I have used."

"Are you alone?"

"Yes."

"Go and see," the mounted man ordered. Fisher took a step forward, hoping this might satisfy them and prevent a search. "I told you I am alone," he said.

"And I believe you are a liar. But we shall soon see." The mounted man waved and said, "Frazier," and the largest of the three advanced.

"I'm afraid I cannot permit him to enter."

"Permit him? No one is seeking your permission," and he signaled the remaining two to take Fisher. Sir John thrust his rapier into the ground close to his hand while raising the pistol. He fired at Frazier who screamed, clutched at his chest, and fell backward. Fisher produced a derringer which was concealed up his right sleeve and dispatched a second attacker. He dropped that weapon as it discharged and grabbed the handle of the rapier as his third assailant made a brutish charge. The man rushed at Fisher holding the sword over his head like a woodsman raising his ax to chop. John braced himself and thrust under the upraised arm. His blade caught between the ribs and the weapon was pulled from his hand as the man fell dying.

"That will be all," said the mounted man, his pistol leveled at Fisher. "You cannot be a revenue agent, otherwise there would be more of you within."

"Custom agent?" Fisher laughed. "You're smugglers, then?" The horseman nodded. Fisher abruptly sat down and could not control his laughter. "I risked my life and took theirs over mistaken identity?"

"Do not unnecessarily distress yourself, Sir. Though they were my tools, I cannot say their loss represents a blow even to myself. There are neither wives nor children to mourn."

"I thank you, Sir," retorted Fisher, "though I fear my conscience is not quite so forgiving as you."

The horseman smiled and lowered his pistol but raised it again as the door behind Fisher opened. Catching sight of Mary, he saluted her and put the weapon away. "My most profound apologies, Sir and Madame. If I can be of some service for having inconvenienced you, you have but to name it."

"It is good of you, Sir, to offer, and we do require direction. If you might lead or direct us back to the main road to Portsmouth, though beyond the closest town to the east where I was obligated to steal a horse."

"Ah, a man after my own heart, I recognized it at once. A man of spirit there, I said to myself. Come home with me. You shall eat, rest, and at your leisure, depart."

Fisher retrieved their horse and helped the Queen into the saddle. "Permit me to introduce my wife, Mary."

"Charmed," said the still mounted stranger who did not volunteer his own name. "I can guess your story. Her parents objected to your love and tried to place barriers between you. So you've run off, stealing a horse to thicken the pudding. Criminals and fugitives and all for love."

Fisher's head bobbed in emphatic agreement. "They left us no choice," he confirmed.

"Let me see about my fellows, and then we shall away." The stranger dismounted and bent over the victim of Fisher's derringer, a notoriously inaccurate weapon. There was considerable blood on his hair, face, and even neck. "Flesh wound – the ball cut a path though the scalp but no real damage. I'm afraid these other two are finished."

Fisher felt sick again. He had seen action and acquitted himself well, but two men were unnecessarily dead.

"John?"

"I'll be all right, Mary." They watched the stranger wash his man's face with snow, lift him, apparently without effort, and carry him to the horse. "We shall go to Hell's Fire," he told her.

The Queen's eyes fired with anger. "Do you suggest we have acted as Paolo and Francesca, that most unfortunate couple of Dante?"

Fisher smiled. "I have nothing so Papist in mind, Majesty. Hell's Fire is the name of our host's estate. He is a coreligionist of yours, Thomas Howard, and belongs to one of the most powerful families of the south."

"Do you know the man?"

"I know of him and have seen him in London, though we were never introduced. He does not go frequently to the capital. The family is believed to be involved in smuggling, though nothing can be proved. The Howards live wild, debauched and ungodly lives, and so flirt with hell fire. The name is something of boast."

Howard mounted behind his man and said, "Let us away."

Fisher wondered whether to show Howard he was recognized and decided it was ill-advised. Then he thought, smugglers have boats. Here was a perfect opportunity for the Queen to escape to France and join her son who must by now have departed Portsmouth. He would propose the plan to her Majesty at the first opportunity. Further thought on the matter was suspended as a fine pile of buildings came into sight. The house was magnificent, noble, as exceedingly well-contrived as any in England or abroad. Roads were cut through the forest, radiating out from the house like the spokes of a wheel. Trees were likewise placed to give the house shade, and protection from the wind. Stable hands exploded upon them as they clattered into the courtyard and halted before the main staircase. Footmen poured from the house to help them dismount.

"Welcome back, Squire!"

"Useful trip, Squire?"

"Trouble, Squire?"

"Take this man to his bed and see he's tended," Howard ordered, "and retrieve the bodies before the dwelling beyond the east pasture." He turned to the indoor servants and commanded, "Draw baths and prepare rooms for my guests." As the servants moved to follow his orders, Howard turned to his guests and said, "If you will excuse me, I must attend to business. I shall join you for a meal," he said, and was gone.

"This way please, Sir and Madame." The Queen was taken by a chambermaid up one side of the staircase while John was conducted up the other. Fisher wondered whether the separation was accidental or contrived. "We shall endeavor to thoroughly clean and iron your clothing while you bathe," Fisher was told. "Here is a dressing gown. Books are here. The lady is in the adjoining room, and while there is a connecting door, the key is misplaced. It shall be found and opened directly." The pace of speech did not permit John more than a thank you. Fisher inspected his room. It was richly furnished. He pushed on the thick mattress and imagined how he would enjoy this night in a warm, soft bed. He peeled off his clothing and felt the bath water. A gentle knock came from the communicating door.

"John?"

"Mary?"

"I'm afraid I shall not see you alone again."

Fisher spoke with a confidence he did not feel, "We shall be able to walk about the grounds together soon."

"I want to be with you," said the Queen.

"And I with you," he responded. There was silence then, and Fisher entered his bath. He had much to contemplate.

Bathed, groomed, and dressed in his freshly cleaned clothes, John felt presentable when he knocked at his "wife's door." She opened the door and smiled at him and then stepped into the hall to reveal a new gown.

"Madame, you are my sun; I look to you for warmth and light, for very life." Mary smiled. Fisher was about to continue when a footman arrived and suggested they dine. "We are being watched."

"Closely," she observed.

At breakfast they were informed their host would not be available until supper. He invited them to explore the house and grounds and to ask for what they desired. Their unwanted guide took them to the formal rooms – the hall, the library, the chapel, through bedrooms of various colors and names, and to the stables. They obtained horses and rode to the village. The church and various ruins suggested at sometime in the past the village had been a market place of some importance. The church was a small masterpiece of medieval construction, Mary insisted, while John argued it was an architectural deformity, like hunchback. Fisher suggested the church was Papist, but was corrected. The living belonged to the Church of England. He was further informed when the holder of the living was about to die, a heron came and sat upon the pinnacle of the spire.

"What, the Church of England professes such an absurd notion?" he demanded, recalling his dismissal of Saint Beatrice.

Mary smiled sweetly and said, "As you have often heard, John, heron today, gone tomorrow."

Fisher rocked with laughter, almost tumbling from his horse.

"May we walk through the village?" she inquired.

"The mud will soil our clothes and require we bathe again before sup," Fisher said.

"Are you most adverse to the mud, the bath, or walking with me?"

Fisher did not have a ready reply. "I am supposed to be something of a wit, Madame, and yet I find your mind races ahead of mine."

"Does the light of the sun not eclipse that of the moon?"

"Aye, Madame, so that the moon never dares to be in the sky with the sun lest he be shamed."

"Then I have no desire to be the sun but the earth, and you my moon."

"That I may have you as my center?"

Mary blushed and turned away. John turned to their ever present companion and inquired about the inn which was far too large for the village. "It serves those who find no lodgings at Tunbridge – fops, fools, rakes and the like who go there for the gaming, racing, and wenching."

"I thought its attraction was the medicinal wells."

"And so it is, Madame, though it is also known as a place where a lady may shipwreck her character more thoroughly than any other in England."

"Have you ever spent time in Tunbridge, John?"

"Oh yes," he said, "though not I trust as fop, fool or rake."

"I should like you to narrate your adventures there; my education is neglected in these matters."

"Someday perhaps I shall take you there, bold wench that you are."

"Am I?"

"I meant courageous and determined, Mary, and you are courageous and determined." Mary blushed and smiled. John was surprised when Howard's footman, their companion, announced he would meet them at the horses when their walk was completed.

"He must not enjoy walking in muddy snow."

"He has not the sun to warm him," John said.

"No conceits, John, let us have plain speech between us. Do you like the country?"

"Very much your, ah . . . Mary." The Queen smiled, and Fisher felt himself blush. "My education and the influence of my father taught me to flee the city for the tranquility and comfort of soul one finds here."

Again the Queen smiled, "And yet you describe the country as a gibbet, a sort of dying, a place to hear no discourse but of dogs and hawks."

"Such is the description, Madame, gentlemen of fashion employ to describe the country."

"Like your father?"

"Yes."

"My husband told me about the Merry Gang."

"Ministers of pleasure, they styled themselves. My father ought to have been a minister of state. He had natural abilities to render the crown great service. He died drunk and penniless in personal property and yet managed my mother's estate with great success and skill to the end. Her wealth increased under his direction even as he fell to temptation."

"I have it on good authority that you honor your father by emulating his career as a drunk."

Fisher displayed neither surprise nor anger. "I do not think your humble servant a fit subject for their Majesties' conversation."

"And what, my Lord, do you wish from this life? Pleasure? The opportunity to serve your king?" Mary's voice was forceful and direct and caught John by surprise.

"To serve my Queen and my country," he responded. The answer was ambiguous; she was disappointed and he knew it.

"Do you remember seeing anything of the village?"

"I could not describe a thing, save the church."

"We saw that before our walk began." She halted and faced him and took his hands. "Will you follow me to France, John?"

"For what purpose, Majesty?"

The Queen was silent. Horses approached. It was Howard's man, their guide, come to return them to Hell's Fire. "I am fatigued and ready to rest," said Mary. Sir John helped her mount and did so himself.

There was nothing further Fisher wished to see on the estate and so he wandered about the house until he found the library. In it was a massive oak device. What was one to call it? It was part ladder, part lectern, and part stool. One could select a book from a high shelf, read at leisure, even take notes without moving from the stacks. Without thinking, Fisher climbed up and scanned the titles. The books were in no particular order and did not seem well-thumbed. The bulk of them were theology, Papist theology. A Papist smuggler, John noted with satisfaction. The lot of them are criminals and fanatics. He placed the volume back on the shelf and took another, lost his balance and almost fell. In his hands, he held a beautifully bound work entitled, *Les Heures Malheureusementes de the Dirty Duke,* attributed to his father. It was copiously illustrated with magnificently executed, filthy miniatures. He had no time to react to his discovery. The door was thrust open and a voice demanded, "Have you had her yet?"

Fisher flushed and slammed the book to demonstrate his anger, but said quietly, "A gentleman would not ask such a question to one whom he has given hospitality, nor can a gentleman who has accepted hospitality answer such a question as it demands to be answered."

"What has that to do with you? Your family contains no gentlemen!" Howard strode across the room and picked up the volume Fisher had discarded. "Oh, found your sire's book have you? Filth drawn to filth like metal to magnet."

Fisher climbed slowly from the lectern and confronted Howard. "My father and yours fought side by side for King Charles."

Howard, red-faced, stated calmly, "That is so. Your father was a brave and loyal soldier however grave and odious his faults."

"Why do you seek to provoke me? Send us on our way if you wish to be rid of us."

"I wish only the Queen were back in the arms of her husband."

"Then send her there with an escort; the country is in arms against their Majesties."

"The King would have her back after she eloped with you?"

"You are a fool," Fisher told Howard, "who knows nothing about her misadventures." He then narrated the events that brought them to the smugglers' lair. "She has done nothing dishonorable; she is incapable of such deeds."

"I beg your pardon," said Howard, "with all my heart. Princess Anne, James' daughter, has gone over to William, as has Churchill, James' best general. Queen Mary was only fifteen when she married the King who is thrice her age. Running off with a young suitor did not seem out of the question for his wife."

"The Queen is devoted to her husband."

27

"It is well someone is devoted to the King," Howard mused and told John, "be seated and tell me what you require."

"It's quite simple. The Queen and I must return to the main road and either go on to Portsmouth or return to London as she desires. We must travel as we began, incognito. What happens after that I cannot say. In either case, she will depart for France."

"You do not believe the King can hold the throne?"

"Do you seriously believe King James can rely upon his loyal subjects, his loyal army or his loyal Parliament to resist William of Orange and Mary, the Protestant daughter of the same king, King James?"

"Can you get her safely to London?"

"I believe so, yes."

"What will you do then? Will you follow the King to France?"

"Will I follow the King to France?" Fisher sighed and stroked his chin.

"There is much to be said against it. He is not an attractive man. He is a religious bigot. He is not intelligent. He does not obey the law." Fisher paused.

"He is King by the will of God."

"If that is so, he certainly does not require my humble assistance; the Lord will provide."

"If the divine right of kings is not to your liking, what about the argument of Mr. Hobbes? Expel the King and all is in jeopardy – our lives, our property, our liberty."

Fisher scoffed. "The question, my dear Howard, is not whether we must have a king but whether we must have this king."

"But this King is King because he was born, as I am Howard and you are Fisher because we were born. To permit an assault upon this King is to undermine the basis for the power, position, and wealth of all the quality."

"That is indeed a serious consideration," Fisher conceded, "although its force is undermined by the fact the House of Lords was abolished by the Puritans and reconstituted in our fathers' day. Our class has withstood the assault of mere ideas."

"Do you doubt society needs us?"

"I do not. Aristocrats are the best men in any society, and society cannot flourish without its best men. But, our right to rule springs from our ability to manage property and govern men. These are practical skills."

"Are you so sure our ability to do these things is not the result of our natural superiority?" Howard squared his shoulders and rose to his full height as he posed this question.

"You are free to believe what you will. I believe we rule because we possess property. The proper management of property gives us those virtues we claim to possess. We command because we are accustomed to give orders to those who toil on our land. We can manage government expenses because we have in our account books, debts and balances to calculate. We can legislate because we study at the Inns of the Law. What has accident of birth to do with all of this?" Sir John put his hand to his head and said almost as if he were in a daze, "It is property indeed. It all rests upon property. It is property which must be defended."

"Then you must follow James, and abjure revolution. Law, class, and property are our holy trinity. James stands between you and the destruction of law. The tissue of law is seamless; cut into the mesh and you sever all connecting strands. Remove James and you eliminate the heart upon which the rest depends. Present the rabble with the spectacle of the Lords rejecting their King, and the mob will assume the right to reject the Lords. Drive the King out and seize his property and soon we shall be despoiled and exiled. James stands between us and the despoilation of all property. You may say birth makes you no different than a field hand or servant, if so you do not know them well. They are filthy, ignorant, and, if not properly tamed, savage. They are animals, no better, who live and die without knowledge of life. I am not as they; I am different. My superiority to them, I believe, is a result of my birth and breeding."

"And are you also by birth and breeding superior to those doughty merchants and tradesmen who defeated our noble fathers in the recent war and took King Charles' head?"

"We go round endlessly. The defeat of King Charles resulted in confiscations of noble property. The House of Lords was abolished and so for that matter was the House of Commons. You cannot risk permitting this to happen again. You must support the King." Howard dropped his argumentative tone and added, There are other considerations as well. Your father served the King, and you yourself have eaten at the table of King James. This must mean something to you. And, in serving the King you serve his gracious lady, the Queen."

"And yet," Fisher responded, "we might better serve our class and property by supporting William and Mary. This is not a revolution of the rabble, by the rabble. Many of the noblest houses in the Realm invited William to come. His Mary is the daughter of King James II. The Lords thought the crown would fall to her before the miraculous birth of the Papist babe. The people will be told the Protestant Daughter is the true sovereign, though what the people are told or think is of little importance so long as the reins of power do not go slack. Property must be defended upon that we agree, but perhaps we all ought to rally around the new king and present a unified face to the world and to the rabble." Howard made a gesture of dismissal, and Fisher continued, "There is one more point, my Lord, and that is the role and power of Parliament. Who do you believe sovereign, Parliament or King?"

"The King rules," Howard asserted.

"But Parliament made King Charles II and permitted James II to take the throne."

"The King rules," Howard insisted, paused and demanded, "And what about the Queen? Will you consign her to exile? Must she become a beggar in a foreign land?"

"The Queen," Fisher sighed, "what about the Queen indeed?"

"You love the Queen," Howard stated, placing his arm on the youth's shoulder.

"To do otherwise is not possible."

"Then you must support King James."

Without warning the library doors opened, and the Queen entered the room. Sir Thomas knelt and said, "Your Majesty."

Fisher remained standing, looked somewhat surprised at Howard, and then went to his knee. "Your pardon, Majesty. I have become confused by our charade."

"Arise both of you. The curtain is not yet descended on our play. There is the necessity of returning to London and the equal necessity of quashing any rumors of intimacy between John and myself."

"No honorable man or woman could doubt you," said Howard.

"To discredit me is to harm my husband, and to raise doubts about my chastity to give credit to the false fable of the warming pan. I am Mary, Sir Thomas."

"How soon do you require horses, eh, Mary? Won't you delay your departure until tomorrow? The roads are always dangerous, but especially so at night."

"John, do you agree with Sir Thomas?"

"Yes, Mary, the advice is sound." Fisher could not bring himself to seek the eyes of the Queen. He looked beyond her, through a window to the courtyard where the journey back to her husband would commence.

"Very well, let us dine. But, Sir Thomas, let it be such a dinner as you would offer unexpected and unimportant guests and go early to bed. We must be in London tomorrow night." The Queen turned and left them together.

"I must see about the arrangements," Howard told Fisher and took his leave. Sir John was left in the room with his thoughts.

The Queen did not appear for dinner. Fisher was not surprised, though he was disappointed. Howard tried to be amusing, but Sir John sank into melancholy. "I would have thought the son of your father and a young Oxford man would be one for talk."

"I apologize, Sir Thomas, but the wit is lacking this night to be a pleasant companion. I would retire, save even my bed will not find me fit company."

"Your mind is overburdened. Do you desire drink?"

"Thank you, no. I think a walk will lighten my spirits."

"A walk? You mean, outside?"

"I have become fond of walks," Fisher smiled, though his heart was pained with recollection and longing.

"Do you wish company or a dog? I can have one of the pack brought."

"You are kind, but thank you, no."

"Wait, I shall have a heavy cloak brought."

"Please, there is no need. Moving about will do me good."

"As you wish."

Fisher walked through the vast structure, seeing nothing, concentrating upon avoiding thought. He ascended the stair, dimly aware of the family portraits which hung there, as they did in his mother's home. The house was strangely silent; servants ought to be about preparing bed warmers and tending the fires. Fisher found that the supply of wood was already replenished and the fireplace filled for the night. He liked Howard now, but was irritated nevertheless there wasn't something about the house and the manner in which it was run that he could criticize. Sir John got his cloak and retraced his route down the steps and went into the night. Gloom hung over the land, but candles could be seen glowing weakly in the windows of houses in the village, like distant stars in the black void of space. Fisher walked vigorously away from the village toward the forest. The wind, already strong, was steadily gaining force. It swirled snow about in the pasture while pelting objects encountered in its way, like Fisher. The cold cleared his head while his body, working hard to stay warm and moving, felt more at ease. Fisher commanded his senses to listen, to watch, and to smell in order to occupy his mind, although he knew the wind would impede his ability to detect any hostile animals that might be about.

"John! John!"

Fisher smiled to himself. He thought he heard her voice. "A trick of wind and hope."

"John! Wait! Please wait!" It was the Queen! Fisher was not about to wait. He ran to her and threw his arms about her.

"My lady," he said, "forgive me," but he did not release her.

"What sort of man asks forgiveness for embracing his love?"

"You are my love," Fisher said.

"Yes," confirmed the Queen, and shook her head. "There is no future for us here, in France, or anywhere."

"The Queen disappeared in that village. There is no reason she need reappear."

"I have a son." There was nothing John could say about that. He released her, and she put her arm though his; they walked together in silence. Fisher watched her. The Queen scanned the heavens searching, he thought. At length she asked, "Did they tell you, Sir John, when you were at Oxford of what elements the soul was composed?"

"It is a great problem, Madame. The soul is an entity which is immaterial but has form and substance."

"Like fire, John, or this vapor we exhale?"

"The Greek for air, my Lady, is pneuma; it is the word for soul as well. Thus," he said, drawing her close, "we may join our breath and our souls." They stood together and breathed two warm streams of air which combined and was one.

> "Where, like a pillow on a bed,
> A pregnant bank swelled up to rest
> The violet's reclining head,
> Sat we two, one another's best.
> Our hands were firmly cemented
> With a fast balm, which thence did spring.
> Our eye-beams twisted, and did thread
> Our eyes upon one double string;
> So to integrate our hands, as yet
> Was all our means to make us one;
> And pictures in our eyes to get
> Was all our propagation.
> As 'twixt two equal armies, Fate
> Suspends uncertain victory,
> Our souls (which to advance their state,

were gone out) hung twixt her and me.
And whilst our souls negotiate there,
We like sepulchral statues lay;
All day the same our postres were,
And we say nothing all the day.
If any, so by love refined
That he soul's language understood,
And by good love were grown all mind,
Within convenient distance stood,
He (though he knew not which soul spake,
Because both meant, both spake the same)
Might thence a new concoction take
And part far purer than he came.
This ecstasy doth unperplex,
We said, and tell us what we love;
We see by this it was not sex;
We see we saw nor want did move
But as all several souls contain
Mixture of things, they know not what
Love mixed souls doth mix again,
And makes both one, each this and that.
But O alas, so long, so far
Our bodies why do we forbear?
They are ours, though they are not we; we are
The intelligences, they the sphere.
We owe them thanks because they thus
Did us to us at first convey,
Yielded their forces, sense, to us
Nor are dross to us, but allay.
Because such fingers need to knit
That subtle knot which makes us man;
So must pure lovers' soul descend
T'affections and to faculties
Which sense may reach and apprehend;
Else a great Prince in prison lies.
To our bodies turn we then, that so
Weak men on love revealed may look;
Love's mysteries in souls do grow.
But yet the body is his book.

And if some lover, such as we,
Have heard this dialogue of one,
Let him still mark us; he shall see
Small change when we are to bodies gone."*

They returned to the house at length, in silence. The very next morning, John and Mary reached the road which ran from Hastings north to Greenwich and found Gunfleet, the nurse and the babe. The Lord High Admiral had refused to take the child aboard ship. Mary, once again the Queen, entered her coach and bade the driver strike for London with all haste. None knew or heard of her adventure. Sir John Fisher rode to his mother's estate and contemplated which side he should take in the coming conflict.

* "The Ecstasy," John Donne

The Philosophe

The Enlightenment (1687-1789) was a glorious period of advancement and flowering in the arts and sciences, and perhaps most importantly in the art of living. The religious intolerance which marked Europe since the Reformation was abandoned when thinkers concluded since religious truth could not be conclusively established, toleration was the best policy. Addison and Steele, among many, tirelessly advocated manners for society. Few spoke for Christianity. Blaming the faith in Christ for centuries of darkness, the persecution of Galileo and the abominations of the Spanish Inquisition, the Enlightenment was viscerally anti-Christian. All forms of the supernatural were debunked. An English judge confronted with an accusation of witchcraft – the accused was said to have flown on a broomstick – consulted his Blackstone, announced he could find no law against flying and dismissed the case. The cup was filled with all of the nations of Europe and America contributing men of genius: Voltaire, Diderot, Montesquieu, Johnson, Hume, Locke, Holbach, Franklin and Jefferson. Men and women conversed and debated in the salons of Madame du Deffand and Madame Geoffrin which served as centers of European civilization. The Enlightenment took the achievments of the Scientific Revolution which included a heliocentric universe, inertia and gravity, and advocated a revolutionary organization of man and society to be based upon universal, natural laws to be determined by the social sciences. These were described in perhaps the most characteristic work of the Enlightenment, the Encyclopedia, which, Denis Diderot stated, should change the general way of thinking.

In **The Philosophe**, Francois and Philippe, two young members of the party of progress, as Enlightened thinkers styled themselves, discover the peril of their convictions. In a society which enjoyed neither freedom of speech nor of the press, Francois has published a scathing attack upon throne, altar and privilege which makes *them hunted men. As he avoids the authorities by disappearing into the working class faubourgs (suburbs) of Paris, Philippe examines the basis for his conversion to the Enlightenment, and whether it is worth the cost. He considers their lofty objectives and the daunting obstacles to reaching them. Meanwhile Francois, also a fugitive, dreams of revolution which will topple the old regime.*

The two young men faced one another like boxers but exchanged only verbal jabs. An older man watched, his expression fluctuated, but the gleam in his eye said he expected this outcome from the beginning.

"You no longer believe in enlightenment!" Francois shouted in Philippe's face, having lost control of emotions. To lose control, that alone was a capital sin against enlightenment.

"I no longer believe," Philippe responded calmly, though his blue eyes glowed with an internal fire, "in the enlightenment of the general population, or that it must be accomplished by our press. We must run this establishment as a business and not a hobby horse espousing causes for cranks and malcontents."

Inspector d'Hemery of the spotless linen and gleaming boots smiled and nodded with approval as he scanned the still wet sheets from the press.

"Have accommodations improved in the Bastille, Inspector?" Francois, tired of arguing with his partner, taunted the policeman. Philippe's eyes flashed a warning, but Francois paid no attention.

"I cannot say, Monsieur, but you may give us a full report when you get out."

"I, for the Bastille, Inspector?"

"If Monsieur does not guard his tongue, restrict his friends to desirables and concentrate on publishing works which improve the mind, the Bastille may become something of a second home." Francois, Philippe saw, was further enraged. In one sentence the Inspector, as he well knew, rejected freedom of thought, speech, and press. Beneath Francois' blond mop of hair, the skin bordered on purple, and the veins in his neck rose against the skin.

"Monsieur, L'inspector is the right man for the job. Not bothering to think he needs neither facility with speech nor a machine which can widely disseminate his non-thought." D'Hemery moved his vast bulk with remarkable agility. He caught Francois by the lapels, lifted and held him aloft. Francois dangled and waited, since any attempt to regain his feet would simply make him ridiculous. The inspector smiled at the young man and lowered his arms. He enjoyed Francois' discomfort for he recognized Francois' contempt for himself and his office. "You, gentlemen, have done well. Comedies, tragedies, even pamphlets advocating reform so long as they are accompanied by the right dedications or paid for by patrons above reproach, or best of all carry the approval of censors from crown and altar, pour from your press. Other documents for which you have no records, of which you have no knowledge, also come off this press, eh?" In fact, Inspector Joseph d'Hemery frequently stood in this very spot making shrewd observations about the legality and the quality of works he knew originated in the shop. Philippe was more disturbed by Hemery's sarcastic commentaries on the style and sense of the contributors than by his denunciations of their impiety or illegality. The inspector was no fool, nor, by implication were his superiors. Philippe understood that M. Berryer, the Lieutenant-General of Police, received daily reports on everything seen in cafes, theaters, and public gardens, in short, in all of those places where men of letters assembled. Such reports permitted the authorities to keep a thorough check upon dangerous subversives. "Yes, you have done well, until now." The inspector slammed a folded document on Philippe's stand throwing the objects there onto the floor. "Fools," he said and shook his head while Philippe examined the paper. D'Hemery heard him gasp and saw him raise his hand to his head in shock. Philippe read the most libelous, blasphemous, scurrilous attack upon Crown, Quality, and Clergy ever issued in Paris. The essay even lacked redeeming qualities of grace, wit, and style.

"Your partner has sold that," d'Hemery flicked his wrist contemptuously, "from this shop while you attended the burial of your father."

Philippe, much to his own surprise, remained calm when confronted with the deed. He removed his spectacles and wiped the lenses with his handkerchief, then turned to Francois and said, "You will go with M. d'Hemery to Monsieur Berryer and report our locks were broken and the press used without our knowledge. He will not believe you, but it may gain some time." D'Hemery indicated it would not. Philippe turned his icy blue eyes upon his partner and stated flatly, "You have sent us to the Bastille, or to death." He watched the face of the other man change. For the first time, Francois realized the serious nature of the act he committed. He was a member of a movement which enjoyed the privilege of denouncing abuses, of lampooning political opponents, and of thinking unthinkable thoughts. Now he had gone too far.

"Philippe, I, I'm sorry."

Philippe snorted, "Much good that will do us. Still, I accept your apology. Now, go with d'Hemery."

"No," the inspector told them. "Your only hope lies in flight. You will receive no protection from the police. Those you have offended have been given carte blanche to deal with you themselves." D'Hemery paused and concluded, sadly, "You have brought this upon yourselves." The inspector straightened himself and went to the door, then turned back and said, "May the God in whom you do not believe have mercy on your souls."

Neither man moved for a time until Philippe ordered, "Go, Francois. They will seek you first. I shall put our affairs in order here. Get Marie and be prepared to flee Paris."

"Where shall we meet?"

"Saint Marcel or Saint Antoine?"

"Marcel," Francois stated, "even the police avoid contact with the tanners." Francois paused before the door and, chagrined by the consequences of his deed, avoided looking at Philippe. "I shall see you soon." Francois retrieved his cane, squared his shoulders and strode boldly into the street. He looked neither right nor left and simply went about his business. He had some regret about the incident, though not much, for Francois believed the time for discussion and debate were over. The time for action had come, and he believed Philippe to be incapable of action. Philippe had his points. As an analyst, Philippe had no equal. He could follow the twists and turns of false logic, spot flaws in arguments, and compose moving prose. Too often, however, he could not see the proverbial forest for the trees. Philippe concentrated upon argument. The point of the matter he either missed, or ignored. The work of enlightenment was to make men free. It was as simple as that. Man must be freed from the old superstition which told them they were naturally corrupt but free from death. In order to live free, Francois knew, one must carry the burden of freedom. One chose to be good and worked to remain so. Or one chose evil and worked at that. The wages of sin were, perhaps, more pleasant. In either case, one made oneself. The mind was a tabula rasa. Death, from which there was no escape, came for all men. Here was a terrible truth to be sure, but one which man must face before he can be free. Happiness must be found here in material and moral terms. Here was the only place man exists, no heaven, no hell, no purgatory, no soul. This was the truth that would make man free. That it would also make them unhappy and hostile were thoughts Francois did not entertain. The enlightened had made their case. The truth was self-evident. Let the struggle begin. Diderot said it best. Let the last king be strangled in the guts of the last priest.

Francois was fearless, but not foolish; it would do no good to languish in the Bastille when there was work to be done. He was committed as well to meet Philippe tomorrow and, doubtless, help him escape. Francois did not doubt his fellow philosophe would run and forgave him for it. Paris would soon be in flames, and Francois could hardly wait for the challenges to come. He unconsciously opened and closed his fists, ready for the action. But first he must send Marie home. The young provincial from his village, with whom he was in love, would be in grave danger when revolution came to the capital. Francois hurried.

While Francois effected his escape, Philippe opened the cash box and packed coins about his person. Some went in his trousers and shoes; some went in his coat. He glanced about the shop wondering what else he should take and how much time remained. "Jean, do any copies of the pamphlet Francois printed in my absence remain?"

"A few, Monsieur."

"Burn them." There were no other portable objects of value visible, and his mind turned to the press itself. Given sufficient time, he could dismantle it and arrange for transport to London or Amsterdam. I might begin again, he thought, noticed the "I" rather than "we" but got no further in his reflections since the barrel of a pistol came through the door first and a head followed. The gun swung to where he was seated. He watched the tug on the trigger, ignoring the head which directed its motion, and saw, or told himself he saw, the hammer moving forward to strike, but this could not be as he had already thrown himself to the floor. The ball hit the back of the chair splintering it and sending fragments in all directions, and continued until it lodged in the wall. The door was pushed wide open and three others, also armed, leveled their weapons. "The ink! The ink! Throw it, Jean!" The apprentice did as he was told and the would-be assassins discharged the pieces while tripping over themselves in retreat as ink could not be removed from their elegant silks. Jean went down hit by a ball in the shoulder, Philippe thought. The boy would not be bothered; he was only a printer's devil, not a philosophe. Philippe was already moving to the back of the shop convinced "his betters" lacked the brains to cover the alley.

The street presented the pageant of life which always afforded Philippe pleasure and in addition today, cover. Prostitutes, the clothing about their shoulders torn and bloody from a judicial flogging, were pushed by bayonets to the nearest gate of the city. They were provincial girls sent home after tasting the hospitality of the capital. Letter writers set up their stalls or sharpened their quills or inspected their paper, while washer women with baskets balanced on their heads walked briskly toward the river. Philippe watched for troops or men who might be police, though he doubted there was a warrant for his arrest. Those who visited his place of business were settling a private score as agents of an Estate, not representatives of the King. Philippe walked beyond Francois' door and stopped to examine a vendor's merchandise with an eye for detail. More carefully, he examined the crowd milling in the street and concluded no one was there who did not belong. He returned to Francois' building, entered, and climbed the steps. Halfway to the top, Philippe said to himself, "But someone may be laying in wait." Francois' door swung open, and for the second time a firearm was discharged in his direction. Philippe vaulted the banister, musing that this day he was personally bringing more damage to structures in Paris than termites. He determined to make haste to those places of the city where neither the authorities nor "the Quality" would venture, and then he would turn his attention to a rendezvous with his confederate. Perhaps it would be best to turn myself over to the authorities, he thought. The Bastille at its worst had more comforts than death. Such sentiments were a betrayal of the cause, he recognized. Science and science alone, which pitilessly destroyed the myths of Christianity, gave inner peace; how often he recited this, the Philosophe's Creed. The man of reason was neither deluded with the hope of heaven nor tormented with the fears of hell. Over and over again he rehearsed these words with others and by himself. He recalled the Sage of Ferney's remark that the immortality of the Philosophe would be guaranteed by the memory of posterity. Posterity be damned! Rameau was right: "The devil take the best of all possible worlds if I am not part of it!" What did posterity matter to one whose being and memory were extinct? Wasn't it better never to be born than to experience a life which could not and would not be prolonged? Philippe thought, during all of those centuries long past, I did not exist. Now I breathe and see and love the experience of seeing and of hearing. I love to love women. I love the flesh. Soon I shall be dead. Until then, I must contemplate my nonexistence. I know future centuries will pass without me; I shall be completely gone. Philippe felt his stomach churn; vomit rose, splashing its sour taste on his tongue. How often he had made sport of his brother Arnaud the priest, dismissing his bigoted superstition, only to find the Cure obstinately insisted that Jesus held his arms open to embrace Philippe. "Though you may have lost faith in your Savior, He has never lost His faith in you." This Second Person of the Trinity, thought

Philippe, was the very devil, tempting men from the true path of science with this contemptible and fantastic promise of life beyond the grave.

It may be that Philippe was too deeply lost in reverie to guide his footsteps, or it may be that the lowly driver of the coach of the most high Duc d'Or had acquired that contempt for the people of Paris so conspicuous in his master; whichever the case the harness of the horses drawing the Duke's coach so recklessly through the narrow, packed street struck Philippe's shoulder and sent him flying through the air. Promptly obeying the law of gravity described by the divine Newton, Philippe landed upon the back of a toothdrawer who was thrust by the blow onto the body of his client. All three landed heavily on the earth. Philippe was the first to rise and said, "I most sincerely beg your pardon."

"I'm damned if you shall have it," exclaimed the toothdrawer, who raised his hand to his nose, discharged the contents into his fingers, wiped them on his trouser leg and finally extended it to his client. The latter remained on his knees apparently dazed. He patted the ground like a drummer, raising the dust, searching for something. Finally in triumph he rose to his feet and shouted, "The tooth! The tooth!" He held it aloft for all to see as the priest holds the monstrance at mass.

"My fee, advance me my fee," insisted the toothdrawer.

"You did not draw the tooth; it was knocked from my mouth by accident."

"You agreed to pay regardless of the instrument I used to extract it."

"Liar! Criminal! You'll have nothing from me," retorted the former patient who escaped in the crowd.

"Stop! Come back!" screamed the toothdrawer, who departed in pursuit.

Meanwhile, Philippe retreated into the crowd and scanned the street again before he walked purposefully to the faubourg Saint Marcel, where Francois had gone to avoid the authorities. He did not realize that he had acquired a shadow, a professional informer who knew his business, and who knew the life history of Philippe Monde.

Philippe, born in 1740, was the eldest son of good gens de bien in the provincial town of Mirabel. He was educated at the local college by Masters educated at Paris. The young man's parents paid for a practical education which would provide Philippe with the skills to supervise accounts in the hotel de ville. The young man's education was entirely conventional. His religious training was thorough, if uninspired, and the circle of parental friends was as solid and dull as trunks of old trees. His parents wanted Philippe to get on, that is to find a position, a wife, home, in short, success. Philippe did not reject these aspirations out of hand but was convinced there was more adventure in life than he witnessed in the experience of his parents.

Arnaud, the younger brother, who attended the same college some years later, entered the Church in 1758. That same year Philippe, bored nearly to death by his profession, left Mirabel to make his way as a man of letters in the capital. In those days, a country bumpkin did not simply depart for the great city but made a connection with a friend, or relative, or at very least a fellow expatriate of his town with whom he would live until other arrangements were made. Philippe's cousin, Suzzette, who had fled an unattractive bridegroom selected by her parents, was there. She aspired to a career on the boards and, in the meantime, worked as a prostitute. Suzzette knew a prostitute who knew a lesbian who knew the lesbian sister of Sophie Volland, mistress of Monsieur Diderot, who brought young Philippe to the attention of the great man. Philippe came as a secretary and remained as a committed convert. Working and socializing with those to whom Monsieur Diderot introduced him, his conversion was confirmed. Their talk was brilliant and, though the young man did not realize it, corrosive. In the rooms of Madame Geoffrin men and women of consequence at court or in the city assembled to listen to Le Kain read correspondence from Voltaire. All laughed when the Master observed: "In general, the art of government consists in taking as much money as possible from one class of citizens to give it to the other"; and again, "Marriage is the only adventure open to the cowardly"; and once more, "Selflove never dies." It was as poison administered in sugar, the taste was pleasant and the effect deadly. Before long that portion of Philippe's tabula rasa imprinted at Mirabel was erased, and the contents of his mind refurbished.

M. Diderot was not the man to permit his young protege to be randomly informed. He introduced Philippe to Francois, another recent arrival at Paris, and introduced both of them to the discipline of learning. Diderot's attraction to the boys was professional and emotional. His marriage was notably unsuccessful and the only fruit of the long relationship – a daughter. The old Philosophe longed for a son, perhaps because he had been rejected by his own father. Diderot grasped the opportunity to set all right at last. He would have sons properly educated by himself and heirs to carry on the great work. Francois and Philippe took rooms together and began reading. They commenced with Bayle and Fontenelle. Bayle was, in Diderot's view, the apostle of tolerance who defended atheism and rejected the contention that atheism must lead to an immoral society. On the contrary, Bayle insisted, a society of atheists would practice moral actions as well as any other, provided it punished crime severely and attached honor to those acts which were so-cially beneficial. Tolerance was practical since ultimate truth cannot be es-tablished; therefore we must respect one another's partial truths. Catholics who persecuted Protestants, or Protestants who persecuted Catholics – all were fools. Truth was the exclusive possession of no one. Descartes and Newton were to be approached through Fontenelle, author of comedies, trag-edies, and operas, whose lucid style illuminated the densest scientific theo-ries. Fontenelle insisted that, regardless of the problem, thought must be clear and cautioned, "A fairy tale remains fairy tale whether a hundred or a hundred million believe it." They learned the history of the world was di-vided between two types of men, the ascetic, superstitious, enemy of the flesh, and those who affirmed the body, knowledge, and generosity. This meant that history was divided between two great cycles – those when big-otry, myth, and superstition reigned, and those ages of criticism and science, in a word, of enlightenment. The task of the little band of Philosophes was to gain reliable knowledge of the past, rational control over the world, and freedom from superstition.

M. Diderot was so pleased with the boys' progress that he presented them with an embossing tool to mark those books they purchased and mastered. The devices printed their names and the Latin challenge "Sapere aude!" Francois and Philippe were invited to dinners and readings as well. Diderot's German friend Holbach, who composed over four hundred articles for the great Encyclopedia, invited them for coffee and pastries. Englishmen like Lawrence Sterne, Horace Walpole and Adam Smith, Doctor Franklin from the New World, and the Italian Beccaria intoxicated the boys with their ideas. It was thus they began to confuse the world in which they moved with that which existed in the streets of Paris and the unpaved roads which ran into the provinces of France. They should have reminded themselves that the first book published by the great Voltaire was condemned as scandalous, contrary to religion and good morals, lacerated and burned at the stake in the very Paris where they now resided, and that the Jansenists, themselves no favorites of the government, labeled the authors of the Encyclopedia, "depraved."

Rene Lucas, the shadow, knew all these things about his quarry and also knew in which faubourg Philippe would seek refuge. Lucas was a reliable informer, reliable in constancy if not accuracy. Since the authorities paid whether the intelligence was accurate or not, Rene did not regard truth as essential. He told his masters what they expected to hear. In his youth, he followed suspect Protestants or regicides, now it was scribblers and printers foolish enough to make their ideas public. Men so stupid deserved what they got. The problem with Philippe and his kind was that their failure to conform to the general notion of conspirators made the authorities less willing to pay, and so he sold them to the Quality instead. The gentlemen of privilege, enraged at being the brunt of jokes and denunciations, took matters into their own hands rather than waiting for the slow grinding machinery of the State. Lucas was almost as glad as Philippe the bullets missed their mark, since alive, Philippe remained a source of income. Rene's smile pulled his lips back onto his teeth and the corners of his mouth upward to his cheekbones. It reminded those who saw it of a wolf. He was tired of playing cat and mouse, especially as this mouse did not realize the game was afoot. It was the smell of fear that made the game worthwhile. Lucas guessed Francois was with his family, the tanners, in Saint Marcel. Philippe logically would seek refuge with his family, brewers, in the faubourg Saint-Antoine. Lucas decided to give him time and turned east.

A crowd watched men in boats who threw hooks into the river. Several people pointed when one of the ropes became taunt; something was on the end of the hook! Prostitutes, Rene thought to himself, so often chose the Seine. Who would believe the job so hazardous? This prostitute, however, had chosen to die because of himself. A towering police officer, whose duty consisted of watching the crowd watch the dragging of the river, saw Rene and rushed him with his arm raised to strike. "You!" he screamed and struck Lucas, who fell heavily upon his back. The officer followed with a vicious kick to the ribs. "You were ordered out of the city. Is Monsieur deaf or stupid?" He grasped Rene by the scruff of his neck and effortlessly pulled the struggling man to his feet and dragged him toward an alley. "I shall give you some reminders that authority is to be obeyed." Pushed against a disintegrating wall in a court filled with debris, Rene's face was presented with a fist the size of a ham, but the officer whispered, "She was exactly where you expected, Monsieur."

"But of course, Captain, have I ever failed you?"

"She was the mistress of Monsieur Francois Girard for whom a lettre de cachet was issued?"

"Yes, Captain."

"And he killed her to prevent her from telling where he is hidden?"

"That is my intelligence, Captain."

"You will inform us when you locate M. Girard."

"At once."

"Good. Adieu, M. Lucas."

Rene was perturbed that he could not view the body; he wondered what the woman's expression would reveal. Lucas, who knew Sophie Volland, investigated her friends and discovered the prostitute friend of Suzzette, Marie d'Etable, who happened to be the mistress of Francois Girard. Rene threatened the young woman with arrest and torture until she divulged the refuge of her lover. Despair over the betrayal of Francois took her to the river. Rene then proceeded to charge Francois with her murder. Lucas found the entire incident lively and instructive entertainment. The thought of it brought a smile to his lips again. Life was indeed diverting and amusing.

Philippe, too, was ruminating on the vagarities of life which took him so high and deposited him so low, a hunted fugitive. While his eyes and some portion of his mind actively watched for signs of recognition, hostility, and pursuit, he was otherwise oblivious to his surroundings and to the men and women who filled the streets. Philippe was a PHILOSOPHE, who loved MAN in general but disliked MEN in the particular. The lives of the men and women who lived in the faubourg Saint Marcel revolved around manual labor. Philippe was disposed to agree with Aristotle that those so occupied are deprived of their ability to think. To care for the indigenous population of the faubourg the Philosophes must demand the rights of the people he conceded, and after they must still protect them against the rapacity of government and estate, though they would never understand the issues at stake. One could only hope they possessed sufficient intelligence to follow their natural leaders. This thought, that the third estate would follow and be grateful, was central to the program of the Philosophes, and yet didn't Diderot often assert that the objective of enlightened thought was to change the general way of thinking? Perhaps the great mass of humanity rejected the ideas of the Philosophes. Philippe contemplated his own journey to "the light." The Ancients invented "criticism," that habit of mind which disbelieved where there was no proof and upheld the dignity of man. At school, Philippe read Virgil and Pliny and Cicero as bits of quotation to drop in conversation or to demonstrate one read, but now these commonplaces had meaning. When Montesquieu stated "a spirit of toleration and kindness reigned in the pagan world," Philippe recognized both that he was right and that he was offering a challenge to a Christian Europe which was neither kind nor tolerant despite Christian love and charity. Next there was the issue of Christianity itself. Galileo entered the school of Plato and concluded with that noble ancient that God had written only one book, the book of nature. Man could understand God through his work, the universe. How, then, was man to understand the Bible, God's other revelation? Here M. Diderot did little but quote approvingly of contemporary Christian theologians who questioned what they considered the "unreasonable" aspects of relevation. The learned Benedictine, Calmet, complained the scriptures were obscure. Toland proposed that the priestly caste had invented the Christian mysteries in their greed for power. Collins' massive "Discourse on the Grounds and Reasons of the Christian Religion," argued all that was miraculous and unreasonable in scripture be discounted and removed from the faith. When Cardinal de Bernis' memoirs noted it was no longer considered well-bred to believe in the Gospels, the Philosophes felt the rout of superstition had begun. If there were no miracles, how could there be a Trinity? If there were no Trinity, what was the nature of God? Oh yes, there was a God, a Creator who made the universe and all it contained and then withdrew to see what man would make of himself. This God manifested himself in the book of nature. He made the laws which govern nature and did not violate them by performing (that was the word all right, performing, like the cheap tricks of a parlor magician) miracles. This God does not command His adherents to slaughter those who do not believe, as happened on Saint Bartholomew's Day. The strategy of attack against the old superstition however was satire and deception; there would be no direct attack upon the church which, like a rabid dog dying, might still inflict a lethal bite.

"We oppose superstition," Diderot told them, and meant Christianity, "not merely because of what it does, which is to conduct inquisitions and assassinations, but because it hates and humiliates man. The Christians betrayed philosophy by despising the resources of the mind. Tertullian proudly announced he believed in scripture because the doctrines of the faith were absurd. But man shall triumph! Look about you and see how the world is changing. The priests have no answer for Copernicus, Galileo, and Newton. They who have so long argued about the nature of the world with no authority save the gospel, and no verification save belief in that flawed book are now confronted with verifiable proof. We accumulate new instruments: telescopes, microscopes, barometers, to better study and know the world. We have begun the conquest of small pox – the triumph of our science soon will be seen on man's clear face. We have not forgotten the practical arts. Tull has improved planting with his drill; a threshing machine has been introduced. The flying shuttle has made man more productive, and hard paste porcelain has made dishes widely available. Here is progress – with tangible benefits, fuller bellies, clothes on the back, coal for warmth – after a thousand years of stagnation under Christ. The Age of Criticism is an Age of

Humanity!" And yet the old order still endured and it was Philippe, a philosophe, who was a fugitive. This made no sense.

At the intersection of two streets Philippe, having no choice, paused. A three sided donkey cart driven by the most remarkably ugly man he had ever seen moved men and vehicles left and right. It was the municipal scavenger carrying the unclaimed dead to the paupers' field. On top of the pile was the body, partially obscured, of a young woman, her hair and clothing still wet. Death again. Philippe shuddered. "I am a failure as an ancient philosopher," he told himself.

Philippe walked until he found himself among the tanners whose clothing was covered with blood and guts, or reeked of curing agents, and who had, quite visible under their fingernails, pieces of flesh from the carcasses. His revulsion was unusual since filth was a common component of life in the city, though Philippe's acquaintances were personally clean, however squalid might be their surroundings. These men and women smelled and acted like pigs. "Excuse me," he said to a great hulk of a man who aggressively and publicly scratched his private parts through his trousers. A dog bounced down the steps and sniffed at him, looked puzzled, and sniffed again. In the midst of this stench, Philippe thought, I must be undetectable to the dog's nose. The fat one, made no more lovely by broken and brown teeth, gave no sign that he heard Philippe.

"Francois. I am searching for Francois; he was to be here."

"Ah, Francois!" the fat one boomed and crushed Philippe against his chest. The young man gagged and felt as though he'd fallen into a cesspit. "A friend of my nephew is my friend. I am Villard – to friends, Le Grosse." He winked at Philippe and pounded his stomach. Then Villard put his arm over Philippe's shoulder and turned him toward the steps, even propelled him up the first. "Go in, second level, third door. Knock three times, wait and knock again." Philippe carefully stepped over and between bodies of men and women drinking, passing bottles, nursing babies, beating children, and simply trying to talk. It was like a scene, Philippe thought, from the fable of Babel.

The door was opened by an old, toothless crone whose nose was so long and bony that it appeared to be a finger pointing at him from between her eyes. She stepped back and he entered the room, empty except for filthy straw, rags and pieces of clothing, small lumps of cheese, cuts from loaves of bread, and empty bottles. Without speaking, she handed him a bottle of wine and gestured that he should find a spot and be comfortable. Philippe produced his watch and noted the time. He would give Francois two hours –

it would be dark then – and flee to Suzzette. To be surrounded by prostitutes was far more congenial than this. He picked up the bottle and worked the cork from the neck and took a deep swig. An hour and a bottle emptied themselves, and Philippe began the new hour with a new bottle.

As he was safe for the first time since morning, his mind and body relaxed and enjoyed the wine, and the wine deepened his relaxation and pleasure. He had worked too hard for too long, he told himself; some time ought always to be reserved for pleasure. Pleasure, that was a subject little considered by the Philosophes. They certainly approved of pleasures, especially since the Christian superstition steadfastly opposed them, but they had not developed an ethic or even a simple position on pleasure. Perhaps this arose from their obsession with virtue. Diderot, his master, examined everything from the perspective of virtue. Diderot questioned, "After reading Seneca, am I the same man I was before I read him?" Diderot insisted over and over, "To do good, to know the truth, that is what distinguishes one man from another. The rest is nothing," and again, "The whole glory of virtue lies in action." One must be virtuous, and one must act. To make society moral at its base, one began with the family. But here M. Diderot did not live by his words. Fidelity in marriage he feigned. Diderot had a mistress. But what could one do when marriage failed and divorce was illegal? Besides, the traditional practice of marriage was really nothing more than a legal device for property management and for controlling the number of paupers. The Philosophes waged war against this legal and religious tyranny. Ah, thought Philippe, but where was virtue in deserting wife and children? Is there not virtue in faithfully fulfilling the obligations one has voluntarily undertaken? Perhaps there was some wisdom in those words of Jesus, "Whom God has joined together, let no man put asunder." Nor did Diderot honor his father who felt his son's attacks upon religion were a personal betrayal. Diderot was not always truthful; none of the Philosophes were. Voltaire advised: "You must lie like a devil, not timidly, not for a while, but boldly and persistently. Lie, my friend, lie. I shall repay you when I get the chance." Diderot did not perform well when measured by the commandments. Of course he would be proud of that.

Another apparent contradiction was in how the great unwashed were considered and treated. The philosophe considered all men equal in value and worthy to be educated, since every educated man could be enlisted in the struggle against ignorance and superstition. This dictated that all men be treated politely, since politics and manners, in the words of his master, hold each other by the hand. Treat all men equally that they might aspire to be equal through education. Make that great engine of learning, the Encyclopedia, available to all. But how many of them could read it, and even if they could read it, would they understand the argument, and even if they understood, would they agree? The philosopes weren't certain. Sometimes they even doubted the ability of the mob to be educated at all.

Philippe would not admit that worst of all was the worm which wiggled and gnawed in his brain. He was not certain that man unaided could know the right course of action. He was not certain that mortal man – that he himself – could face the tormenting power of death. "I am worse than Peter; he merely denied the Master thrice; I deny two Masters."

Philippe lost track of hours and bottles, sights, smells, and sounds. He was vaguely aware that bottles appeared as he needed them and was pleased that a lantern provided light. A candle burning in the straw would be dangerous. It became difficult to maintain a train of thought as he drifted toward sleep. This does not really matter, he told himself, as the Philosophes' program was as unclear as the processes of his mind at this point anyway. The central problem in the grand scheme was how to bring about general enlightenment without which there could be no general progress. The advances in science and philosophy were no better than the secrets of free masons if they could not be introduced into the general thinking and acting of the man in the street. The problem was the Philosophes were known to themselves and to their natural enemies. There was a warrant for Rousseau's arrest in Geneva; the chevalier de la Barra was burned at the stake for blasphemy; and the Hapsburgs issued their own Catalogue of Forbidden Books. The Bastille threatened the Philosophes in France. Merchants and artisans read the Philosophes with approval but lacked wealth, power and prestige, and numbers. Numbers, that was the problem. The people, that imbecile crowd, that ferocious and blind monster must be elevated. "But," he said aloud watching the light fluctuate, now bright, now dim, what progress can society make when the bulk of mankind, even in France, is no more than two-footed animals living in virtually the state of nature, with hardly enough to live on and clothe themselves, barely enjoying the gift of speech, barely aware that they are miserable, living and dying practically without knowing it?" What could be done with them? They were illiterate and there were no schools. They did not go to the theater. They were not invited to salons. What was to be done? Diderot did not know; Voltaire did not know; Holbach did not know; Hume and Gibbon did not know. Philippe suddenly saw the light.

The enlightened must accept responsibility for their inferiors by inspiring employers to follow the example of Josiah Wedgwood in England who had organized a model village for his "hands," (That term itself revealed how the ordinary man's intellect was viewed.) and by influencing those final arbitrators of human destiny, the monarchs of Europe to provide money to educate the people. But could one join the establishment and remain a detached and active critic? Experience suggested the Philosophes might be more readily co-opted by the rulers than the rulers converted by the Philosophes. "Lead us not into temptation," Philippe said bitterly, sliding into the straw to sleep.

When Rene Lucas was a young man, the stocks, in which he was displayed for impertinence, were jumped upon by the nobleman of whom he had been making sport. The wood gave way and his arms were crushed. He regained some use of them in time, but his fingers remained rather rigid, partially closed, reminding those who saw them of claws. Not many saw them, however, as Rene developed a number of habits, like drawing them into the sleeves of his great coat to reduce their visibility. The young man also formed a life long loathing for the nobility he so faithfully served. He was contemptuous of them as well. These fools who owed all to accidents of birth were constantly victimized by charlatans, adventurers, and impostors, like Cagliostro and Casanova, who were exposed and ruined by Lucas. The Physicians Royal, deceived by Mary Tofts and convinced she gave birth to rabbits, were humiliated when Lucas demonstrated her ruse before the King. An indispensable man, Rene loved only himself and trusted not even that widely. Lucas feared his contempt for all he encountered might lead to his downfall and so he watched himself even more closely than those he pursued. And now Rene, like God, contemplated the fate he had arranged for the prostitute Marie; he had transformed her into a fish. "Ha! An excellent joke!" he exclaimed, while consciously maneuvering his blighted fingers to scratch behind his right ear. It was time to manipulate the life of Francois Girard as well, he decided. One of his two birds must be taken lest he do something unexpected. Philippe lay in the house of "Le Grosse" waiting for Francois who was hidden in a whorehouse by friends of his Marie. Should he turn his captives over to the Church, the Police, or the Quality? The latter would be more generous, but the gratitude of altar or crown were not to be dismissed. "Pierre!" Rene shouted. No sound came from the antechamber but the harsh, coarse breathing of an animal. "Pierre! Pierre! At once!" The guttural sounds ceased. "Drag your worthless bones here or I shall cane you within an inch of your life!" Immediately the dragging, flailing sound of a wounded beast was heard, followed by the crudest, most blasphemous oaths ever uttered in Paris.

"Do you never sleep, Monsieur?"

"If I thought as little as you and slept as much, bah, no man can possibly do so." Pierre's tiny pig's eyes displayed no offense. "I want Francois Girard taken tonight, now. Get Henri and Claude. Send one with the message that Marie d'Etable is incarcerated in the Salpetiere, the hospital, not the prison, and that she may only be released in the custody of a man. He will come willingly first to his Marie, and secondly, because the Salpetiere is located in the faubourg Saint Marcel where he expects to meet his friend Philippe."

"What force may I use to bring him here?"

"Do whatever is necessary to extract him from the Rue Mouffetard without attracting the attention of 'the Watch.'" Lucas examined Pierre's heavy blank face, the features of which might be animated by sex, food, sleep, and brutality, though not in any set order of desire or need. "Do not kill him, he has no value dead. Men are the only commodities of flesh that cannot be sold dead, even freshly dead."

"Eyes?"

"I do not want him to be in a condition that will receive sympathy from his enemies. Enjoy yourself in the capture. Inflict such pain as you will, but quit before severe damage is done to his person. Leave that pleasure for his declared enemies." Pierre was as vicious and inhumane a creature as Paris knew, and yet the smile of Lucas was enough to send chills through him. He received his words of dismissal and left the presence gratefully.

Francois did not like the looks of his companion or his choice of streets. The eyes lacked the light of intelligence, but in them lingered the dim gleam of cunning. He was built like a heavy laborer, with massive shoulders and chest, and thick and solid arms. There were no calluses on his hands though, and there ought to be if work was done regularly. What did he do, if not labor? Perhaps the question was better unposed. It was an unusual man who ventured on the streets of the city at night, and he was probably the only one Marie could find to carry the message. He was certain the message came from his beloved since no one else, not even Philippe, knew where to find him. Francois recognized in his heart of hearts that he must meet with Philippe. To maintain their status as Philosophes, the two men must agree to go their separate ways. They could not simply do it, although the break had already occurred. They must discuss their breech and take formal leave of one another. Francois saw two men approach whose appearance gave him no comfort. He was also aware that his companion was loosening his coat and rotating his shoulders anticipating action. The cane Francois carried contained a sword and he was skilled with the weapon. Like other members of the bourgeoisie, his father insisted the youth be given an education which equaled that of the Quality. Francois received instruction from a dancing master and, more to the point, a fencing master. He glanced at his companion and decided he was probably in league with the approaching ruffians. Francois' left hand grasped the base of the stick while his right drew the sword and continued the motion with a thrust into Pierre's left eye. The blade, though sharp and deadly, was thin and delicate, and he could not risk a thrust to the body which might have deflected or even damaged the weapon. The two thugs halted, disconcerted by the sudden change in the odds, and drew razor-edged knives. Then they charged. Francois retreated into a corner where his back was protected but not so far as to lack room for maneuver. He was confident of his ability to ward off if not kill his assailants. He challenged them with his sword and taunted them to attack. Then came the sound of boots on the cobblestone; someone was coming! Francois smiled and advanced against his opponents. They retreated cautiously at first, and then displayed confusion. First they seemed happy to see the person with the boots, then they ran. Francois did not give their reaction a second thought, or ascribed their reaction to the peculiar features of the man who approached. His long nose and mouth presented a wolf-like appearance. Girard faced the newcomer, his sword at the ready, the point dark with coagulated blood.

"Please," said wolf-face, "state your intentions. Is this a robbery?"

"It was an attempted robbery, Monsieur, with myself the intended victim. However, the prey became the predator."

"Well done, Monsieur."

"Thank you, and I bid you good night."

"Wait," said Rene, "may I accompany you for safety sake? We seem to be going in the same direction."

"You must pardon me, Monsieur, but my experience this evening makes a companion unwelcome."

"Yes, I see that. Very well then, good night Monsieur, and may you complete your journey without further incident."

"Thank you, Monsieur, and good night." Francois watched the wolf-face who walked in the direction of the faubourg Saint Marcel. He did not remember making any comment or gesture to indicate his destination. The wolf-face may have been an agent of the police, Quality, or church. Francois wheeled and retraced the ground he covered earlier that evening. It was best to be safe.

When Philippe awoke the following morning, his skin tingled, though whether the vermin were real or imagined he wasn't certain. His head ached and that was no illusion. "A rare vintage," he said to the bottle he held in his hand, "two or three days at least." Sitting in the straw disgusted him, and yet he did not rise; he required concentration, and the unfamiliar surroundings were not conducive to thought. Francois was not in the room. Where was Francois? His sluggish brain recalled that Francois was to be here to plan their escape. They were hunted men! Philippe staggered to his feet and over to the window. Animals were being herded through the streets, were being inspected by butchers and tanners, were being led away after money had changed hands. Women with baskets moved purposefully between the animals and men going to or coming from the market. Philippe did not believe the building was watched.

"Francois has broken our agreement," he said, "let him fend for himself. I owe him nothing; it is he who is obligated." Philippe realized at that moment, he could leave the other man without regret. Once this would have been unthinkable. When Diderot brought them together, as secretaries compiling and correcting articles, he would also assign them problems which required solutions to promote the cause of the Philosophes.

"To advance the work and assert the greatness of man, it is necessary to dismiss God, and undermine those subjects which claim knowledge of Him, His works and attributes. But, my children, this must be done in such a manner as to assure the authorities we have advanced the cause of God and upheld His dignity. Otherwise, the Bastille or the stake await us."

"The stake, Monsieur? We do not live in Spain."

"Fanaticism," said Diderot, "is to superstition what delirium is to fever, and rage to anger. The superstitious man may be ruled by the fanatic, and turn into one. Our Voltaire, whom I have just quoted, has opened his campaign against "L'infame"; do you believe they shall not strike back? M. Arouet at Ferney sits astride the French-Swiss border and keeps his bag packed. We, however, shall cross a mental border to engage and defeat Christianity, and not give the appearance of doing so."

Francois and Philippe questioned how this was possible but recognized the dexterity and ingenuity of the minds of Diderot and d'Alembert. "What you must see," d'Alembert explained, "is that classification gives power; he who classifies exercises power. Meat goes to waste because we have determined geese may be eaten, but not swans, and rabbits but not squirrels, even though both are rodents. Do you see?" They did, vaguely. "Hair, finger, and toenail clippings and other bodily fluids, what can be done with them?"

The two pupils were stunned. "What can be done with them, Monsieur?"

"Who makes use of them?"

"Fingernail clippings, Monsieur?"

"Do not look at me as if I were mad. Who uses fingernail clippings?"

"Magicians?"

"Yes, now we're getting somewhere. A magician employs them because they represent a border area. They are part of you and yet not quite. Your arms, your legs, head and trunk, now those are solidly you and impart no suspicion. Where we place things determines, to a certain extent, what we think about them."

"Guilt by association?" suggested Francois.

The Master continued, "We shall develop a tree of knowledge for the Encyclopedia illustrating all branches of human learning. There shall be major branches, minor branches, and finally twigs. We shall set boundaries between the categories, 'known and unknowable' so that most of what man considers sacred shall be labeled unknowable. The great branches shall include knowledge of man and knowledge of nature. A tiny, stunted branch shall be knowledge of God. From that shall arise Revealed Theology, which we condemn, and knowledge of good and evil spirits, which we shall condemn by association with black magic and divination, thus." D'Alembert displayed the page covered with beautiful script to his proteges with a flourish.

The Unknowable

    Knowledge of God

        Revealed theology

                                   ─── black magic
        Knowledge of good and evil spirits ─┤
                                   ─── divination

"Such a scheme will hardly redound to the credit even of the old superstition."

"Beautiful."

"Magnifique! And there is more?"

"Yes, Francois, much more. Our articles on Christianity, and the Mass, and the Sacraments and the various Christian sects will blend Descartes and Locke, Calvin and Luther, Saint Francis and Saint Paul, so that all Christian thinking will be seen as inconsistent and contrary to good thought and even good morals."

"How will you arrange the last?" Philippe inquired.

"Historical vignettes. We shall highlight the gluttony and hypocrisy of Pope Leo X, and the orgies of Alexander VI. We shall introduce Augustine as a debauched African. Oh, it shall not be difficult. Lastly we shall conquer with cross references. We shall associate religion and superstition, communion and black magic, prophets with astrology! The reader will confuse down and up before we are finished." Philippe gazed in awe at such an achievement.

Even now he could remember doing so. He and Francois shared so much then, even prostitutes and mistresses. Excitement was the dominant note of their lives. They talked about their work when they rose and before they went to bed, when they ate, as they walked, and even as they fornicated, since both believed the mind of women should be improved. The prostitutes were not as enthusiastic about their schemes as Philippe and Francois hoped.

"You put them out by what you say." Madame La Porte, proprietress of their favorite house, told them.

"It is only fair," said Philippe, "we put them out, which exercises their mental faculties, and they put out to exercise their bodies. That way they end up well-rounded."

"They shall end up well-rounded if you forget your sheaths."

Philippe saw the three of them convulsed in laughter; those were good days before he lost his faith in man. Philippe sighed deeply and shook his head. That the Philosophes were men of genius could not be doubted. They were right on most matters, that too was beyond question. Equality before the law must be established for all men, even the lowest of peasants. Torture is inhumane. War is barbaric, and worse, absurd. And yet. And yet.

Disillusionment is like erosion, a gradual wearing away. It is not like a flood where the torrent comes but gradually recedes, leaving things as they were before. It is not a wind storm which strikes but in the aftermath leaves damage which can be repaired. Erosion cuts gullies which endure and widen and are cut to new depths. It began, he remembered, with his discovery that Diderot was a pensioner of Catherine the Great, barbaric Empress of the wilderness of snow, murderess of her husband Tsar Peter! Philippe saw letters M. Diderot sent the Empress. "Great Princess, I prostrate myself at your feet; I reach out my arms to you. I would speak to you but my soul faints, my mind grows cloudy, my thoughts become confused, my heart melts like a child!" He wrote this paean for an introduction Catherine wrote for her proposed new law code (a law code which never was written). "In her new code the best of codes!" his master effused, "She has reformed everything!" Philippe was shocked by such extravagant praise. Catherine proposed a code to improve the lot of the serfs, but the condition of their lives grew worse. Voltaire, too, was a paid lackey of Catherine and of Prussian Frederick as well. For years those two danced a minuet of insincerity, flattery, praise and hypocrisy. War, denounced in Candide, was praised in secret letters. "Madame," Voltaire told Catherine, "Your Imperial Majesty restores me to life by slaying the Turks." He approved her slaughter of Polish Catholics as well and begged Frederick, "in the name of the human race to whom you have become a necessity, take care of so precious a health!" Diderot and Voltaire waged war against L'infame, and yet said nothing to Catherine who acted as defender of the Orthodox faith. Here was yet another cause of his breech with Francois. For Francois, the last laugh belonged to the Philosophes who were subsidized in their assaults upon the monarchs by the very monarchs they attacked. Philippe was not at all sure this was the case. It appeared to him that the Philosophes were being used to legitimize the activities of Monarchs who were less than enlightened both in their political and moral activities. Worse, how could anyone take the criticisms of the establishment and the general reform program of the Enlightenment seriously when it was clear that leading Philosophes were in bed with the very culprits held responsible for the dismal conditions of man and society?

Philippe refocused on the street scenes. There were sharp pains in his stomach, the usual aftermath of too much alcohol and too little food, which he desired to quell with breakfast. And he craved coffee! He went unsteadily down the steps and shouted for Le Grosse. "I shall return directly." The fat man nodded. Another time, Philippe would ask himself why the man was not at work, but he was occupied at this moment by thoughts of breakfast. He sought a boulangerie which did not appear too squalid, the baker too dirty. Finding one to his satisfaction at last, he ordered bread, cheese and milk, which he drank on the spot. He took the chunk of cheese and the fresh loaf and began to walk, searching for a place to take his meal which would contribute to his mood and his digestion. Philippe's peregrinations took him finally to the bank of the Seine. He sat and watched the myriad activities conducted here – poor women drawing their water, others bathing, washer women rubbing clothes with rocks and, within their sight, municipal scavengers discharging the collected refused of the chamber pots into the river. Why wait for Francois, he asked himself? Why not leave the city and take ship for England? Two men and a woman would make flight far more difficult. Philippe tossed bits of the loaf into the water and watched carp rise and snap for the bread. Their blunt ugly faces and aggressive behavior reminded him of too many people he encountered in the street. What did he owe Francois? Their differences were not superficial; they were profound.

Francois believed, really believed, that men would shed their old values and adopt those of the Philosophes as easily as a snake sheds its skin. Christianity was completely discredited in his eyes. The Bible was inaccurate as history, the theology absurd, the clergy corrupt, its practices dangerous to men and to the thought of men. There was one simple thing to do, as Voltaire suggested, "Ecraze l'infame!" Simple indeed. Christianity would not be so easily defeated. Whatever the abuses of faith were, it offered men the hope of eternal life. The persistence of that radiant hope was more important than some minor difficulties. A Christian culture could not become an unchristian culture overnight. Grimm wrote: "It has taken centuries to subdue the human race to the tyrannical yoke of priests: it will take centuries and a series of efforts and successes to secure its freedom." The dead hand of Galen thwarted advances in medicine for fourteen centuries until the great Boerhaave and Sydenham brought Newtonian insight to the healing arts. But prejudices in favor of the ancient and familiar die hard, and the extended hands of the dead Christ contained a more soothing balm than Galen.

Philippe scratched his ear and yawned and finally smiled. "I have a terrible time keeping the faith," he said to himself. "First I break with the Church, then with the Philosophes, and now with Francois. Is it right to look to myself and not consider the fate of my friend and partner? Perhaps he is searching for me. No decision will be made until we have talked." Philippe strolled, enjoying some scenes, criticizing others – the lack of sanitation, the physical mutilation of criminals, the professional writers, symbols of the abysmal igornance of the average Frenchman haggling with their customers over price and realized his most immediate fear was that he would be embraced by the proprietor again. He was surprised when "Le Grosse" followed him up the steps. Philippe heard someone moving about inside the room and assumed it was Francois. He entered, ready with a cheery greeting and found a wolf-faced man whom he recognized as the most loathed and feared informer in France. "M. Monde, we meet at last. A pleasure, Monsieur."

"What do you want with me, Lucas?"

"Want with you? I assure you, nothing. The worthy Inspector d'Hemery is eloquent in your defense. He insists you have nothing to do with the appalling filth which spews forth from the presses of Paris and from your press. It is all your partner's doing, the Inspector insists. Now I would prefer to see both of you named in warrants, or to have both of your names circulating as men sought by the Quality – they pay cash, you understand – but d'Hemery insists you receive different treatment. You are to tell me where Francois Girard may be located and agree to prepare a document listing his crimes, and you will be permitted to leave France without interference."

Philippe demanded, "What crimes must I specify?"

"Only those," Lucas smiles, "which he has actually committed or it can be made to appear he has committed."

"Will he be sentenced to death?"

Lucas replied, languidly, yawning, "That I cannot say. He shall certainly die if the Quality find him before he can be arrested. You will perform a service for him, M. Monde, and for yourself as well. My men, and the inspector's men and other spies and informers of whom you have no knowledge are watching the gates, the coffee houses, theaters, and homes of patrons. There really is no escape possible."

"Francois is an active man, Monsieur Lucas, and there are half a million Parisians. Surely among all of these one may lose oneself."

"Surely," Lucas smiles, "and yet, here I am. And, until last night I knew the location of Francois as well. He has not returned to the brothel."

"What guarantee do you offer that the betrayal of Francois will result in my being released?"

"You have my word."

Philippe convulsed with laughter. "Pardon me, Monsieur, that was rude."

"Not at all, Monsieur, I did not take you for a fool." Rene withdrew a document from his breast pocket, which he unfolded and showed Philippe. "You are guaranteed safe passage from Paris by Inspector d'Hemery himself."

"May I have some time to think?"

"No, Monsieur, that I may not permit you. Hesitation puts your friend's life at risk. He will be shot dead or knifed should his enemies find him before the police, and worst of all he will be of no value to me. Compose the document. Be accurate in what you write; give him the benefit of the doubt where you can. Plead his case effectively and all may yet go well for him. I will even suggest to him that he blame the blasphemy and libel on you, and since you will not be there to defend yourself, the court will listen. Most importantly, remember, he has done this to himself, if Inspector d'Hemery is correct. You need not feel ill at ease. Now, however, you must write. Prepare the document or submit to arrest." Lucas rose and signaled "Le Grosse." The two men advanced upon Philippe.

The Loyalist

Revolutionary America

The American Revolution frequently appears in the pages of history texts as a kind of immaculate conception. The English national debt doubled during the French and Indian War (Seven Years War in Europe), and much of the expense was generated by war in the Americas. To ask the lightly taxed American colonials to contribute to their own defense was hardly the act of a tyrannical government. The American response, however, caught the mother country offguard. Meanwhile, as we tell the story, Americans of vision – Adams, Franklin, Jefferson and Washington – realized English rule of the colonies could not long be maintained. Here there was no aristocracy, and no established church; the franchise was broadly distributed and English mercantile regulations were largely ignored. Then came the Tea Act which provoked the Boston Tea Party, and that the Coercive Acts which lead to the calling of the First Continental Congress, and the rest followed like gears meshing in a machine bringing the inevitable revolution. Such an interpretation ignores the fact long known by historians that about one third of Americans supported the Revolution, about one third opposed and about one third didn't care. It ignores the machinations of revolutionaries, like Samuel Adams, who actively provoked revolution and were willing to intimidate those who failed to support them. As free born Englishmen, the colonists had rights guaranteed by English law and constitution; a revolution was a great leap into the constitutional dark. Revolution would disrupt trade. Most Americans, independent farmers, probably would not have been directly affected much. Taxes would have increased without a revolution, but their tax burden after independence was greater than ever since the British taxpayer was no longer subsidizing the army and navy. In those days of small professional armies, limited movement, and rural isola-

59

tion, *the great events of the day could occur without affecting much of the population. Why, then, become involved in the affair? What moves some individuals to forsake the routine and be swept into the great acts of history? In addition to exploring these questions,* **The Loyalist** *examines daily life in the North American colonies.*

  The Loyalist *tells of Jeremiah Roote and his family, working their farm on the Massachusetts frontier far from the contentious and belligerent citizens of Boston. His sons, however, have caught the contagion, calling themselves Americans, denouncing the King, and rejecting their fathers' politics. Josiah Roote, the oldest, lives and works in Boston, and admires Adams, Hancock and the rest. He is informed by his employer, Mr. Thomas, that British authority may punish Boston and that war is a possibility. Meanwhile, in tranquillity, Jeremiah's family continues through the cycle of the agricultural year until an event occurs which teaches him perhaps the great events of the day cannot be avoided after all.*

"Damn!" Was the share of the plow broken or had it simply been deflected? "Probably broken," he said in disgust. "New England," he scoffed, looking across his rock strewn fields, first, then raising his gaze to the distant Berkshire mountains. "All the stone of England broken in pieces and distributed on and under my land, maybe." He took some pleasure in recalling Berkshires back home, were swine. The mountains, he mused, must have been named by some other transplanted Englishman who cursed the stones which filled his fields. His oxen stood still waiting for him to indicate his pleasure with the reins. Jeremiah waited too. A thorough examination of the share would require unhitching the team; since there was nothing for them to graze on, he would have to take them to the wood lot and tie them up. It would be better to take the share back to the shed, feed the beasts, and begin again after supper. Pork was in the pot with the potatoes, carrots, turnips, and onions. Lots of onions, he hoped. Jeremiah flicked the reins and clucked, and the ponderous beasts turned back toward the house.

  "Pa's coming!"

  "Something must be wrong," Sarah told her son. "Go and see to your sister, Jared. She's at the Baxter place, and I don't want her coming back alone. Bears 'ill be hungry after their winter in the caves."

"Yes, Mother." He came in through the shed, deposited an armload of wood near the great orderly pile, dry and drying, then entered the kitchen and took down the long rifle from its rack over the fireplace. He picked up a powder horn and the skin bag which contained wads and ball from the top of the cabinet. "Ground could be too wet, or Pa might just be hungry today."

"More reason to get your sister. And take this gingerbread to them."

"Why's Miz Baxter teaching Annie to quilt, Ma? You do it well as she."

"Prudence Baxter's stitching holds better than mine, but she takes fewer stitches. I asked her to teach Annie so the child can work on them, like a trade, and contribute to the family. She can teach me the stitch, too."

"You better teach Annie all you know, too, Ma. She's pretty, like you, and they'll be paying her court soon."

"Just who will be paying her court soon, some of your friends?"

"No, well, none definite. I just hear compliments paid her."

Jeremiah's boot thumped, one, two, in the shed.

"Be off with you, now, Jared." The boy swung the rifle up over his shoulder, nearly knocking the candle molds filled with cooling wax from the table. "Be careful, boy."

Jared exited through the shed, without speaking to his father who cleaned the share with a shovel and was closely examining it for damage. The boy breathed deeply, filling his nose with the wonderful smells of spring. He smiled at the turquoise sky, whistled at a robin, and walked as quickly as he could toward the Baxter's. There was no sign of older brother Jonathan who should have been checking the orchard for winter damage and mending the fence. Beyond the orchard were other farms and beyond those, the Berkshires. Unlike his father who viewed them as an inconvenience to travel and ugly to boot, Jared thought the mountains beautiful. He loved to watch them, when the sun moved over them in the west, change colors as the light struck here and now there, picking out certain trees, or illuminating rock formations. Rocks. Damn the things. Instead of hunting in the Berkshires, Jared was doomed to spend the next weeks ruining his back picking up the rocks and moving them to the waste. One might suppose the things were alive and that they migrated back to the fields from which they'd been removed. Every year they picked and piled, and the following year they would pick and pile again. "Cursed be the ground because of you; in toil shall you eat of it all the days of your life; thorns and thistles shall it bring forth to you, and you shall eat the plants of the field." Jared wondered that the Lord forgot to mention the rocks. The boy climbed upon the wall which separated their land from the Baxter's place and saw, gleaming in the sunlight, the barrel of a rifle pointing east. Jared froze and his eyes followed the barrel across the Baxter's arable, past their meadow and into their wood lot. He saw nothing; at what was Jonathan taking aim? Suddenly his brother shouted, "The Redcoats! The Redcoats are running!"

Jared cupped his hands and warned, "You'd better not let father hear such talk," but then continued his journey to the Baxter's. Father and mother expected their children to be prompt in carrying out their chores.

Jonathan reckoned he killed forty of the sheep, or Redcoats he got in his sights. The others withdrew in not very good order before his withering fire. He put his piece over his shoulder and marched parallel with the wall. It was in remarkable repair this year. Winter and critters had hardly touched it. There was little damage to the orchard as well. A few major limbs were broken, but the younger trees especially were intact. Someone would have to cut down the oldest, remove the stumps, and seed and then nurture the young seedlings. But really, Jared could do it without him and he could join Josiah in Boston. They needed men like himself in Boston, now that it was coming to a showdown.

Back at the house, Sarah found the quiet eerie. Oh, there was Jeremiah banging about in the shed, but the children were all gone. The children were all gone. Soon that might be true. She shook her head rejecting the thought. Annie and Jared were babes yet, and the betrothal of Patience Baxter to Jonathan, though certain, was not fixed in time. Jonathan wanted to visit his brother in Boston, to see the great city for himself, and to hear about the great issues of the day. "Sam Adams, Mother, and John Hancock, Josiah sees them every day! He knows the men we sent to the Stamp Act Congress. Great men, Mother."

"Traitors," his father corrected, "disloyal to their King and contemptuous of the law. The lot of them ought to be arrested." Sarah shook herself again. It was surprising how often she found herself thinking rather than working. Here was the table unset and the broadcloth for her husband's new coat on the loom, and she pausing for thought.

For nineteen years, she had risen before dawn in winter, with the sun in summer, to clean, launder, iron, mend, and watch the children. She made candles and soap, combed and carded wool and flax, spun, weaved, dyed, made sausages, baked, brewed beer, helped bottle the cider, pickled and preserved, worked in her garden, and taught the children their letters and their Bible. She prepared their main meal at noon and a simple supper about six. In the evening she sewed, knitted, and supervised her growing children and lastly kept them in order while her husband led the family prayers. The chickens and geese and bees, too, she tended. It was a hard life, Sarah thought, but a good one. "My Annie will find it so." Josiah suggested his parents send Annie to visit him in the city. Jeremiah objected that a decent girl wouldn't be safe there. "Lead us not into temptation." It might well be an easier life for her there, wife of some great man with servants to direct. She looked about her own kitchen. They had four chairs about the table which matched and two which did not. Sarah cooked over an open hearth and had to revive the fire first thing each morning. Annie could invite us to visit, she thought, and felt guilty about having secret complaints about her lot in life.

Jeremiah, too, was deep in reverie. He found the share was not broken, not even damaged. He was happy at the discovery but disgusted at having lost half a day's work. After twenty years work at farming, he remained distrustful of the land, the seed, and the weather. Jeremiah peered from his window and saw all; there was nothing here that was more than the eye could absorb. He had known such days. The Rootes were a family from the west coast of England, bred to the sea. He followed his brothers to the merchant service, started as a cabin boy and worked his way to seaman. He had passed through Gibraltar and walked streets in the Holy Land. Voyages had taken him from the icy Baltic where furs and timber were traded to the Cape of Storms where his Captain, finding the ship not fit for the long voyage, turned back from the Indies rather than ask help from the Dutch at Cape Province. He returned home after each voyage and gave half his pay to his parents, rested, and took another ship. Then came the day he approached his village he could see it still – and wondered at the lack of activity on the road. The only sounds were the harsh caws of ravens and the fierce growls of dogs. In the field, the animals grazed as though no one tended them. On the village streets, he saw waves, black undulating waves, which shifted right and left as he watched, and rose in waves as the dogs charged at them. Their flight uncovered the bodies, or rather the remains of bodies, being devoured by crows and dogs lying about the street. Plague had come. Jeremiah wheeled and walked away. The bodies of his parents must remain where they had fallen. He would risk neither beasts nor infection. That failure tormented the man, though it was far from certain he made the wrong decision. He spent the next year trying to find his brothers, making inquiries at each port, but without a central home it was not possible. He took ship bound for America, though it was late in the season and sailed west across the Atlantic. Not one day was clear. The swell stood her almost perpendicular on her stern, then dropped her, and the bow dived toward the bottom of the sea. Up and down ceaselessly she was tossed. Men not roped to the deck lay tight together in the cabin for comfort, crying and praying that God would grant them release by taking the ship for the sea. They reached Boston, but Jeremiah never returned to the sea. He tried to live in the city, but all of those souls packed so tightly together reminded him of that cabin. And so he bought some land, found a good woman, and began a new life. In retrospect, settlement in Virginia or the Carolinas would have been better.

From a purely practical perspective, the soil was better there, and from a political perspective, there were more Anglicans. As relations with the Mother Country deteriorated, members of his creed were suspected of a conspiracy to install the established faith in the colonies. Jeremiah understood the Quebec Act which legitimized the Papist Creed in Canada arose from the recent war with France. Canada, now British territory, was Catholic. Parliament acted in the best interest of all concerned and even demonstrated religious toleration by the passage of the Act. New England interpreted the Act with calculated perversity, as Parliament asserting its authority to establish religion wherever and whenever it decided to do so. "New England would interpret the King sneezing as an insult."

Jared and Annie came in view, and he watched them wave to Jonathan, who joined them. The three walked to the house. It was a relief to see them all here under his watch and care. He wished Josiah was here with them, working the land, but the lad was different, ambitious, determined to be someone in the colony. His parents possessed the good sense not to try to hold him back. Jeremiah went with his son to Boston to find a place as an apprentice in a printer's shop. Immediately he sensed the danger there. Printers and those who associated with them were the worst of the radicals and malcontents; ner-do-wells hung out there making a penny delivering the slop spewed forth from the bowels of colonial Grub Street. The arch-devil Samuel Adams himself wrote a newspaper, and even wrote letters to himself in his capacity as editor, though he never signed them, of course. Adams was stirring up the rabble for no good purpose. Josiah would become involved in all of it, that was plain. His son insisted upon calling himself an American, despite his father's objection that there was no such creature. "We are all free born Englishmen, there is no other thing." The boy, man, he corrected himself, insisted upon interpreting every act of Parliament as an evil. When Josiah was but six years old, Pontiac's uprising occurred, and Parliament wisely responded with a Proclamation Line. The logic was quite simple. Since the colonists objected to taxes which paid for troops deployed in the colonies, and the taxpayer at home was already heavily burdened by the cost of past colonial wars, and since without a law to the contrary the colonists would follow the savages into the wilderness and seize their land, Parliament created a boundary for the colonies and a refuge for the Indian nations so that both could live in peace with neither threatened. A great squeal arose from certain colonial criminals and speculators, men from Virginia and Connecticut, who had established fraudulent land companies to sell Indian land to yokels. Good solid farmers, like himself, applauded the restrictions since competition from new lands, doubtless more fertile than New England, would be reduced and, besides, less land meant a greater supply of hired hands. Among the speculators and miscreants who damned Parliament was a land surveyor named Washington. Josiah could not or would not see that the world was far more complicated than he chose to believe.

"Franklin, your hero, obtained commissions for his friends to be Stamp Duty Collectors. He changed his mind only when he saw which way the wind blew. You regard him as an honorable man?"

"You don't understand these things, Father; the world is changing."

"The change makes it possible for you to revere a flagrant turncoat like Franklin?"

"Doctor Franklin is a great man and a patriot."

"But during the Stamp Act controversy."

"That, Father is past history," Josiah told him, with the condescending smile one reserved for the village idiot.

"And what about your hero Adams? I know a man who was in Boston in 1746 when his father was denied a seat in Council because of his seditious views. It was then young Sam entered the legislature and began his scurrilous policy of attacking Governor Shirley. Not from principle do these Adams act but from the disappointment of office seekers."

"That is your opinion, Father." Jeremiah remembered that he could feel himself flush as the blood surged into his cheeks. Even now he clenched his fingers. "Father. Father," Annie gently pushed his shoulder. Mother has the table ready. You're to come." Jeremiah nodded and received his daughter's kiss on the cheek. He followed her into the kitchen, dipped his hands in the warm water and soaped them, dried them and then sat down at the table. He performed the grace then sat back and smiled at each member of his family in turn.

"Father," Jonathan began, "the orchard is undamaged and the wall stands upright. Do you think I might visit Josiah in Boston? He invited me, you know."

Mr. Samuel Adams considered the grievances of Boston which had festered for forty years. The origin of the present discontent lay not ten years ago, nay not even twenty. The British had mistreated Massachusetts for two generations and more. While Bostonians huddled in their homes before empty hearths during the long winters; while Bostonians denied themselves the warmth and joy of a good fire; while Bostonians scrimped on food and piled on clothing because fuel was so dear, royal navy press gangs continued to take sailors from wood boats so that contractors refused to send them to Boston. The government at London refused to hear complaints. Parliament's arbitrary actions ruined colonial commerce and colonial merchants. In 1740, London suddenly restricted the use of paper money, and many businessmen never regained sums they were owed by customers. Further manipulation of the currency occurred in 1750 and again just a few years ago in 1764. Without money, and there was never enough gold or silver, colonial commerce was reduced to barter, which prevented expansion. All of this was done at the behest of London merchants and bankers whom WE exist to serve, who complained about the "cheap paper money" they received from the colonials for payment of debt. Grenville's regulation of commerce, the enforcement of the Molasses Act, the hated Stamp duties, and then the Townshend taxation of necessities, all demonstrated the Americans must suffer under the economic direction of the British. Massachusetts's men were generous and forgiving. Financial grievances could not melt the ties of blood, but callous disregard of blood could. New England men came forward to fight in campaign after campaign. One Yankee out of ten survived the disastrous assault on Cartagena; five vessels carried the Massachusetts men to Jamaica; one was sufficient to bring them back. New England reduced Louisburg at considerable sacrifice, and London returned it to France. Colonials, like colonial trade, were expendable. And now there were British officers in Boston, whoring and seducing innocent girls, fighting on the streets, and openly ridiculing the idea of heaven. Why should New England have truck with such as these? Adams smiled and sipped his flip; his newspaper articles would reduce these issues to a basic formula, easily remembered and cleverly recited. The colonials must be made aware of past abuses and fearful of future British grabs of wealth and power. He would inform them, inflame them, and finally direct them to the creation of a new nation. Adams studied his list and penned his article, then he tore the compilation in two and lay the pieces on his fire. Sam Adams was not a man to leave evidence of his activities.

Josiah Roote loved Boston and told all he knew it was impossible not to love Boston. It was the most beautiful city in the whole world and one of the most modern. Bostonians taxed themselves to place drains and sewers under the streets. Streets were paved. Had the streets actually been paved with gold, the effect upon Josiah, when he first entered Boston, could not have been more profound. The roads which led from his father's farm to Boston and now from Boston back to the farm were dirt and gravel. There was no maintenance performed to regrade them, or cut back the brush which threatened to reclaim them for the wilderness. Country roads were empty; Boston streets teemed with life. Chimney sweepers, wood sawers, merchants, ladies, priests, carts, horses, and coaches clattered over the pavement. It was impossible to think on such streets. His mind was diverted by new objects of sight or sound.

In Faneuil Hall, the central Boston market, one could find the produce of the entire Bay Colony and townsmen plying the stalls for the best quality fruits, vegetables, cheeses and meats. Everything was tended in the city. Farmers' carts and trucks were of standard weight and size less the pavement be damaged. Chimneys were required to be swept, and the law vigorously enforced after the fire of '60. Property was protected while Bostonians were abed by the Watch which also maintained ten fire engines. The Boston companies were famous throughout the colonies for prompt arrival and competent work. Josiah loved to walk about the outskirts of Boston as well. In quaint villages like Cambridge where Harvard College was located, the mansions of the Olivers, Lees, Borlands, and Vassalls stood on five or ten acres of land. The houses were grand, graceful, solid. The life there, too, must be grand, Josiah concluded. Over the roads were trees leaning (need it be said?) gracefully, lending shade and proper dignity. The roads were so wide that those walking had room even while carriages charged past. He could not imagine a more perfect spot in the entire world and had the opportunity to enjoy it often since Christ Church was there. Josiah's one regret was that he would never be able to sit on the benches in Harvard College and hear the learned discharge the contents of their minds to their students, empty vessels, waiting anxiously for the intoxication of learning. "But my children will be there someday. My children shall be schooled in Boston at the South Grammar, one of the most distinguished institutions in these colonies." Who could possibly mind paying taxes to such a community as this?

"Josiah! We cannot print until you finish composing the text and it's a lengthy piece. Get to it, lad." Mr. Thomas smiled at him and returned to recording his orders, or keeping his accounts. Josiah picked out the letters, one by one, spaced them, punctuated with his composing stick, and then locked them into the form. He quickly rechecked each letter, knowing well that Mr. Thomas would recheck them one last time before he inked them, and would examine the first copy for errors. "Tommy Thomas, you busy yourself, too. The shelves need stocking and arranging." Josiah finished the word "Danger" and glanced at Tommy, happy that he was freed from laboring on the stock. The printing office carried stationery, legal blanks, writing paper, ink, inkwells, sealing wax and wafers, slates and slate pencils, pocketbooks, razor straps, quills and even wallpaper. There were volumes on every subject, some of which Mr. Thomas printed himself, and on the walls engravings for sale! Josiah had purchased two of the engravings for himself, one of Mr. Adams, another of Mr. Hancock. He sent "Adams' likeness" to Jonathan who, he imagined, kept it hidden from his father. He wanted his brothers to know these great men of Boston and Massachusetts who were leading their fellows toward the creation of a new world.

Timothy Thomas Esq., proprietor of the shop, was constantly surprised by the ineptitude of the British authorities whose offenses against the colonials were, more and more frequently, the subject of his editorials. Since the last war against France, it appeared the intention of His Majesty's government was to enrage his American subjects. Historically the home government never enforced much of the law by which the colonies were, in theory, regulated. Authority winked at smuggling and at colonial manufacture which produced pots, pans, and most household goods, though these were supposed to be imported from England. Then, for reasons of which he was only dimly aware, a Pandora's box of legislative plagues spewed forth from London. The Royal Navy was charged with monitoring the coasts for smugglers. The Proclamation Line was decreed to force the colonials to hug the coast where they could be supplied with British goods and punished if they manufactured themselves. Currency acts from London devastated colonial trade and forced many to resort to barter. Then came that colossal piece of foolishness, The Stamp Act. Parliament with one stroke united the most prosperous, best educated, and most articulate men in the colonies – lawyers, merchants, publishers and printers by requiring a stamp on every newspaper. Here was subtle censorship, disguised as a revenue act, which smacked of the French monarchy! True, London backed down, but then came the Townshend duties and finally troops arrived in Boston in 1768. No step threatened LIBERTY more seriously than this establishment of a standing army among them. Yet this was not the end. The new Board of Custom was empowered to issue writs of assistance and general warrants! A man's home might be searched and his goods seized at the whim of foreign magistrates. Here was tyranny indeed. Proof of all such accusations was in the pudding, and all of these ingredients blended by George III produced a massacre in Boston. Mr. Thomas involuntarily shuddered recalling Mr. Adams' action upon that unhappy occasion. He had the bodies placed upon a cart and driven throughout the city that all might witness the fruits of British rule. "Tommy, those shelves are not yet stocked. See to it lad. You may not go out until you have finished." Timothy pushed himself back from his desk and rose. "Josiah, is the copy ready for my inspection?"

"One moment more, Master Thomas."

Tim Thomas was especially interested in the document about to come from the press. It was about tea, India Company tea, which was now bobbing on the waves of Boston Harbor. The broadsheet which urged Bostonians not to purchase the tea had been written by Samuel Adams before the 'red Indians' dumped it overboard. Now there was no tea to purchase. Samuel Adams and his Sons of Liberty were the chief suspects, but the printed piece was evidence of his innocence. Why pay for printing a plea against the tea if you knew there would be no tea? Still, when he saw Adams the evening before, Sam winked and asked if he were turning over any new leaves.

Timothy didn't understand, then.

Later that afternoon Mr. Samuel Adams was in a public house, listening to the good natured jibes about Indians come to Boston and sipping his rum punch. There was nothing out of the ordinary to be seen. The Teneriffe, Vidonia, and Madeira wines were flowing, as were the domestic ciders, beers, applejack, and the house specialty, a particularly potent peach brandy. Games of backgammon, billiards, and darts were being pursued with typically Bostonian daring and good nature. Some drank coffee and read newspapers. Others, like Mr. Adams, came principally for conversation.

"But what will they do now, Sam?"

"What will they do now? They will give in as they have before." Mr. Adams paused and took a deep draught of punch and wiped his mouth with his hand, a common touch appreciated by his audience. "What did they do when we rejected the Stamp duties?"

"Backed down," said William Sheaffe.

"When Governor Bernard told the Assembly not to convene, we resisted and he. . ."

"Backed down," said Cadwallader Colden.

"And when we refused to buy their goods while the Townshend duties were collected?"

"They backed down again," concluded Ebenezer Mackintosh and a chorus of voices, who began to enjoy the game.

"And they'll do so one more time," insisted Adams. Benjamin Edes of the *Boston Gazette* led the conversation while Adams went to have his glass filled. Privately Sam wondered whether the British would act as he calculated they would. The King never pushed events to a major confrontation with his subjects. The colonists employed force, beatings, tar and featherings, hanging officials in effigy, even burning ships, and learned from the results the restrained use of force overawed authority. Concessions were wrung from Parliament without much cost. The lesson which Parliament might draw, then, was that sufficient force to coerce the colonies must be mustered in order to avoid having to exert too much force. Give them a real show of power, though do not actually employ it, and they will back down. But what would happen if both of the parties misread the resolve and intentions of the other? What if they confronted one another and left no ground for either to maneuver away from the confrontation? What would happen then? Mr. Adams knew. He had worked toward such a conflict for fifteen years. Sam returned to his table, slapped Cadwallader on the shoulder and proclaimed, "They'll never hold their ground against us."

About the time Mr. Adams was making that observation, Jeremiah announced, "It will be a longish trip, this six miles."

"It would have been faster with the horses," Jonathan stated flatly with the impatience of youth.

"Aye, but the rain reduced the roads to mud and ruts. Do you choose to be the one pushing behind the wheels and lifting the frame in your best clothes if we get stuck? Trust the oxen and your father."

"What compels Squire Dobbs to have an open house at this time of year, when the first work of the season is to be done and the weather yet inhospitable?"

"Tis an ancient custom we honor, the May Day. At home it was the time for games and sports and the setting of the Maypole. People gathered flowers and hawthorn to decorate their houses, and a Queen of that May was crowned. That would be you, Annie dear."

"Oh, Father," she said blushing.

"May from Maius, Latin, probably Maia, goddess of growth and increase."

"Well, well, Jared, you are mastering your lessons indeed."

"Yes," he retorted, "though what my lessons have to do with plowing, or milking, or fencing or hunting, I don't see."

"Father plans to send us to Boston to join Josiah, Jared, so that we may make our fortunes. Don't you, Father."

"I do not!" Jeremiah shouted at Jonathan, "as you know from past conversation." The boys were startled by his vehemence since he rarely raised his voice. "The city is a place of sin, ill-gotten gain, drinking, whoremongering, and who can guess what other abominations. I like not having Josiah there. I'm damned if any of my other children shall set foot in the place!"

"Jeremiah, hush, the children."

"The children know my mind on this matter and like dutiful children must obey. We shall divide our land and find place for Jonathan, Jared and their wives and children. If we need more land we shall save and purchase it. We shall all be together here, as was intended for families to be, and hope that Josiah comes home to us."

The oxen were slow in their movements at the best of times. The mud caused them to work hard, grunting as they lifted one leg from the mud and placed down another, lugging the cart which itself squeaked and cracked. Birds were excessively communicative, sending such messages as they judged necessary before finding their nests at the close of the day. All of the Rootes were grateful for the cacophony since silence after Jeremiah's explosion would have been dreadful. "Explain the Squire's conduct to your children as is your duty, husband." Sarah had considered her question well. It distracted Jeremiah from his anger and drew him back to the virtues of life on the land."

"Squire Dobbs has no obligation to entertain us all, but in so doing he continues one of the ways by which this country is held together. Oh, formally we are bound by law, but what makes a real community is people linked together by admiration and affection and by a recognition that when an act of providence or a man's industry carries him to a height above the common lot of men, we ought not be jealous or spiteful. The good fortune of one man is the good fortune of us all; for the community prospers as each of its members prospers, and the advancement of each man leads to the advancement of all. It is like those beautiful sweaters your mother knits where all the yarn is worked in individual segments but interconnects to form a perfect whole. By insuring good law and good order, Squire Dobbs promotes the welfare of us all."

"You are a thoughtful man, husband."

"Thank you, Sarah."

She smiled at him. "I was thinking of the extra hay in the cart; the children will want to crawl down into its warmth on our return."

"We will probably be asked to stay the night, as is his custom."

"Perhaps, but Mistress Dobbs has not been well, the flux it is said, though it may be worse."

"Here come the Redcoats attacking the wagon! Fire!" shouted Jared. Jonathan pushed his brother under the hay. "Hush," he ordered. "Father will be furious." Jeremiah turned with anger on his lips, but Sarah put her hand on his shoulder. "Tis but the game of youth. They do not understand."

"Do you understand," he said crossly, "that they take the part of traitors to their country?"

"They do not understand which is their country. They are children, Jeremiah, who have not been to Boston. How are they to understand that England, weeks across the sea, is their country?"

Annie, her voice thin and pure, began a lovely English ballad which she learned from her mother, who had learned it from her mother in an unbroken chain which stretched across time and the very ocean which separated the vast new continent and the mother country. The song, thought Jeremiah, demonstrated the falseness of the assertion that the ocean was a barrier. The best parts of people were easily transported across time and distance for thought and feeling knew no barriers. The other children joined in the singing and so did Sarah. His wife's voice was a distant reflection of his daughter's, not so clear and precise an instrument as he remembered it once had been. He squeezed her hand and wished the apple blossoms in the orchards that dotted the way were open to fill the air with their potent perfume. It was a sweet moment.

The circular drive which led to the Squire's house was already filled with carts and carriages. The hobbled animals fed together, grateful to rest after their arduous work. Sarah and the children, the boys wildly screaming, Annie waiting demurely for her mother, went up to the house, while Jeremiah unyoked the team and took them into the paddock. Jeremiah greeted his neighbors, lent a hand where he could, and then went to find his host. Though he had been coming to the house for years now, Jeremiah was impressed again by its size and quality and remembered the configuration of the rooms. The main door entered upon a central hall which ran from front to back. There were six large chimneys on the roof reflecting the existence of a fireplace in each of the sitting rooms and each of the bedrooms on the second floor. The parlor, about the size of his entire first floor, contained a pianoforte from London, a mahogany secretary – the center of Mistress Dobbs' social and charitable functions – a card table, sofa, silver tea set, and child's tea set. This, though a formal room, was nevertheless a cheerful room, not a showpiece. Then there was the sitting room, the everyday gathering place, with the chairs drawn close to the fireplace and open books on the tables. The arrangement of the furniture here was less formal, far more work-a-day. Presiding over this room was the portrait of the family patriarch, Salem Dobbs. In the dining room was a splendidly carved table and chairs, a matching sideboard, and English bone china and silver. The last room on the first floor was the ballroom with the curious figure of the All-Seeing Eye painted upon a pitch black ceiling. Jeremiah understood that Squire Dobbs, like his ancestors whose portraits lined the lower hall, was a Mason. The sound of a reel spilled from the ballroom, blending with and yet distinct from the laughter of children in the sitting room. A strange raucous voice shouted; the sound of pounding followed, then more laughing. Jeremiah stepped into the room and picked out Jared and Jonathan sitting in rapt attention before Mr. Punch and Judy. He guessed Sarah and probably Annie would be in the kitchen, though his daughter might well be on the arm of a suitor in the ballroom. His place was in the parlor with the men. The room was crowded but quiet he thought as he acknowledged the winks and nods of friends and neighbors whose attention was given to a stranger. "Mr. Robert Hewes," he was told, "is traveling through the colonies to prepare an accurate report for Parliament."

"Your best cultivated lands here," said that gentleman, "cannot be distinguished from those at home. They have a cheerful, enclosed prospect. One difference is that I never see beggars here; all your inhabitants seem well-fed, well-clothed and well-lodged. My host," he bowed to Squire Dobbs, "lives in the style of an English gentleman, though better since there are no titled aristocrats to bother him, no church tithes, no poor rates. You have increasing trade, navigation, fisheries, rising population, and plenty of land. You have a high price for labor and this makes your young men industrious. They may take a wife and begin their families with excellent hope for advancement."

"You make it," said Jeremiah, "sound like a paradise."

"A paradise with red Indians and other minor discomforts."

"Even a picnic's plagued with red ants," remarked Ebenezer Goodrich, and the room filled with laughter.

"Why, Mr. Hewes, does Parliament afflict us?" inquired John McClellan.

"Sir, Parliament does no such thing. Parliament expects all Englishmen to obey the law. What does she find in these colonies but smugglers, like your Mr. Hancock, who flouts his illegalities in the face of authority. It finds men like your Mr. Adams who make spurious arguments about taxation, King, and Parliament. Parliament, Sir, granted a charter of liberties to Massachusetts and may, by an exercise of authority, cancel them. And yet, Mr. Adams would have you believe this same Parliament cannot do so simple a thing as create a tax for all Englishmen. You seek the protection of British arms, but you evade payment of the taxes which keep them in readiness against the Catholic powers, France and Spain. What government, Sirs, can afford to grant its citizens the right to decide which laws it will choose to honor and which it will choose to reject? There was silence in the room.

"Where then, Sir," inquired Jeremiah, "comes this discontent in New England? Surely reasonable men will consent to taxation when the benefit is so clear."

"I will tell you, though it will not make me popular amongst you to do so. You have a black regiment here of dissenting clergy who are active for rebellion. They prefer talk to hard work and so became men of the cloth and from that status look down on their fellows every Sunday and have gained from that experience such overwhelming self-importance they look down on all men every day. Dependent on the mob for their daily bread, nonetheless, they have taken the view of the rabble and the worst of the rabble at that, those at Boston. In the streets they have gleaned sedition, and from the pulpit they sow the seeds of further sedition which bears fruit in the streets." Voices though low, were clearly expressing their disapproval with Hewes' appraisal.

They gathered volume, like the thunder of an approaching storm, until Peter Edes virtually shouted, "Do you deny there is a conspiracy to impose upon us the Church of England, to strip us of religious freedom, and to accustom us to rule from above? Do you deny that a bishop is selected who will be sent to New England for this very purpose?"

"I do deny it," Hewes calmly replied, "with all my heart." Fists were shaken at the Britisher and more denunciations hurled. Liar was the least offensive. Men rose and left the room after demonstratively turning their backs, backsides in fact, to the speaker. Hewes smiled through it all and remained perfectly polite.

"There has been talk of a bishop for the colonies, Sir," Jeremiah stated.

"I did not deny that. There are many Church of England men in New England and in the southern territories Virginia, Carolina – the brethern constitute a majority of the citizens. Do they not deserve the same spiritual leadership which their counterparts have in England? Is that not a cause for dispute between us, that the Mother Country treats you unfairly?"

Jeremiah smiled, but he was alone. Those about him, his friends and neighbors, grumbled, "Pettifogger," at Mr. Hewes, who was not gaining popularity.

"It is time to go and dance with our ladies," Squire Dobbs announced. The parlor cleared rapidly. Dobbs took Jeremiah aside at the doorway and introduced him to the traveler. "Mr. Hewes, Mr. Roote."

"A pleasure, Sir," said Jeremiah.

"The pleasure is mine, Sir, I assure you," insisted Hewes. "You did not seem offended by my remarks."

"I was not, Mr. Hewes. Your views and my own are in agreement."

"And conform to my own," added Squire Dobbs. "We must speak of this again."

Jeremiah excused himself and went into the sitting room to check upon his boys. The stage was there, the puppets lay before it as though exhausted by the performance, but the children were gone. Roote went back into the hall and was informed, "The youngsters are outside playing Indians. The Master assigned members of the household to watch them. Reassured, Jeremiah went to find his wife. Sarah was in the arms of Tom Dulany, who was their nearest neighbor. Dulany, a bear of a man, was called upon by the whole community for help in removing stumps. Susan, his wife, watched the two whirl about the room until she found herself in the arms of Jeremiah and on the floor.

"May I have the honor, Ma'am?"

"You have already taken the liberty, Sir," she told him laughing. "The line has formed all evening about Annie, Jeremiah. Squire Dobbs' boy is regularly among her partners."

"Who is that pockmarked runt she dances with now?" he inquired. "Oh, it's that Daniel Dulany. She must have given that poor dull boy a turn from pity."

Susan pretended to look cross. The music stopped, the dancers applauded and thanked one another. Then Susan said, "Excuse me, Sir, I must go and cut your wife."

"Permit me," he extended his arm, "I wish to speak to the wench myself."

"If you please," Susan addressed Sarah, "I wish to trade this man for a better one."

"And if I will not trade," Sarah clutched Tom Dulany's arm, "what then?"

"Why then your parents and children shall be disgraced and your husband cast into the wilderness. Would you be the cause of these manifold misfortunes?" Hands clapped; feet thundered on the floor; the fiddle commenced, followed by the other instruments.

Jeremiah took his wife in his arms and into the very center of the floor. "Let them eat their hearts out when they see me with the most graceful dancer and the most beautiful wife."

"How many women have you brought with you tonight?" Sarah teased.

"Only one, the only one." Sarah kissed him, raising eyebrows throughout the room. "You have one rival."

"Annie." Sarah shook her head in wonder. "Remember that awkward child who was all arms and legs and could not coordinate them?"

"Blast!" he exclaimed.

Squire Dobbs stood at the door and proclaimed, "Come and seat yourselves at the table." Jeremiah and Sarah stood together as the room cleared, watching their daughter decline invitations and seek out her parents with her eyes. She joined them but continued to glance over her shoulder.

"Watching for Indians, Annie?"

"No, Father," she said and appealed to her mother with her eyes.

"They're waiting for us, Jeremiah," she said. "Let us join our friends," and she led him from the ballroom while Annie, safe from her father's teasing, followed.

"Here, we have saved space!" Jeremiah and Sarah sat, as expected, with their neighbors – the Dulanys and Frothinghams, the Hunts and Evelyns, the Gridleys and Hawleys. After some talk about weather and crops, the conversation turned to the metropolis.

"George wants to go to Harvard, next year," announced Samuel Gridley.

"Do you think that wise, Sam? I hear Professor Winthrop explains that earthquakes, lightning, and hale are caused by nature rather than being Divine in their origin."

"Tis but vexatious rumor and no more," retorted George. "No man can imagine free thinking at Harvard."

"What do you want to do with your life, George? Study divinity? The law?"

"I would rather be brought up to a profession where there was a chance of being honest than to the law," the young man responded.

"My son shall never go to Boston. I have heard," John Hawley's voice became a whisper, "they have taken to cards and dice on the Sabbath, and one can even find drunks on the street on the Lord's day."

76

"While we prepare beans on Saturday that we will not even have to cook on Sabbath," Elizabeth Hawley added, not without a note of satisfaction.

"Damn their impertinence!" shouted Gil Frothingham. "You are treating them too lightly; they treat us with contempt. Rustics, they call us, bumpkins. They put on airs in their speech. 'Naishur,' they say for nature, and 'susetem' for system. Holiness is no longer numbered among the words they employ; all is now virtue."

"Virtue has to do with man, not God," Hawley observed.

"They have abandoned God in Boston," Elizabeth concluded triumphantly, and anticipated a chorus of "amens."

"Boston is the great sewer into which all of the filth of this colony drains and festers," said Jeremiah.

"But your Josiah is there, and there are other good men there as well. You are being intemperate, Jeremiah," Tom Dulany stated. The conversation now swung in the praise of Boston. Streets drained by sewers and lighted after dark, goods from around the world gathered in one market, and night life, these were the attractions of the great city. And one had to admit Boston was well-regulated. The Watch patrolled the streets; the lighters had the lamps burning at dusk and extinguished at dawn. These were formidable undertakings. "And," Tom Dulany noted, "Masters Otis, Hutchinson, and Adams have made our case fairly and well to ourselves and to Parliament."

"Aye," Frothingham agreed, "we must not and will not permit the King to crush liberty in this land."

"King and Parliament threaten not our liberty. Adams is a dissembler, and Otis a madman as you all know. Imagine the babe new from the womb who seizes and cuts the cord which binds him to his mother, spattering both with blood. This is what these men would have you do in breaking with England."

Sarah placed a restraining arm upon her husband. "Your opinions are not popular in these matters," but Tom Dulany clapped him on the back, "We are all proud to number Jeremiah among our friends, now and forever. His opinions be damned, among us are ties that bind." Sarah smiled with pleasure both at the sentiments Tom expressed and because she had never seen her husband blush.

Squire Dobbs walked to the front of the room and raised his hands for silence. "Friends, the hour is late. I regret our hospitality must be curtailed this year for reasons known well to you all. Please carry the prayers and best wishes of my good wife and I as you plant your seed and nurture your crops until we gather again to celebrate the harvest. I have asked Doctor Chauncy to lead a recessional."

That hoary man of God took his place next to Dobbs and began, in a thunderous bass, "Now thank we all our God! With heart and hand and voices!" All joined Chauncy and were moved with joy and fellowship. The warmth remained with them as the children huddled under the straw, or squeezed together on the seat, speaking softly, while fathers guided the teams.

Rain again. There was rain and chill for eleven straight days. Josiah imagined his father, standing at the window, watching his furrows become rivulets, drowning the germinating seeds, breaking the fragile roots, or carrying them to barren ground. Jeremiah would open and close his large, hard hands in impatience and anger but could do nothing. The young man was himself angered by the articles he was composing. The city fathers accused farmers, like his father, of selling dead meat – sheep, cattle and fowl – in Boston at prices charged for properly slaughtered animals. "The bumpkins," it said, "take advantage of us at precisely the time when the commodities we sell them, the salt, sugar, molasses, and cotton are less dear than ever. Businesses are closing in Boston as merchants are caught between customers, usually rustics habitually delinquent in their payments, and creditors in England who ruthlessly press their demands for payment." Josiah could not imagine why Mr. Thomas would choose to publish such a piece now. There were rumors flying in the city about the intentions of those who commanded the British regulars. Surely this was a time for all AMERICANS, the term was circulating and gaining popularity, to unite. On other issues as well, Mr. Thomas was pressing forward with the customary concerns of Bostonians. He congratulated the community on its determination to retain the schools at the present level, even though they absorbed more than a third of the town's entire budget. "The education of the children is of the greatest importance to Boston," the selectmen affirmed, and Mr. Thomas proudly agreed. He pointed out how much circulation of the written word had increased in Boston and its environs. There were more booksellers to distribute sermons, pamphlets, almanacs, magazines, and broadsides; there were post riders and carriers to circulate newspapers which were read aloud in taverns, coffee houses, and parsonages. Then came the sobering news.

Boston Alms House was filled, as were virtually all of the city churches, with men who had been thrown out of work by the closing of the port of Boston and their families. The closing of the port was the British reprisal for the destruction of the tea. "Boston has long served as an example of public benevolence to her sister colonies, but we can no longer do so until the crisis is passed. The selectmen recently authorized the investigation of all strangers to prevent the overburdening of the taxpayers of Boston. All ablebodied men will be returned to their native villages. In addition, our sister colonies have rallied to our aid with gifts of money, grain, and livestock, though even that may yet prove insufficient. Boston which has known hard times shall, we fear, do so again. Drawing upon those same reserves of strength and virtue as our Fathers, let us put our backs to the wheel and make the best of it. Let's go forward!"

Josiah shivered with pride and determination as he completed reading the piece. The attack upon rural New Englanders angered and perplexed him still. Mr. Thomas sat at his desk as usual, his face darkened by thought. Such looks usually betokened he was at work on the accounts, but that could not be the case today. Josiah knew it would be best not to disturb him, but he felt compelled to understand his Master's motives for running that piece at this time. "Sir?"

Mr. Thomas looked up, removed his spectacles, rubbed his eyes and responded, "Yes, lad?"

"What you wrote here?"

Mr. Thomas smiled. "You want to know why I denounced your sort of people?"

"Yes."

"It may be difficult for you to grasp, Josiah, and you won't like it. I don't like it myself."

"Then, why, please?"

"Listen closely, Josiah, and interrupt freely. In the summer of 1768, Mr. Sam Adams, in the name of our liberty, called upon the merchants of Boston to boycott British goods. We were defending our liberty by demonstrating how loss of our commerce would hurt their merchants. Do you follow me, boy?" Josiah nodded. "The boycott, to be effective, had to be complete." Adams and his brawnier lieutenants visited merchants and asked them to observe voluntarily. There were those who were loyal to the crown and told Adams so. There were others who wished to be permitted to make an honest living. Many, perhaps even the majority of Bostonians, saw Adams and Hancock, Rowe and Malcomb as dangerous fanatics. It mattered not. Those conservative, law abiding gentlemen who wished simply to be left alone, or to honor the crown, experienced suspicious fires in their warehouses, mysterious accidents broke windows in their homes, and hitherto unknown currents sunk their merchant men, or carried them to the open sea. The glorious cause of liberty was advanced by the most grotesque forms of intimidation and harassment. Have you followed me so far?" Josiah again nodded, and opened his mouth as if to speak but did not. Mr. Thomas continued, "Events, great events, do not simply happen, Josiah. They are caused by the actions of men. Sam Adams, Patrick Henry, and the others have led us, and are leading us to a break with England, and to independence for these colonies. Few men could, and fewer still would, think that far."

Josiah's head jerked as though he was struck in the face. Mr. Thomas halted. He saw the lad struggle with these new ideas. Josiah thought that the events which occurred since 1768, events he could recite well, happened, just happened, and that the path the colonies took was ordained by God. That this path was the consequence of men, rebels or demagogues their opponents called them, that made everything different. "I understand, Josiah, you must think about these matters, but let me continue for now and be done with it. Some years later, Mr. Adams circulated a rumor that kindling was being gathered that Boston might be burned rather than occupied by British regulars. There were no such plans, but no one knew whether the rumor be true or not. We armed and assembled before the Governor's mansion as a warning. It was done to impress the Governor and his generals and to demonstrate our resolve. So it is with my attack upon the rural folk. Boston is about to suffer for her acts done in the name and interest of the thirteen colonies. How long the oppression will continue, and who will rally to our aid, only time shall reveal. I shall travel to Philadelphia tomorrow to make some inquiries at the behest of Mr. Adams. Meanwhile, the duty of this paper is to unify Boston by voicing our concerns, like our being victimized by 'bumpkins'," Mr. Thomas winked at the youth to disarm the sting of the word, "and celebrating our strengths. We tell our citizens they are like Horatius at the bridge, a tower of strength standing between the other colonies and British tyranny."

Josiah could not concentrate on Master Thomas' words. Events which happened seemed inevitable and therefore right. Events which happened because of God or fate, or circumstances or whatever could not be otherwise, and that bestowed upon them acceptability. "It was meant to happen," everyone said. But here were men taking upon themselves to create, what, thirteen new nations? They were conspirators against King, Parliament, governor, and judges. Could all of these authorities be in the wrong and Masters Adams, Hancock, Henry, and the rest be right? Did mere men have the right to wreck governments? Could men do so without bringing chaos to society? Who would respect law once the source of law, King and Parliament, were overthrown? The law protected the weak against the strong. Who would perform that function? Would Massachusetts become a jungle where men killed or were killed? And what would happen if the rebellion were successful? Might not the colonies turn upon themselves to establish which would be dominant, dictating orders to the rest after the parent country was expelled? Josiah was frightened.

"I'm sorry, Josiah," Mr. Thomas put an arm about his shoulder, "but you'll have to work now, and think after this piece is finished. We must have this off the press and distributed before I leave the shop this day."

"Yes, Sir. Sorry, Master Thomas." Timothy moved beside the youth and began to assemble the letters. "You go home for the three weeks I'll be gone, Josiah. Go home and be with your parents, brothers and sister. Talk with them about what you know and what you have heard. When you return to Boston, well, the world may have turned upside down."

"What do you mean, Sir?"

"I will be blunt. You may find, upon your return, that we are at war with England. If that be the case, Boston will suffer. It may be no gay, prosperous city when you return. It may be occupied, completely occupied, by British soldiers, governed by British generals, dominated by British men-of-war, their guns trained upon us. If you return, you may be caught in a struggle which must afflict you. Loss of life and limb is possible if you fight with the Americans; loss of your father is certain. I know his opinions. Your father will argue that you should remain with your family. Perhaps you should. I would mourn you as I would my own son." Thomas paused and drew in a deep breath. "And now, let us have a competition to see who can set more words." For the rest of the day, his master was uncharacteristically silent. That evening, he gave the youth wages for the weeks he would be in Philadelphia, and bid him take care on his journey home. Josiah did not hear Master Thomas leave the next morning.

Home was about one hundred and thirty miles from Boston. If he walked for ten hours, allowing time for rest and refreshment, he should be home on the fourth day. Josiah rejected traveling by coach; he sought conversation on the great issues of the moment from a variety of his fellow citizens. When he left the shop, after securing the shutters and checking the doors, the streets of the city seemed normal. A habitual drunk had been sentenced to walk about in a barrel, the drunkard's cloak. Mr. Symthe, found guilty of selling spoiled fish as good, wore a necklace of dead smelts as he wrote out the sign announcing the catch of the day. Josiah even saw Mr. Samuel Adams on the street talking with laboring men, doubtless Sons of Liberty. The rumor circulated, as ever, that Adams would soon be arrested and sent to England for trial. This be a slow pace for a long journey, he thought to himself, and quickened his steps.

Josiah slowed again while he walked along the banks of the Charles. Here were the homes of fashionable Boston. Thick and verdant lawns could be seen through dense clumps of woods, spared the axe to guarantee the privacy of the inhabitants. Graceful three story mansions were surrounded by outbuildings – servants' quarters, stables, barns, and other necessary structures. Nothing short of the New Jerusalem could be so beautiful. Josiah heard the clatter of a coach and team coming toward him from Boston. As there was plenty of room for himself and the vehicle, Josiah continued to observe his surroundings. The coach slowed as the horses approached him, and the driver carefully gave him room. Then, much to the youth's surprise, it stopped. The driver looked down and smiled at Josiah. "It's Master Roote?" Josiah nodded. "Well, Sir, you might as well ride with me and your handiwork. Mr. Adams has paid to circulate these papers you printed yesterday."

Josiah said, "Thank you, Sir," and joined the driver. "How far are you going?"

"Mr. Adams wants the paper distributed to towns and villages and public houses within twenty miles of Boston. I'm going fifteen miles yonder before I turn north. I'm Wheat that grows in town. Donald Wheat."

"You're a Son of Liberty?"

"Proud to be," Wheat affirmed, and they spent some pleasant hours in political discussion. The sun was well up in the sky, and the youth's thoughts turned to dinner. There was a public house he knew about two miles further, The Cross Roads, which prepared an ordinary at a fixed price and time, as well as meals cooked to order. With three weeks' wages in his pocket Josiah felt rich, but he would not be extravagant. The ordinary was the working man's choice. "A penny saved is a penny earned." Josiah thanked Mr. Wheat for the ride, and carried a load of papers into the inn. He found the meal was excellent, the conversation was not. There was no interest in Boston or in the events which were transpiring at breakneck pace. The talk was about the difficulties of travel, of the delays the weather created in planting the crops, and of the mating of prize bulls. Josiah was happy to go back to the road. The land through which he traveled was not wilderness but well-cultivated. There were woodlands to be sure, but these were integral to the farms of which they were part. There were also villages irregularly located and inhabited. Some had grown up about the intersection of rivers or roads, others about a commercial enterprise like a water mill. Josiah was nearly through one such village when the church bells suddenly rang in unison. Within minutes, the commons were filled with armed men of all ages, more than half of whom came from the countryside on horseback. Josiah counted fifty. The leader, Captain Parker, congratulated them and then sent them back to their work. About half of them lingered, and the youth discovered that these were related to the Captain by blood or marriage. Resistance to the British or the Indians was a family enterprise. He thought about his own family and determined to add a few extra miles before settling down to sleep.

Had it been one month later, Josiah would have slept under the stars, but spring nights retained some of the bite of the long winter. He would seek shelter in a barn along the way. "Tis not too early to inquire," he said. Pink and white dogwood, magnolia, and forsythia were in bloom while the elms showed only a trace of bud. A preacher might well derive a homily upon the dazzling but short life of the impudent which flower and are gone, and the long, stately, powerful development of the patient, from the trees. How varied was the commonwealth of trees: elms, maples, oak, birch, aspen, pine, tammarch. Yet they dwelt together in peace. How different was man. What was to be done with the Catholics? Sam Adams feared them. Their recognition of the Pope, he argued, introduced an imperium in imperio, government within a government, which must lead directly to the worst anarchy and confusion, civil discord, war, and bloodshed. New England Protestants feared Anglicanism but did not trust the intentions of rival Protestant sects. A sharp breeze come suddenly from nowhere suggested to Josiah the trees did not favor being compared with humans who acted far less reasonably than they and prodded him to find accommodations. A mile back from the road, a house surrounded and dwarfed by great elms stood on a gentle rise. Josiah left the road and headed for the house.

It was almost evening the following day when he acquired a traveling companion. Josiah was resting. His muscles, though strong, were accustomed to life in the city which did not include walking such distances. The blisters on his feet developed that first day did not help either. He was seated, his feet dangling over the water into which he lowered them periodically on a covered bridge. He breathed deeply, taking air through his nose, filling his lungs and realized how he missed the salt and fish smells of the sea, and the sea.

"Do you live hereabouts?"

"Beg your pardon," Josiah said, responding to a voice. He could not see the person asking the question who stood under the cover of the bridge in the shade.

"I said, do you live hereabouts?"

"No, about twenty-five miles from here, as the crow flies."

"What if the crow is walking?"

"The same," Josiah smiled.

"Would the crow like company? My name is Peter, and Bennington is my destination." The youth sat next to Josiah. Peter wore his blond hair rather short. His gray eyes looked alert enough and Josiah liked his ready smile.

"Bennington lies directly north of my parents' farm by one hundred miles and more. I'm grateful for the company, Peter," he said.

"You can't have been shopping since you come back with your hands empty, and therefore you must either have been visiting relatives, or you've lost your job."

"My master is traveling, and he released me for some weeks."

"Ah," said Peter.

Josiah wiped his feet and pulled on his socks and boots. "Shall we begin?"

"I'll follow you," Peter told him.

They were not walking long before Josiah observed, "You're a seafaring man." He thought a fearful look came into the boy's eye, but it may have been a reaction to the light.

"Why do you say that?"

"Your sea legs are pretty obvious."

"I followed the sea for some time, but now long to feel solid earth beneath my feet."

"As did my father."

"Aye?"

"Yes, he'll enjoy talking with you. You're English?" That look appeared again.

"Aren't you?"

"Not the same way." They maintained a rapid pace, and the miles passed unnoticed. Peter enthralled Josiah with his tales of the sea and of the lands he had visited until late in the evening. Near sunset, they came to a stone wall Josiah remembered well. On the other side of the fence were three trees which stood as a triangle with the tree at the center pointing toward the house.

"Yours," said Peter.

"Why do you say that?"

"You wear the expression sailors get when they spy the home port."

"Come on." There was musket fire, but Josiah was not alarmed. "Father is teaching the boys and probably Annie to shoot. He likes them to practice at this time of day when the shifting light plays tricks on the eyes. Teaches better concentration, he says." A dog barked from behind the house then made an appearance on their right and charged now, barking frantically.

"He'll twist his tail clean off," said Peter.

"Not old Nobbs," Josiah said, as the dog planted his feet firmly on the youth's chest, knocking him down.

"Nobbs! Nobbs! Get away, blast you," shouted Jeremiah. "Get him off the man, Jared."

"Father, it's Josiah!" Annie, who held a rifle, slammed the stock against the ground in her excitement, and the hammer snapped forward discharging the piece."

Jonathan and Jared took up the cry, "Josiah!

"Jonathan, go tell your mother your brother has come home," Jeremiah said.

Nobbs ran back and forth between Jeremiah, the cluster of his children, and the stranger. Jeremiah waited for his wife and watched his younger children throw their arms about Josiah. Sarah, still wearing her apron, came through the door and joined her husband. Together they went down to greet their son.

"Mother," Josiah said and with unusual formality hugged and kissed her.

My son is maturing, thought Jeremiah; he behaves with restraint as a man should in the presence of strangers. His boy then extended his hand and said, "Father."

Jeremiah took the hand solemnly, then laughed and caught his son between his arms, lifting him off he ground. "Welcome home, Lad!"

Josiah, his feet again on the ground, introduced his companion. "Peter Sudbury, meet my family. I'm certain their names are familiar to you by now."

"Mistress," said Peter to Sarah. "Sir," he said, bowing to Jeremiah. "Jonathan, Jared, and Ann," he smiled at each of them in turn. Annie, Jeremiah noticed, flushed and looked at the ground; he did not remember any young man ever having such an effect upon the girl.

"You must be tired and hungry," Sarah stated, and neither of the travelers disagreed. "Take your guest to the house, Josiah. Children," she continued, "see the farm is ready for the night." Jonathan, Jared, and Annie went to attend to their chores. Then she turned to Jeremiah and warned, "Your son is here to visit his parents and family. Don't you talk of Boston or England.

And do not try to convince him to remain with us. Your son is old enough and man enough to make his own decisions. And."

"Enough wife! You do not want me to talk with the boy at all; you want him all to yourself." She put her arm through his as they walked to the house. "But what are we to feed them? It is too late to slaughter the fatted beast."

"Fetch a ham from the smoke house. I'll tend to the rest."

"Put on the kettle," he said, as she entered the house, and he went to retrieve the meat.

As Sarah bent over the hearth to stir the soup, she realized it would be difficult to speak with Josiah and his friend until the younger children were abed. Jonathan and Jared wanted to hear about life in Boston and the possibility of war. "We'll lick 'em easy enough," Jared concluded.

Peter shook his head. "Your cities, I've seen them, are pretty and bustling, but they would all, buildings and people, disappear in London. You have no idea of the reserves of manpower and money that would be pitted against you."

"We'll lick 'em anyway," Jared insisted.

"No more about wars," Sarah ordered.

"Tell me about life in Boston, Josiah. I hope to join you there."

"What, Jon? I thought you were one foot down the aisle with Patience Baxter."

"Indeed, but Patience and I want a different way of life. She will wait while I serve an apprenticeship, then we shall marry."

"And to whom are you apprenticed?"

"Mr. Harbottle Dorr, the baker. He's agreed to send me to night school as well. Education and trade are arranged."

"Congratulations, Jon! It's a splendid plan and an excellent trade! Why didn't I hear about this before now?"

"And I," demanded Sarah.

"Heard about what?" asked Jeremiah, placing the ham on the table. He smiled at Sarah and at his children gathered safely under his roof.

"I have arranged to move to Boston, Father. I am apprenticed to Mr. Dorr, a baker."

"You have planned! You have arranged!" Jeremiah's face darkened, and he straightened his shoulders. His fingers were fists. "I forbid it!" If a display of parental fury was supposed to move the child to break and back down, Jeremiah was disappointed.

The youth stated flatly, "Father, I love and respect you, but I must make my own way. This life is not the life my wife nor I desire." Jeremiah's open hand was drawn back to smite his son.

"No!" Sarah screamed. "Husband, don't! Please," her voice became a whisper.

"He that spares the rod, hates his son," her husband retorted but did not deliver the blow. Tears covered the eyes of both father and son. Jared began to cry.

"Tis a good thing you don't come often, Josiah," observed Peter, "or you would have no family left." It was a gamble, breaking a tense deadlock that way, but Sudbury had seen it work many times aboard ship.

Jeremiah placed his arm upon Jon's shoulder and softly stated, "We shall speak more about this decision of yours." The tea kettle lid exploded upward and flew across the room, discharging boiling water. Peter grabbed a shawl from the back of a chair to cover the open top of the kettle and removed it from the flames. "You are a right, lad," Jeremiah told Peter. "Do you need employment? It seems I need help on the farm." He turned to Jonathan and added, sternly, "Do not think you have heard the end of this yet."

"But your father is wise enough to know," Sarah observed, "his sons take after himself, pig-headed and stubborn, and you have to make the best of a bad lot." She watched her husband smile from the corner of her eye. "And now, if all is well, I'd like to feed these boys before they faint." Annie jumped to help her mother, setting plates, then silver, placing the cups and filling them with cider. Mr. Sudbury came first in each of these operations, a fact overlooked by neither parent.

"Father, let us begin the discussion we must have so no cloud shall hang over the rest of my visit. Let me observe that you do now what no person in Boston will do, drink East India Tea."

"And why is that?"

"The reasons are twofold. First, because even now it floats on the ocean; it was taken and dumped in the sea. Second, because it constituted an illegal tax which we would not pay."

"A good Englishman loyally pays his taxes levied legally by Parliament."

"WE are not Englishmen; we are Americans. Father, the ocean stands between us and London. Here we have liberty: no king, no noblemen, no established church. We are not and can not be Englishmen."

"Your father is an Englishman."

"That," said Josiah, "is only because he has not yet become an American.

He shall, in time."

"You treat loyalty as if it were a bit of fashion one discards after a time. It is not so, especially not so with me. Let us assume, however, that I was capable of such an act, the critical question would be why should I give up a familiar King and Parliament which must and shall restrict their acts and respect my liberties as required by the Ancient Constitution, by Magna Carta and Bill of Rights for a new government bound by neither law nor tradition? Who shall see to the preservation of our liberty then?"

"We shall make a new government that does so?"

"And which of these men you so admire, Mr. Adams, Mr. Henry, shall be a new Cromwell?"

Josiah hesitated. Sam Adams intimidated his political opponents, and when that failed, employed force against them. These were bitter facts. Certainly it was done for a good cause, but was this not the logic of all tyrants? "No general shall rule here; it will not happen that way."

"So you hope."

"The King, Father, is become a tyrant. He pays governors who send home our legislators and will not permit them to act. This is tyranny! He declares legal writs for searches and seizures of unspecified objects and dispatches hordes of placemen to enforce them. This is tyranny! Why don't you see this, Father?"

"Your Boston merchants smuggle, and your Boston citizens protect them. The law is not enforced by local authorities. What alternative do King and Parliament have but to act in this manner?"

"Father, it comes down to this. We in Boston and most of the citizens of Massachusetts believe King and Parliament are seduced by power and mean to destroy our liberty. There shall be a war, and we mean to defend our liberty. The Redcoats are not sent here to fight Indians. Father, to save their empire, the English will raise the savages and the slaves. They will give them license to kill us. The Redcoats will terrorize our towns, the slaves and Indians the countryside."

"Josiah, the British soldier is disciplined and civilized. He does not rape, loot, or burn. You are conjuring demons who do not exist. Remember the alleged massacre in Boston. The individuals responsible were put on trial for their lives."

"This is different, Father; this will be war."

"Josiah, even if I agreed with you about dangers from the soldiers, which I do not, we are one hundred and fifty miles from Boston. We shall not see even one British soldier. As for savages and slaves, how many slaves are there in Massachusetts?"

"Savages?"

Jeremiah rubbed the stubble on his face. "Your father is not an unlettered man. I read books and newspapers and maps. Indians may, may mind you, pose a threat to the upper valleys of New York, but this is Massachusetts. A war will not affect our frontier, and that is why I ask you, Josiah, to stay home until this has passed from us. Then if you must go and live in the city, I will offer no objection."

"Father, since I am to recognize and to respect your love and loyalty to what you believe is your country, you can do no less for me. You may serve your country by not taking arms against her, and I must serve mine by taking arms against yours." The candles were burned to stumps below the tops of the holders. Sarah, hours earlier, had carried Jared to his bed. Both men became silent. Jeremiah turned to Peter and inquired, "What about you, Master Sudbury? It appears my sons are determined to leave me short of help. Would you be willing to stay through harvest?"

"Well, my uncle, in truth, does not expect me. He pledged his brother, my father, to look after me, and doubtless will do his duty. I have sailed half my life on English ships and only recently been discharged here, so I have done my duty to one, cannot yet owe the other. Gladly will I stay through harvest."

"That's settled then," said Jeremiah. "And now, having temporarily resolved these and other grave matters, to bed. You will find a bed, Peter, on the platform over the stall we keep empty for calfing and foaling."

"I'll show him, Father," Josiah stated.

"Good night, children," responded Sarah and her husband.

If ever a man had right to rejoice and to mourn, it was Jeremiah Roote. With his sons at home, the major work of the season was completed without strain and the time lost to spring rain recovered. They turned to preparation for the long winter and cords of wood were cut and stacked. Repairs Jeremiah had long contemplated for the house and barn were undertaken and accomplished. The boys turned then to hunting and fishing and the fruits of their endeavors were smoked or salted. Another half acre was cleared from the wood lot and more fruit trees planted. "If ever there were ungrateful children," Jeremiah told them as they rested from pulling stumps, "I am surrounded by them. They get me accustomed to their labor, I grow soft from inactivity, and then they leave me. You will bare the responsibility for making your mother a widow."

"We shall leave a full larder, an expanded orchard, and a superior worker you may entice to stay on."

"Or Annie may entice to stay on." Josiah winked at his father while Peter blushed. "Did you think we did not noticed how you stare at our sister, and how she returns your attention?"

"I can pack and be gone, Sir, if you think I have been forward with Mistress Ann, or if I displease you in any way."

"Peter, you cannot see a joke where Annie is involved," Jeremiah said. "If you are as serious as you appear, you shall have the opportunity to take the measure of your rivals when our neighbors arrive to celebrate the new orchard. Many have designs upon the lass, though she shows no interest in the lot of them. Go on now all of you and look sharp when the company's here!"

And they did look sharp. Jeremiah thought his boys, and he included Peter, were the likeliest looking of them all. Josiah teased Patience and Jonathan, Annie and Peter. It was good natured, though the victims were not amused. Again and again Annie rejected partners, reserving her dances for Peter. Finally her mother intervened, insisting such conduct was not proper. Annie danced with boys she had known all her life, but her attention remained on Peter. The caller, at the prompting of his host, demanded that Peter, recently of the Navy, come forward and demonstrate his skills in a hornpipe. Space was made and the youth found himself the center of attention. The musicians began and Peter's rapid, vigorous, but agile steps won their approval. The assembled company were surprised when the music stopped to hear, faintly at first, drums. Someone was, apparently, coming to join the party and bringing more musicians. No, this music was official not joyous, military not civilian. Jeremiah was distressed to find the troops appeared ready for action. Their bayonets were fixed; their eyes were cautious. Jeremiah went to greet the officers.

"Good evening, Captain."

"Good evening, Sir. I'll come right to the point. We are searching for deserters from the Army and Navy. I will interview the men assembled here."

"There are no such persons here, Captain. What is your name?"

"Forbes. I see no reason to engage in pleasantries. I do not have a pleasant mission. Be good enough to have the young men form a line now, otherwise I shall deploy my troops and conduct the interview under more rigorous conditions."

"Sir, I must protest. Those assembled here are my sons and my neighbors' sons. There are no deserters amongst us."

"That's one there," said a voice from the ranks. "He was in the sails of the ship I come over on."

"Which one?" demanded Forbes.

"The tall one, next to the girl," the soldier pointed at Peter Sudbury.

"Take him," said Forbes, "in irons until the charge be proved or dismissed."

"No!" Annie held him until she was knocked away. Jonathan and Josiah went to his aid and were cracked with rifle butts and barrels. At Forbes' command rifles were leveled on them all.

"Do you see any others here whom you recognize as deserters?"

Another voice said, "One of them you knocked down, the young one, might have been a cabin boy on my ship."

"That is my son, Jonathan; he has never left this farm in his life."

"You previously informed us that you harbored no deserters, isn't that right, Sir? Take him," Forbes ordered. Sarah shouted and rushed the soldiers, hitting and scratching them.

Jeremiah went to the defense of his wife and was cracked on the skull with a rifle butt. "It's a mistake!" he shouted before the blow, "a mistake!"

The horses' front legs scraped at the earth, anxious to depart. Jeremiah and Josiah too were ready for a hard ride. "We shall find the proper authority in Boston, Sarah, and secure Jonathan's release. They have made a mistake."

"And Peter? What if they haven't made a mistake in his case? What shall you say to your daughter?"

"I shall bring them back. Both of them," Jeremiah said, grimly.

"And don't forget to bring me a volume on the rights of free born Englishmen," his wife called after they spurred their horses.

Resurrection

The Resurrection Men and Doctor Knox

Since the description of gravity, Enlightened Europe awaited a Newton of medicine, but progress in the healing art came slowly. When the news of Waterloo arrived in England, Sir Charles Bell, her most distinguished surgeon, departed for Brussels. For the next week, he performed all the capital operations daily until "his clothes were stiff with blood and his arm powerless with the exertion of using the knife." Robert Knox, then a Hospital Assistant, observed that only one of Sir Charles' secondary amputation survived and there was a low opinion of English medicine. Consequently, after the peace of 1815, there was a demand from the Navy and Army Departments as well as the general public for an improvement in medical training. The Royal Colleges of Physicians and Surgeons advocated an expansion of anatomical courses within the medical curriculum. While Parliament approved of the plan, it did not act to make an adequate supply of cadavers for study available. Professors of anatomy continued the practice of buying corpses from grave robbers known as 'resurrection men'. In 1825, Doctor Robert Knox, one of the most original thinkers and gifted teachers of the nineteenth century, began his lectures on human anatomy in Edinburgh, Scotland. Knox took pride in having a 'well stocked table', which translated to a sufficient supply of cadavers for his students to dissect, and the shortage of these specimens meant the Doctor would do business with anyone, no questions asked. In November, 1827, corpses began to be delivered to Knox's assistants at Surgeon's Square by two Irishmen, William Burke and William Hare. On November 1, 1828, Burke and Hare delivered their sixteenth corpse, and were promptly arrested for murder. Because the chest in which the body was delivered had not been opened, neither Knox nor any of his assistants were examined by the Court which *tried Burke and Hare. The citizens of Edinburgh drew their own con-clusions, aided in part by a pamphlet published by Knox's discharged doorkeeper, David Patterson, which stated Knox dealt with Burke and Hare and complemented them on the freshness of their specimens. As the medical profession stumbled toward competence, a panic gripped Europe and America – the fear of burial alive. The attempt to clearly define life and health convinced many that signs of life were being overlooked, and untold numbers were victims of premature burial. In this, argues Philip Aries, we see the first appearance of the great modern fear of death.*

In **Resurrection***, Dr. Alloway, Professor of Anatomy, and cu-rator of the Museum of the Royal College of Surgeons, requires ana-tomical specimens for his students. Unfortunately, the law denies him sufficient supply. The Doctor turns to resurrection men as did his pre-decessors and contemporaries. Two of them, Hodgkins and Brodie, supply corpses which display none of the usual signs of having been secured in the churchyards. Should Alloway and his assistants, espe-cially a committed Christian named McGinty, take their suspicions to the authorities?*

Two sons of Scotland, Duncan and Ferguson, and a foreigner stood for a time in silence until the latter observed, "Surgeons' Square is as pleasant a prospect as one may discover in Edinburgh." He pointed to the great pile of building behind the ornate wrought iron railing, the Royal Medical Society, with its classical columns and pediment over the door. On its left was the famous anatomist Doctor Alloway's quarters and to the left of that was Sur-geons' Hall where the great man delivered his lectures. A variety of trees and shrubs and flowers planted around the semi-circular drive enhanced the beauty of the building and demonstrated the improving effect of the hand of man upon nature. The speaker, obviously a man of some means, wore im-maculate white linen trousers, a blue waistcoat and top hat.

"My name is Duncan, Sir, and I take it you've come for the series of lectures."

"McGinty is my name, Mr. Duncan. I'm pleased to make your acquain-tance. And yes, I've come for the lectures."

"You'll be wanting other britches, bloodstains you know. I'm Ferguson."

"We begin immediately with dissections?" inquired McGinty.

"Indeed," responded Ferguson, "Dr. Alloway prides himself upon keeping a good table."

"He means by that," Duncan explained, "has a sufficient number of specimens for his students to dissect."

"Odd chap, Dr. Alloway, from what I've heard," said McGinty.

"A very great man, Doctor Alloway, as you shall soon discover. Shall we go on to Surgeons' Hall?"

"By all means, Duncan," said McGinty.

They went down the drive, through the fence which enclosed the complex, and into the vast, rambling, open room around which milled several hundred students. Duncan and Ferguson, who were senior students, pushed their way to the front, and McGinty followed them. Scattered about the room, hidden by the throng, were the tables where the students would work directly upon real human structures. It was curious, McGinty thought, how the word "body" was so carefully avoided. They were working on corpses, dead human beings, though one might never know the truth of the matter from Alloway's handbills or from the students themselves. Anatomical specimens was the favored verbiage. McGinty looked at the large gold watch his father, the General, had given him before he left for the foreign, to an Englishman, north. It was eleven o'clock exactly. Anticipation was high. Eyes focused on the various doors through which the great man and his assistants might make their appearance. The students were not disappointed; Alloway and his apostles burst through the door armed with fat volumes and wooden stands, from one of which hung a skeleton, while others held charts or pictures.

"Gentlemen," said the doctor, bowing slightly at the waist. He was a distinctly odd looking person. No hair grew upon the top of his head and that gleaming dome intersected the features of his face almost perpendicularly. The eye sockets were deep, set under the forehead like caves in a cliff. The nose was irregular and the mouth misshapen with the lower jaw, and consequently the lower lip jutted beyond the upper. The short, thick neck was invisible, covered by Alloway's velvet collar and gaudy muslin cravat. His coat and trousers might be worn by a dandy rather than a doctor. "Practical anatomy, gentlemen, that is our course of study here. The structures of the human body, the history and uses of its parts and all with continuous reference to practical medicine and useful surgery. We shall consider the organs in health and in disease. You shall learn by the art of dissection, which in the hands of too many practitioners, some in this city, nay this university, is mere butchery. You shall discover that each tissue has its own sensibility and contractility, its own vital properties which means, gentlemen, that life is the sum of forces that resist death. And now that my assistants have prepared the lecture theater, I shall commence."

Benches set against the walls abruptly filled. Inkwells were perched precariously next to elbows which flailed wildly, scratching the lecturer's words, then rose, dipped, and returned to the paper. The lecturer peregrinated as rapidly as he spoke, now to the right of the hall, now in the center, thumping a chart, now grasping the skeleton to point out a bone, then to the left, back to the chart, and back to the right of the hall. Alloway's eyes burned, and it was clear the lecturer was far away, intoxicated by his subject and his performance at and around the lectern. "And now, gentlemen, we shall have some inquiry into why you have selected to pursue the art of healing. Mr. McGinty, I believe that is your name, Sir. Why are you in this course of lectures?"

McGinty, already impressed by the lecture, was further impressed by Alloway's recollection of his name. He was, it was true, an imposing figure. Darkly handsome and unusually tall, McGinty carried himself like a military man. "My family tradition is service in the Army of India, but my Christian conscience will not sanction killing. I hope to become a regimental surgeon to do my duty to God and country."

"Well done, Sir," said Alloway.

"Here! here!" sounded through the hall.

"You, Sir, why such a sheepish demeanor?"

"Ross is my name, Doctor," said the man so quietly that the students strained to hear his words, "and I am here because of Frankenstein and the clash between the forces of life and death." Laughter filled the hall.

Alloway's eyes flashed with anger. "Is it so foolish, gentlemen, to seek the boundaries between the states of life and death? Today's fiction, even sensational fiction, may be tomorrow's medicine." From the back of the hall a voice observed that there was no mention of reanimation of corpses on Doctor Alloway's prospectus for the course. The doctor himself joined in the laughter. "And yet, gentlemen, any of your forefathers who suggested that the scum of the pox be gathered from sufferers and injected into those lacking the disease in order to ensure their health surely would have perished with witches in the flame. All for science, gentlemen, that is our motto here. Tomorrow for your convenience we shall divide this class into three sections, one of which shall report in the morning, another in the afternoon, and the last at early eve. Good afternoon, gentlemen."

McGinty found himself and his fellows applauding wildly. Doctor Alloway bowed and strode from the room followed by his assistants. "Masterful performance, Doctor, as always," observed Mr. Jeffreys.

"You might approach that Christian soldier fellow and see if he wishes to join our band, Mr. Jeffreys. Mr. Carlisle must be replaced."

"We received a letter from him this very morning," Jeffreys noted. His appointment in London is confirmed, St. Bart's Hospital. Our former colleague's career in the metropolis is well-launched."

"As we who have the privilege to labor here shall experience in our turn," observed Mr. Burns.

"As you deserve, Mr. Burns," Alloway said. "You are the best and the brightest, the hope of modern medicine." At Alloway's door, they found a young serving woman looking wild-eyed and demanding the doctor come at once. "The mistress has need of your services."

"I am not in regular practice, young woman."

"That's all right," she retorted, "as the Master's beyond regular practice anyway; he's stone cold dead."

Doctor Alloway drew himself to full height. "Explain yourself fully. Who do you represent and what is it, exactly, I am called upon to do?"

"Lord Whigmore, Sir, has died, and Lady Whigmore is carrying out his Lordship's instructions. He insisted upon being examined after death."

"Most extraordinary," said Jeffreys. "Will you go round, Sir?"

"Go and tell your mistress I shall be there directly," Alloway ordered, "I must get my bag." The doctor watched the servant curtsy and depart.

"What can this mean, Doctor?"

"You shall observe for yourself, Mr. Jeffreys. Gentlemen," Alloway addressed the others, "please return the exhibits to their accustomed places and take refreshment. Then attend to your duties in the museum. Jeffreys and I shall fully acquaint you with the case upon our return." Doctor Alloway's bag was kept in the study where it was an exhibit rather than a common tool of his trade. Jeffreys retrieved it, and they set off to the home of the apparently extinct Lord Whigmore. "This is not a Scottish gentleman we are called to examine," said Alloway. "Do you know Edinburgh, Jeffreys?"

"I know the streets about Surgeons' Square."

"There is more to it than that. You must get about and see the old and new towns. There is much to learn about man and the doctoring of man in where he lives and how he buries. You shall also find our ablutions on the honorable Whigmore of interest, I'll wager. But here we are."

Above them at the top of a flight of stairs a large black wreath was fixed upon a highly polished oak door. The two men ascended and knocked with the discretion appropriate to this mournful hour and were admitted by the butler, already wearing the black armband, who noted the bag and instructed them, "This way please, gentlemen." There was frantic activity throughout the house. Black crepe was being draped everywhere. Gentlemen, whom Alloway took from their dress and demeanor to be undertakers, sat in the parlor surrounded by boxes of their wares – black edged mourning cards and envelopes, black sealing wax, black ink, brooches, and rings with tombstones, urns, and weeping willows depicted. There were also thick black catalogues which displayed the available coffins and headstones.

"Come on, Jeffreys," Alloway commanded from the landing. "The show cannot go on until we have certified the guest of honor." A flicker of surprise crossed the lips of that otherwise composed gentlemen's gentleman at this illconceived levity. They were led up a beautiful marble staircase and down a long hall carpeted with thick Persians and filled with classical statuary. "Don't look so impressed," Alloway commanded, "he didn't know anything about art, though he may have spoken to them. They provided a shoulder Whigmore could lean on when he was in his cups, a warmer shoulder than Lady Whigmore's, so I've been told."

Lord Whigmore's butler's disapproval was clear in the face he presented to the medical men when he announced, "Her Ladyship is within."

Alloway entered the room and bowed his head perfunctorily to Lady Whigmore then went straight to the body. His deceased Lordship in a splendid dressing gown was propped upon pillows. "Do you wish to observe?" Alloway inquired of Lady Whigmore.

"No, but my son."

"Where is his new Lordship?"

"We have sent for him."

"My obligations, my Lady, dictate that I proceed at once. You may call upon another medical man if that is not satisfactory."

"It is not at all satisfactory but begin if you must."

Alloway placed his bag upon the bed, opened it, and selected a gleaming probe. "I suggest, with respect, your Ladyship withdraw herself temporarily." Alloway waited until the door was closed then thrust the probe into the veins of the upper arm.

"No reaction," Jeffreys observed.

"No blood," said Alloway. The doctor next took a mirror from his bag which he placed under the nostrils of Lord Whigmore. The mirror did not cloud. "No breath either. We may conclude Lord Whigmore is, indeed, dead."

There was a sharp rap upon the door which swung back and a tall, severe looking man with sharp disturbing features and the collar of a clergyman entered. "Ah, the magician has arrived," said Alloway.

Lady Whigmore, standing to the rear of the clerical gentleman, gasped in surprise at this apparent disrespect, though Reverend Milne remained entirely composed. "Your apology at once for Doctor Milne."

"No, no, Lady Whigmore, not at t'all. Mr. Alloway and his habits are wellknown. I take no personal offense."

Doctor Alloway beamed. "That's the spirit, Merlin. You're not here, I assume, to guarantee the resurrection."

"Resurrection of the body is as much your business as mine, I'm told, Mr. Alloway." Alloway's eyes narrowed and his teeth ground together, but his recovery was swift. "Lord Whigmore is yours, Reverend." He turned to Lady Whigmore and stated, "Your husband is unquestionably deceased. You may begin preparation for his interment immediately."

"No Sir, I may not. My husband's instructions on this matter are quite explicit. He is to remain in this room until the evidence of his death is beyond doubt."

"Madame, your husband shall begin to stink directly and to rot not long thereafter. You may, of course, choose to ruin a perfectly good mattress. That is your affair. Lord Whigmore is gone. Of that, there can be no doubt, I stake my reputation upon it." Milne coughed, deliberately and loudly, when Alloway mentioned his reputation and drew a look of hatred from that gentleman. The doctor started for the door but paused to examine a model to the right of the deceased's bed. It was an ornate, high detailed mausoleum, the top of which was covered with a series of bells and mechanical contrivances to assure they would ring. "I see now," said the doctor. "Your husband is one of those who cannot bring himself to believe in his own death. He sleeps but does not die and consequently will awake in his tomb. He shall, what, pull on a string or chain and summon aid, lest he suffocate."

Jeffreys, surprised, inquired, "What do you mean, Doctor?"

"There is a strange delusion in the land which many have come to believe, that their death is the appearance of death only, and that they shall recover in the tomb. Lord Whigmore is one of these I gather."

"You have finished here, Doctor. Give no further offense! Take yourself away!" Milne ordered.

"With pleasure," retorted Doctor Alloway. "Come Jeffreys."

The two medical men were not through the door before Milne crooned, "His time will come, m'Lady. His time will come."

The iron bar had torn his trousers and entered his leg just below the groin, and the wound was bleeding freely. The wound was not deep. He could put weight upon it and was angrier at the damage done to his expensive clothes than to his body. "Damnit all. Damnit all," he repeated to the noseless angels, grinning skulls, and decomposing bodies depicted so well upon the marble and limestone slabs between which he navigated with difficulty. The soil, so often overturned, from which protruded a sufficient quantity and diversity of human bones for an anatomy lesson, clung to his boots and forced him to drag his feet forward. The loud sucking noises from that action disturbed the vast tribe of cats which claimed Greyfriars Cemetery for their own and fed on strange meats. The rain and mist were cold and, when he looked to the cliff and above to the castle upon the cliff, he feared the moon might become visible, and in turn make him visible. Few were as familiar with the church yard as Toad and yet even he was often lost until, as now, a definite point of navigation could be found. It was the still handsome tomb in which, according to tradition, John Knox had taken refuge when chased by the Papists. The new grave was not far now, and now too Toad knew he was not alone. Usually he did not come unless fortified with drink, his mind too numb to contemplate an encounter with a specter wrapped in abhorred garments come forth from the ground. In his haste to be the first one to the grave, he arrived almost sober. Toad raised his dagger shaped wooden shovel to strike a blow.

"Bluidy Mackingie, come oot if ye dar!" chanted the unmistakable voice of a child who stood before the mausoleum of Sir George Mackenzie, the butcher. Toad had often seen this test of nerve administered to younger children, the required initiation into the society of their betters, that is, older children. "Bluidy Mackingie come oot," said the voice again, with rising terror clear in the tone.

Toad gave voice to a howl, a long moaning call of the dead, and in delight heard the child scream, fall, and run. He laughed and slapped his thigh and the pain which shot through his head staggered him and brought him to the ground. "Damn them for their fences to keep out honest men plying an honest trade." So Toad denounced the new barriers placed around Greyfriars for the purpose of excluding men like himself. Then he grunted in success. To his left was loose earth on the fringe around the raised, rectangular earth and the imprints of boots at the center where it had been heartily trampled. Toad laid a canvas sheet nearby to receive the earth and make possible its rapid replacement. Then he dug with the efficiency of experience and the terror of discovery. It was not the law Toad feared, since it was a point of the latter there could be no commerce in dead bodies and hence no prosecution of those who stole them. What he feared was watchful relatives who would beat him with zeal, as had happened before. The wooden implement turned over the earth without clicking or chinking as iron does when it strikes stones. Toad was well-named. He had massive shoulders, chest and arms, though in this last category he had to admit a deficiency of length, like the front legs of his namesake. His legs too were short. In fact, he was all trunk and head. Toad grinned at the top of the coffin and reached down to place two broad iron hooks under the lid. He pulled vigorously upward and was pleased to hear the cracking of the timbers of the lid. Toad stopped and climbed out of the grave and stood upright and walked about. His back and neck would be fully exposed during the next operation, and he wanted neither the watch, nor relatives, nor rivals to find him so. "Nobody about." Toad pulled away the top of the coffin and embraced the corpse which he drew out of its resting place, straining his heavy muscles, bringing it back to the earth it had so recently but not finally departed. He dropped the body without hesitation, stripped away the winding sheet, and replaced it in the coffin along with rocks he'd brought to give the coffin weight. The body was stuffed into a sack. He replaced the coffin top and the ground over it by pushing the soil back into place. Toad hefted the sack over his shoulder, retrieved his tools, and made for that section of the churchyard wall where Mowatt would be waiting with the gig. The moon made another unwelcomed appearance which forced him and his burden to take refuge in a monument where there were three piles of black earth. One of these presented a fibula to unnerve the weak of heart. Toad spoke to the remains with some familiarity, having availed himself of their society upon other occasions. "You're looking well," he observed to mistress Meg, or what he took for that lady, she being the most recently laid to rest. With darkness he again took up the sack and moved as quickly as possible.

"What are ye doing there mon?"

"Resting my horse," replied Mowatt's familiar voice.

"Move along, now." It was an order. The watch with his light and club had found Mowatt. "Get on with you I said."

"He'll be lame because of you," Mowatt whined.

"Ha! Look at the back on that horse; he's raw as meat for the pot. You'll beat him t'death before his legs go. Move or I'll bind you for the Parliament Close and let the gentlemen advocates decide what t'do with you."

"All right then," said Mowatt. The gig creaked as he mounted, and Toad heard him click to his horse to move on. He knew his partner would not go far and walked in the direction the gig moved. Soon the gig would be out of sight of the watch, the body passed over the wall, and the two enterprising gentlemen riding to make their delivery. He thought about the pleasure he would receive from the money, plenty of food, drink and women.

Life was good thought Toad, who heard the gig stop and Mowatt softly call his name. "Here," he said, and then, "clear?"

"Yes, let's have her."

"Coming over," Toad announced and passed it, like sausage in a casing passed across the counter at the butcher shop. Mowatt placed the sack in the gig and climbed into his seat while Toad lifted himself over the wall, smiled at his partner, and joined him.

"Eight pound," Mowatt said, and Toad knew exactly what he was thinking. They conducted their debaucheries together. Mowatt held his horse in check. The gig made a tremendous clatter on the cobblestones which, in the dead of night, was not muffled by the usual commotion of the city. They drove through the deserted streets of the old city into New Town. Rain began to fall as it often did, but neither the gloom nor their cargo bothered the partners at all. They passed the dwellings where the people of fashion sleep as secure as they thought the dead slept in their tombs, past the respectable shops of merchants and tradesmen and the great public buildings on Prince Street to Surgeons' Square where they had business to transact.

Solomon Leith turned in his sleep and hit out with his hand to ward off a blow aimed at his head. What troubled his dreams this night or any night, if his dreams were troubled, he does not remember. He did believe, and often repeated to those who chose to listen, that he could hear the sound of the gig long before it arrived at the Square. The rhythmic cadence, "loud enough to wake the dead," he amused himself thinking, terminated at the door and was followed by footsteps and finally the knock.

Three long spaced blows, heavy enough to shake the stout door, were delivered by Toad, who always smiled and announced "dry goods for the doctor." This night the partners were not kept waiting since Solomon had taken to sleeping in his clothes at the beginning of the term when deliveries were regularly made. Toad entered the cellar and looked around as he always did, then took the parcel to the table, and stretched the sack and its contents out straight.

"Want 'er to be comfey while I gets 'er out," he told Leith, who stood behind the table holding a candle. Toad repeated the same line delivery after delivery, obviously as pleased with himself as if he had written a long, complicated work of literature. Leith advanced to the table and examined the corpse briefly; if it was too badly decomposed, he would reject the specimen, if not he would summon Mr. Jeffreys. That gentlemen, who promptly appeared, made a detailed inspection to determine the price of the goods. He was wearing an elaborate dressing gown but went immediately to the table.

"Good evening, your Honor," said Mowatt.

"Don't forget to check the teeth," Toad suggested. "She had a lovely smile that one did." His smile, which followed the observation, displayed black gums and rotting, broken teeth.

Jeffreys said nothing and apparently took no note of their presence. He moved the candle about the body while he manipulated the limbs and studied the flesh. "Excellent, Leith. Nine pounds for this one. Don't forget to enter the transaction in the book. Clean it, and put it in the whiskey." He went back up the steps, paused, and said, "Good night."

When the door closed, Mowatt and Toad laughed uproariously. "Invisible men, we are. Mr. Jeffreys don't see us." Leith took large skeleton keys from a hook, opened a closet, and retrieved a strong box which he opened with another of the keys. He removed a leather bound account book and made a notation which he then indicated Toad should confirm by making his "X." From a leather purse Leith counted out nine pounds which he placed in Toad's hand. Before he could withdraw his hand, Toad was shaking it vigorously and smiling his ghoulish smile. "You're not too good for the likes of us, are you, Mister Leith? You'll have a drink to our continued relationship." Toad drew a bottle from his greatcoat pocket and passed it to the porter.

"Long life," said Leith, "or we'll end up here." Mowatt and Toad found this jest irresistible and flopped upon the floor. "And now, gentlemen," he said in dismissal, "I have business." The two resurrection men, still smiling, made their way to the door. Leith waited until he could no longer hear the gig before he moved to prepare the body.

"Before commencing today's lecture, I should like to call to your attention the treatment afforded a patient by a colleague of ours, a professor at the university. This learned gentleman has dispatched, by timely rendering of his professional services, a legion of sufferers, maimed others, and impressed in all a well justified fear of medicine as practiced by himself and those he trains. My subject, gentlemen, has recently published a book which proclaims the major organs function independently of one another. The disease of one, says the good doctor, need have no impact upon the general health. Moreover, he seems incapable of distinguishing between aneurysms, abscesses, boils, and tumors in his clinical demonstrations. It is not unusual, gentlemen, to find those laboring in our field of medicine, ignorant of anatomy, physiology, pathology, and surgery. We are not so far from the time when tooth drawers performed operations, and, indeed, in the countries of the Latin races, that circumstance persists even to this day. But it is the obligation of those who profess to teach to first rid themselves of error." Cheers resounded throughout the lecture hall. "Yes, Mr. Grundy, what is it?"

"Have you ever considered accepting patients, Doctor Alloway?"

"I was in practice, as you may know, for many years after my graduation from the great university of this city. From the first, however, anatomy has been my passion. I made my first contributions to medical journals immediately after commencement, but the practice of medicine and the study of its disciplines are incompatible. As your teacher, gentlemen, I hope to advance by my study and lectures your art."

"Besides," suggested a voice, "your subjects never make demands or render complaints."

Alloway's face flamed. "Who dares utter such sentiments?" Students shifted away from the culprit so that he was soon visible to all. "Your name, Sir?"

"Rosyth, Doctor Alloway."

"You are not a student."

"Indeed not. I am a journalist. It was suggested to me something interesting might be said here this morning and was. There are adages about speaking well of others or saying nothing at all."

"Let me warn you, Sir, that I have been a soldier, a military surgeon. I was at Waterloo and have ridden alone but armed about the Cape of Africa. I have no aversion to the exertion of force to remove unwanted, noxious growths either from the body or my lecture hall." Jeffreys and the other disciples began to close upon the intruder.

"Edinburgh, Doctor Alloway is as interested in your 'subjects'" – he pointed to the specimen ready for dissection – "as your students, though not for the same reason to be sure. Would you care to comment about that?"

Alloway launched himself toward the offender, and his students braced to catch the doctor before he thrashed or even killed the journalist, who chose discretion rather than valor and raced for the door. "Follow him," Alloway ordered Jeffreys. "Find out who he is." Alloway returned to the center of the theater and began to lecture, became lost in his subject as he always did, and the flush faded, gradually, from his cheeks. He strode about the body making acute observations on the condition of the flesh, physical abnormalities, the aging process, consequences of drink and evidence of previous diseases. He, with a flourish that produced a hush of excitement among the students, took up the scalpel and made a primary incision. He proceeded slowly with the knife, his words coming in torrents but his movements displayed conscious precision. He paused to accept questions. He sketched tissues. "Science, gentlemen, science is your profession; the acquisition of knowledge is your obligation. Our art is making rapid progress toward perfection and among you may be the man who can claim that prize." His words were noble and yet there remained about him something of the sideshow barker. At noon he dismissed the class for rest and refreshment, and doubtless because he verged upon exhaustion, but directed the specimen be left for examination and study.

"Soon we shall be working on a body of our own," said the would be Frankenstein.

His partner, who aspired to nothing more than the post of assistant army surgeon and a pension, observed, "I've heard the old boy nearly bankrupts himself keeping us in specimens."

"He could do it the way Mrs. Shelly described – taking down the bodies of condemned criminals, claiming corpses at the morgue, and even robbing graves."

"I'm sure Doctor Alloway explores all possibilities," said his practical companion, "all possibilities."

Meanwhile in the cellar, an argument continued between Mr. Toad and Mr. Leith.

"It needs tending and Jeffreys is gonna tend it," said Toad belligerently. "I got hurt performing a service for Doctor Alloway and you owe me." Leith considered violently expelling the man, but violence might rouse the neighbors and, besides, he was not completely sure he could do it. "I deserve it of 'im I do. The risks have gone up. Take them fences, like the one t'got me. And those damned sealed coffins."

"Sealed coffins?"

"Made of lead and sealed with solder. They blow up as the stink comes out of the body and has nowhere to 'cape. The explosion killed one grave digger and covered the other with filth so as he wished he was dead. And those crazy graves with the bells all over. Gives a body the creeps to hear them bells ringing."

Leith made his decision. "Wait here. I'll inquire for Mr. Jeffreys," he said, and climbed the steps. Toad looked about the room and his eyes fell upon the keys. If only Leith were called away and Jeffreys slow to appear, he could have the strong box and be gone. He heard the sound of the latch and the squeal of the door opening above. Jeffreys carried his kit. He was going to treat him without an argument. This was a real gent, thought Toad, and then he saw the stranger behind Jeffreys.

"Whose 'e?"

"I beg your pardon. This is Mr. McGinty who has just joined our little family."

"How do you do," inquired McGinty and extended his hand to Toad.

"All right, man, let's see it," Jeffreys ordered.

Toad let his trousers drop. Jeffreys involuntarily pulled away from the filthy, stinking carcass but steadied himself and examined the thigh. The wound was black, and dry blood covered the flesh down to the ankle. "Water and cloth, Mr. Leith, if you please. I must see the extent of the puncture."

"This is good of you, Sir."

"Not at all, my good fellow. Not at all. We must keep you healthy. You can't work in this condition."

"Hardly slows me down, Sir."

"Then you've been working."

"No, Sir. Truth is me and Mowatt been enjoying the fruits of our labor. We have a devilish strong need for whiskey."

"But you'll return to work as soon as you're able."

"Yes, Sir, and the money runs out."

"We have more money for you, all the money you want. And you know how to get it. We need more of your wares."

"We do our best for you," Toad said, summoning as much sincerity as he could feign.

"I know you do," said Jeffreys in his soothing bedside tone. "But you may also tell your friends about our little business without fear that there shall be no market here for you. We shall always have business for you. But don't forget to tell your friends." Jeffreys finished dressing the wound. "There, that will do." Jeffreys rose and went immediately to the steps. "Don't forget our little talk," he told Toad, who nodded in agreement.

"He done for me like I knew he would," Toad said triumphantly as he limped to the door.

"Yes," said Solomon Leith, "he's accomplished a lot this day." More than you know, he thought, bolting the door behind the departing grave robber. More than you know.

Toad went forth in search of Mowatt and drink. His partner had taken the gig passed Greyfriars several times that day to discover whether any new burials had occurred. The angel of death had not called in Edinburgh, however, which was all right since they still had coins in their pockets to purchase grog. Mowatt had been drinking heavily when Toad joined him. Toad, being a considerably smaller man, did not take long to equal and surpass his partner's inebriation. It was not the congeniality of the inmates nor the appointments of the tavern, a bar assembled from packing crates, a few rough tables, and chairs over dirty planking, but simply drink which encouraged their effusiveness. They bought a round for the other denizens of road and gutter – the women of easy virtue, the casual laborers, the beggars – most of whom were filthy and already sodden with drink. The man who took a place next to Toad was respectable in appearance, at least for the Odds and Inns tavern. He had thick black hair which fell over a deeply lined forehead, irregular eyebrows which appeared to be raised in perpetual questioning, mutton chop sideburns which covered the sides of his face, a pointed chin, and a rather prim mouth. His body was large and well proportioned but not muscular either in limbs or trunk. "Inherit money, did you?" he inquired jocularly.

"Might say that," Toad stated and winked at Mowatt.

"The lamented dead are providing," agreed his partner.

"There is a joke here which I do not understand. Speak plain."

The partners straightened, more sober suddenly, and examined their interrogator closely. "Go on!" ordered Mowatt who was larger and more powerfully built than the stranger. "Get on with your business."

"I mean no harm to ye. My name is Charly Brodie, and a tinker's what I am. But there's no trade here for me. We lived on what we made cutting the harvest, but that's gone now and we're threatened with expulsion from our lodging."

"Good luck to you then, but get away from us." Toad stepped away from Brodie to join Mowatt. As regular as the clock, they ordered a glass, emptied it, and reordered. The crowd dwindled while Toad and Mowatt drank, and Brodie watched.

At last when all were gone or sleeping, their heads upon the tables, Brodie approached them again. "I'll do anything for money," he told them.

"You'll not do what we do; there's few enough have nerves or stomachs for it." Drink had converted their wariness to boasting.

"Try me."

"We rob graves."

Brodie did not react with shock or revulsion but calmly inquired, "You mean they bury the dead with enough jewels to make it worthwhile?"

"We don't steal jewels; we steal corpses."

Brodie bit his lip and advanced, fists clenched, at the larger Mowatt. "No man makes a fool of me!"

Toad thrust his arm straight on Brodie's breast and said, "Tis true. We take the bodies and sell them to the school men."

Brodie halted and placed his arms on his thighs. "School men, tis daft. What school men buy bodies?"

Mowatt gestured for Brodie to come closer and whispered, "The doctors, man. They cut them up in front of others who watch."

Brodie displayed no interest in what was done with the bodies. "Someone pays for corpses?"

Mowatt pushed him back and drew Toad close and the partners exchanged thoughts. "No harm to tell you. There's never enough of them to satisfy Mr. Jeffreys. You ask for Mr. Leith at Surgeon's Square. Find the back cellar entrance or they'll treat you like you don't know what and won't have no dealings. Tell 'em Toad sent you. Mind though, Greyfriars is ours. You compete with us there, and you'll end up on the table."

Brodie did not react to the threat but shook the hands of his benefactors vigorously and disappeared into the rain and darkness. He prowled the night under the cover of the lands – story upon story of Edinburgh tenements wherein the poor slept over the poor ten deep in vertical direction. Through this black labyrinth, he went unmolested since he showed by his clothes he was not worth assaulting, and by his face that he feared not a fray. In fact he was preoccupied with a scheme for making money and scowled at those who approached, even tarts. Ten pounds, ten pounds, the words reverberated in his mind with the cadence of the anvil chorus. Before his door an old woman, dressed in a shabby cloak and apparently worse for drink, rocked her body back and forth in an attempt to fend off the cold. Brodie gave her scarce a glance but flew up the flights of stairs, pushed his door open with considerable violence, and went to the bed he shared with William Hodgkins. "Come with me now!"

"What?"

Brodie gave the bed a vigorous kick, spilling Hodgkins on the floor. "Up and come with me." Hodgkins, more asleep than awake, stumbled down the steps as he was bidden then halted as Brodie indicated that he should go behind the old woman. "Hold her," he told Hodgkins, who placed his arms around her shoulders, pinning her arms, and lifted her. Brodie stepped forward and placed his hands over her mouth and nose. Hodgkin's eyes remained blank, either from sleep, stupor, or indifference. Even the weak flailing of the woman's arms and legs failed to rouse him. He responded more to Brodie's sharp commands to keep her head still. Neither the warm breath and fluids which he felt upon his palm, nor the muffled squeals and moans moved Brodie, who heard nothing but "ten pounds" and clamped his hands ever more tightly until it was done. "Upstairs," he directed his henchman and Hodgkins obeyed. He laid the corpse on the bed and the two watched it sink into the straw. Charly sat down on the single chair and pondered what he should do next. "We're in business now, Bill, a supply company. Bodies is the goods, and the doctors is the ones who want them. Problem is how to get them there." There was a pile of rags in the corner of the room but none long enough to cover a body.

"Wants a box?" Hodgkins observed.

"Aye, but we haven't got a box."

"There're some crates before the dry goods store, big ones."

"Big enough for this?"

"With some bending."

"Go and fetch one then," Brodie said, and watched Hodgkins lumber out and make his return known by bellowing, "the door," and slamming the crate against it.

"The very thing," Brodie confirmed and busied himself removing the victim's clothes, explaining to Hodgkins. "They don't wear nothing in the grave." The partners then proceeded to push the various limbs about until the body was in the box and the lid secure.

"Don't look comfortable," Hodgkins said.

"She don't care none. It'll be harder getting her out after she stiffens. We might as well get some sleep now; there'll be no porters about to help us 'fore morning."

That very morning, Doctor Alloway stood just inside the imposing iron railing which surrounded Greyfriars. At his back rose the great bell tower of Old Greyfriars Church, thrusting forth into heaven, carrying men's aspirations to rise above this vale of tears and strife, while at his feet were holes cut into the earth to house the dead. Alloway pointed to the houses which bordered the cemetery. "Just there are families sitting at tables into whose windows seep the vapors of petrefying bodies. To improve the health of the working man in this community, Greyfrairs ought to be closed. The bones should be carted away as was the practice for centuries, as you well know. The new custom of sealing coffins endangers the grave diggers. When they penetrate them with shovel or pick, they are blown to kingdom come by the gases trapped in the coffin. Diseases are spread by rats. Here on the surface you see cats, but below in the kingdom of vermin, rats thrive. How many more must die from the great epidemics before preventive steps are taken? Improvement, gentlemen, is the battle cry of our century! Knock down these ugly structures, these morbid monuments, these testimonials to an age of ignorance and superstition. Make a park here."

"But Doctor, what shall be done with the bodies of the dead?"

"They should be consumed by the flames, Sir, a thoroughly rational and economical, and most importantly, hygienic method of disposal. Before being consigned to cremation, they might be of some use to science." Alloway discretely refrained from enlarging on that topic.

"But Scripture calls for the resurrection of the body; to destroy the temple of the Lord is sinful."

"You people believe in an all-powerful God, I'm told, so it shouldn't be too difficult for him to pick your atoms out from the other muck and dust. As a man of science, it is the condition of the living, not the fate of the body after death, that concerns me."

There was a murmur of indignation which increased in volume as it spread through the crowd. "What you propose to do with these temples of God after death is obscene!"

"And what you subject these temples of God to before death is equally obscene and more. Illness and death are my sworn enemies. I have no truck with any place or any set of ideas which give them aid and comfort."

"We know about you, Alloway!"

"Congratulations, man. I was afraid you knew nothing whatever; that you know something, however little, is a consolation."

"That man has blood on his hands!" shouted another.

Doctor Alloway's response was to raise his arms and rotate them so that all could see, despite the increasingly ugly tone of the crowd. "There is no blood on these hands," he said calmly but with sufficient force to carry his voice to all. "I wash them. And just now," he continued, "I wash my hands of you all." With that Doctor Alloway turned and strode through the angry throng.

McGinty and Jeffreys, fascinated by the performances of the doctor and his adversaries, watched and waited. "Doctor Alloway tries the patience of God," McGinty observed somberly.

"Alloway professes no interest in the problem of God's existence."

"Why is that, Jeffreys?"

"Think about it, McGinty. If an intervening God controls our destiny, what need is there for medicine? Why not simply resign ourselves to His will and be done with it?"

McGinty was troubled by the question and felt the answers he composed – for example, God allows man some say in his destiny – were mere rationalizations. As they returned to Surgeon's Square, he continued to ponder the problem.

The business prospered through late summer and fall, and continued to flourish during the winter. The partners' technique became more systematic, and the victims were dispatched in less public surroundings, most often in the partners' rooms after the potential merchandise had been rendered incapacitated by drink. They were not overly greedy. Ten pounds was a considerable sum of money even in the hands of Hodgkins, and no more than two sales were required per month. The general appearance of the two improved. Their trappings became those of the middling sort, fewer holes and patches, but still dirty. They ate more regularly and drank constantly. One may well wonder whether those upon whom Hodgkins' eyes strayed – those dull, dead, blackish eyes, wide apart, one set higher than the other in his sloping forehead – ever quivered as he measured their trunk and limbs for fit into the chest. Mr. Leith appreciated the arrangement since the firm sent its wears during the daylight which preserved his sleep, and in considerably better condition than Toad's merchandise. Leith remained the soul of discretion. If he wondered why the goods were never damaged in extracting them from earth and coffin, why decay was never begun, why weeds, flowers, and grass were never found in their hair, he kept these thoughts to himself. Of course, some men never think to ask questions and some think never to ask questions.

Doctor Alloway completed his first set of lectures and sent his students on holiday, recommending that they spend some time visiting surgeons or observing in the public hospitals of the great cities. Each student who made a request was equipped by the doctor with a personal recommendation to the local authorities. Temporarily relieved of his responsibilities in the lecture hall, Doctor Alloway went to visit those from whom he had correspondence regarding scientific, but especially human anatomical curiosities.

Though Doctor Alloway might decline to examine a beached whale, the body or skeleton of a human giant was sure to bring him running. No medical man scoffed as he did when reports of prodigies surfaced – of babies born with two heads, extra limbs, no thumbs or superfluous internal organs – yet he must go and see for himself. "All for science, gentlemen," he insisted when his disciples warned that he worked too hard or that he must not waste his valuable time upon such quests. "Something may be learned that will recompense us." It was upon one such excursion, while passing a cemetery containing a series of bell laden monuments, that Jeffreys posed to his mentor what the strange constructions actually meant.

"You've forgotten Lord Whigmore?"

"We were interrupted, Doctor."

"Ah, but you should have deduced the meaning for yourself my boy. Science has reduced the credibility of religion. Astronomers find no heaven when they scan the sky, and we find no soul when we dissect. Questions have been raised by Voltaire and others about the authenticity of scripture. The old magic has fallen upon hard times, even as that transpires science increases our life span and gives us better health."

"True enough," said Jeffreys.

"But you don't see it yet? We have made life better and consequently increased the terror of death. When you have more to live for, you have much less to die for. Men now have no desire to die at all, but the prospect of being entombed before one is really dead is horrible beyond their ability to reflect upon the unlikelihood of the event."

Jeffreys stroked his chin and said, "I see, I see."

"And worst of all," Dr. Alloway continued, "by raising issues of death and life we have made them more mysterious than ever. If there is no soul, what animates the body? Perhaps in some twilight time, death and life can be confused. Perhaps the dead can walk and the living sleep like the dead."

"And can they, Doctor Alloway?"

The great man smiled and observed, "It's an interesting problem."

The year turned, as did the weather, and Alloway's four hundred students made their way back to the "Athens of the North" for the second course of lectures which emphasized student participation in the anatomical aspects of medicine and, consequently, increased the demand for merchandise. Masters Leith and Jeffreys were, as always, very appreciative and constantly noted that every corpse, unearthed, as it were, would be happily purchased, but never did either of those gentlemen say a word that could be construed as encouraging the practice. Never would they suggest "watching the cemeteries for bodies," or worse. Nor were formal reports of their activities ever made to Doctor Alloway. What the doctor knew only the doctor knew. The ever enterprising firm of Brodie and Hodgkins increased productivity by ingeniously exploiting the resources at their command. Relatives were invited to spend time with their devoted kin in the famous city and converted into cash. Street women and their children were turned from an embarrassment and a burden to the city fathers to an asset, since the flourishing medical colleges brought paying customers to pubs and lodging houses. Brodie would occasionally confess some conscience in the matter of strangling children but did not hesitate to actually perform the deed. Through all of this industry, the partners' lifestyle remained as it had always been, with drink absorbing more and more of their income.

February came to Edinburgh with its accustomed gloom; the joys of the Christmas season sustain one through January, but by its second month, winter sets like rigor mortis. The indigent disappeared from the streets or froze to death there, or froze to death in the empty, fireless habitations in which they took refuge, supplying Toad and Mowatt with merchandise. Their goods were acquired through brutally hard work. The frozen ground resisted the brittle but silent wooden tools of the trade. The longer it took, the worse the pain in the fingers, toes, and nose. Toad lost the tip of two fingers that winter. Corpses too were frozen and more difficult to maneuver. Often bits – the odd hand, leg, or neck – got broken and the principles found themselves haggling over the price. Business was booming, however, while Brodie and Hodgkins looked on in envy and desperation. The obvious solution was to search for merchandise down under, the way Toad and Mowatt did, but the partners rejected that. They were above squalid grave robbing, and, besides, their product had a reputation for freshness and quality which they refused to compromise. It was the size of the woodpile next to the hearth, and the nights of marginal sobriety dictated by a dwindling purse, which prompted a decisive act.

"We are agreed."

"Perfectly agreed," Hodgkins answered.

Brodie led the way into the street and was greeted by a wind which rocked the lands, causing them to grind and creak and whistle and thump like persons buried alive trying to escape the coffin. Huge chunks of ice were dislodged and fell, crashing and shattering against the street, or crushing the skulls of those unfortunates foolishly abroad. The partners had not far to go and kept their back against the walls which gave them some protection against the falling ice. Gratefully they slipped into the light and heat of the Odds and Inns where Toad had just purchased a round of drinks.

"Gentlmen," Toad said, bowing.

"Your servants," the partners retorted and observed, "Mr. Mowatt is working this evening?"

"No," said Toad, "Mr. Mowatt suffered an accident today, a broken hand, which has not yet been tended by a doctor."

"I know a good doctor, the best in Edinburgh who should be consulted," said Brodie.

Toad smiled and whiskey ran down the corner of his mouth onto his chin and neck, the liquid clearing a path through the dirt, like a plow cutting a furrow. "I'll wager we have the same man in mind."

"How is friend Mowatt to take himself there? He cannot risk a fall on one hand."

"Christian of you to ask, Mr. Brodie," Toad replied, weaving toward the larger man. "I must soon return and escort him."

"Why, man, you cannot hope to do it alone on this night. Let us come with you to be certain all goes well."

"This is most Christian of you, Sir, most Christian. I accept your offer."

"Then let us be about it before we get comfortable," said Brodie, who took Toad's arm and directed him to the door.

"One more wee dram before we go," suggested Toad.

Brodie leaned down and whispered, "We'll take one for fellowship from our bottle; it's on the way."

Toad's empty eyes reflected the candlelight like polished black buttons, and he smiled back at Brodie and winked. The three companions paused at the door in deference to the wind, then threw it open and drew together, Toad between them. They were not gone half the block when the partners fell upon Toad in the usual manner. Hodgkins, however, had trouble both with his footing and also with the Toad's not inconsiderable strength. Rocking his body with violence, magnified by the fear of death, he broke Hodgkins' hold upon his shoulders and Brodie's over his mouth and nose and scrambled madly toward the door of the Odds and Inns. He wasted no breath shouting since he could neither be heard over the wind, nor was there a soul afoot to come to his aid. Hodgkins hurled his bulk against him, but Toad nimbly evaded the man who crashed heavily against the ice covered stone. As his hand reached for the door, Brodie brought down against his head a jagged piece of the paving which penetrated the skull and sunk into the brain. Toad dropped, his eyes still open, though emptier than before, and was dragged away.

"Dead?" asked Hodgkins, his mouth against Brodie's ear.

"Couldn't be deader," Brodie shouted. "But it don't look like he died by hisself. Let's get a drink," he pointed to the tavern, "and think on't." The partners dragged the dead man into an alley, carefully searched the pockets for money, and then watched a light cover of snow and the shadows of the night make the corpse invisible amidst the rubble and debris. Charly had a smile on his face even before they took refuge inside. "Whiskey," he told the bar man and threw down Toad's money. He motioned for Hodgkins to bend, and whispered, "We tell Leith it was ice that got 'im. We was walking to have a friendly glass when the wind brought a chunk o'ice straight and sharp as a sword down into his skull. We didn't have nothing to do with his death."

Hodgkins choked down vast quantities of air, enough wind to send a clipper across the Atlantic, then began to expel it through bursts of laughter, as though his mind grasped and enjoyed the jest, then forgot the cause of his laughter, then grasped it again. He tossed two whiskeys down and moved to the fire, took another from the hands of his partner and was told, "Finish now, we have work." Hodgkins nodded and turned his front to the fire, scratched his private parts, and looked content, while Brodie scanned the other patrons to see if there was a back sufficiently strong among them to carry the body to Surgeons' Square. A huge Irishman who sat at the fire, and apparently lacked the money for drink, seemed likely enough.

"I have some work that needs done," Brodie said, "if you're willing."

"Willing 'nuff."

"Come with us then." The partners said their civil good night to the land-lord and led their Irishman to the alley where he exhibited considerable hesitation to follow them. "I have no money and no valuables."

"We have work for you, man, something to fetch."

"What?"

"A dead body." Brodie expected because the man was Irish and papist he would turn and run but desperation made him bold.

"You killed him?"

"Ice killed him, but we have use for the body. It carries a price."

"You're daft," said the big man, turning away.

"You may have his clothes, his coat anyway. It will be short on you, but his shoulders were large. Yours will fit in't. And money you may have now." Charly took some coins from his pocket and held them out.

"Show me," he said.

Toad's body was stiff and straight, and the Irishman carried it on his shoulder, like a board. They partially wrapped it in canvas stolen from a wagon. It was a long and arduous trudge through the icy streets, blasted by the wind which whipped snow into their faces. Buildings shuddered and seemed ready to fall upon them. All souls were abed in fashionable Edinburgh, and no one slept in the streets which decreased the risk of discovery, but buildings were regular and streets straight, and the light of the moon reflected off the snow focused attention upon these three abroad at such an hour in such conditions. Still, luck was with them, and they made their way successfully to Surgeons' Square. Their recently acquired porter looked extremely dubious about carrying a corpse to the door of such an obviously respectable establishment, and his anxiety further increased when Brodie began kicking the door to gain admittance.

Leith was ill-tempered. He had gone to bed early with visions of the next day's work. Fires would be required in the lecture and dissection theaters. Walks would require shoveling and icicles knocking from the roof. Leaks would develop and he would be expected to putty them closed. The curious howling of the wind disturbed his sleep by inducing images of the grave or required repairs. The sudden concussions which reverberated in the cavernous room drove him toward cold fury. He quickly placed a shawl kept by the fire over his shoulders muttering, "Tonight of all nights, damn them," crossed the room and threw open the door. Brodie did not wait for an invitation but strode into the room and indicated the bundle should be placed upon the examination table. "We will have further work for you," he told the Irishman, "if you have the will and stomach for it."

"You can find me at the Odds," he started to say then looked at Leith and said, "at the tavern." He placed his hand in his pocket, taking comfort in the feel of the coin and left, not looking back.

Leith struggled to control himself. He could not order these insolent fellows to be gone as he was under orders to treat them well. "I'll get Mr. Jeffreys," he said. Brodie yanked at the canvas and pulled the corpse upon the floor. Its eyes stared up at Leith. "My God, it's Toad. You've killed Toad!" Leith did not move. He could not take his eyes from the extinct grave robber. "Mr. Jeffreys! Mr. Jeffreys!"

The door at the top of the stairs swung back and the landing was illuminated in the ring of candlelight. "You're making enough noise to wake the dead," he said and thought, who would get a better chance to observe that than we? Jeffreys chuckled. He was politely tipsy, that was clear. "What's the trouble?" Leith, who had witnessed much since entering the employ of

115

the eminent Doctor Alloway, looked sick and said nothing. Jeffreys acknowledged the presence of the partners, then turned his attention to the corpse. "It is Mister Toad?"

"Yes, Governor."

"Well, Brodie, get him on the table and tell me how he comes to be here."

Brodie took the arms and Hodgkins the legs, and they raised the body rather awkwardly to the table. "This is how it was, Sir. We and him live in Tanner's close and runs across one another, and as gentlemen of the same calling invite him to join us in a drink. Well, Sir, you know what it's like out there. We was running to find cover when we hears a sound like the crack o'doom. Hodgkins and myself keeps runnin', but Toady there stops and looks up, and this icicle drops from a roof and strikes him down. There was no use letting a perfectly good body go to waste when it can be put to good use."

Jeffreys examined the wound. It was inflicted by a broad jagged instrument, perhaps even a piece of ice. There was dirt around the wound, and even inside the wound, which was curious, but men such as Toad were always filthy and the dirt in the wound might have come from his hair. Jeffreys said, "All right," and to Leith, "Get out your book." Leith continued to move slowly, as if in a trance, and he did not react when Doctor Alloway appeared at the top of the staircase.

"What's all this about, then?" he asked Jeffreys.

"It's rather awkward, Sir. Two of our regular, ah, suppliers have brought the body of another of our, ah, clients. Mr. Leith was taken by surprise and reacted with extreme emotion."

"Anything irregular about the proposed transaction?" Alloway came down the steps and walked about the table examining the corpse. Brodie and Hodgkins stood as close to the wall as was possible, and Alloway took no notice of their presence.

"The cause of death is rather unusual, but that is all."

"You never thought to see, Mr. Leith, that those who provided the grist for our mill might someday become the very grist, is that it?"

"Yes, Doctor Alloway. But if I may speak, Sir?"

"Of course, dear fellow."

"The students have cause to know this man by reputation and many of them by sight. He is the chief rival to Andrew Merrilee. There will be talk among them when he is discovered on the table."

"That is an excellent point, Mr. Leith." Alloway turned to Jeffreys and ordered, "Take off the head and see it is not preserved in the same vat as the body. You and I, Jeffreys, shall keep the pleasure of examining it for ourselves. There must be some defect which stunted the development of that body vertically. In fact, if you are now sufficiently awake we might begin our investigation of the brain and spine. Opening here and following the spine upward to the brain, I'm certain we shall find the abnormality responsible. Then we shall publish our results that other physicians can recognize the malady and treat children while they are small, so that they may reach their natural heights. I shall just go and get my instruments. All for science, eh Jeffreys."

Jeffreys waited until Alloway departed then said to Leith, "Quickly now." Leith retrieved the strongbox while Jeffreys made an entry into the account book. "There," Jeffreys said, "everything present and correct." He turned to the partners and dismissed them with, "Good evening, gentlemen, I trust we shall see you again soon." They heard Alloway's footsteps on the stairs as the door closed behind them.

A week later the young and dissipated, extremely dissipated, Lord Chatsworth, who was known to take his pleasure incognito in the aforementioned lands of Edinburgh, was abroad. He found making love to women who were desperate for money in the rooms where their children slept, who would perform whatever acts he demanded, and who would never see him again to shame or reprimand him, confirmed his superiority. It was equally true that he would never recognize them either, as he was always thoroughly drunk before he began his reveals. Indeed, no one would take the red-eyed, dirty and badly dressed man staggering through the close for a member of the nobility. Had they done so, the firm of Brodie and Hodgkins would have stuck to their original plan of further reducing competition by sending Mowatt to the next life. But here was God providing their rent, drinking, and table money. "Mind," said Brodie, "no marks this time. We'll do what we talked about on the way." Hodgkins nodded, and the partners closed upon the fallen Lord who sprawled before them. They went forward and spoke softly to the man, then each took a shoulder and suddenly a leg. Holding Chatsworth like a wishbone, they pushed his face down through a crust of ice which cracked and collapsed leaving his lordship's mouth and nose under water. Between the surprise of the attack and his physical state, there was little resistance. "We'll take him back and get the porter to fetch him tomorrow," said Brodie. And so each of the partners got one of the deceased's shoulders and carried him, like a debilitated friend up the stairs, and deposited him underneath the bed where they lay down to sleep.

Toad's skull, stripped of flesh, sat at Doctor Alloway's right hand, while on the doctor's left a pan contained the brain and spinal cord submerged in whiskey. Students examined the torso and limbs, asking questions of Mr. Jeffreys and responding to those posed by Alloway's chief assistant. The students emitted a cheer when the second body was wheeled into the dissection theater. Jeffreys moved to the second table and withdrew a scalpel from his inside pocket and slit the eyelids of the second corpse to expose the eyes. "Examine those orbs carefully, gentlemen. The doctor will expect you to predict the condition of the internal organs from the information written upon the face." Jeffreys was conscious of a reaction among the students, many of whom had drawn back from the table. He dismissed the possibility that it was his gesture with the knife – these were experienced men – but something was amiss. His attention to the question was distracted by doctor's sudden burst of speech.

"I shall reserve my commentary upon the physical consequences of spinal abnormalities until after you have all had an opportunity to work upon the subjects. Mr. Milton, will you please come over to the table." Milton worked his way through the students and stood opposite Doctor Alloway. "Examine that face carefully and tell me to what you would attribute the cause of death."

"There are a number of possibilities," Milton stated. "The color and character of the eyeball suggests acute alcohol poisoning which means a damaged liver. The body is malnourished. I see nothing to indicate the ravages of other diseases. The condition of the body is the most remarkable point. The fingernails are regular and clean. There are no scars which one would expect from a member of the lower orders. There are no indications that vermin have lived upon the body." Milton continued and Dr. Alloway beamed. This was a model of the type of clinical analysis he hoped his students would be capable of delivering after they completed his lectures. Jeffreys, however, was alarmed. The lower orders do not have bodies like this, he thought, and recalled the students' reactions to this corpse. Jeffreys moved, causing as little disruption as possible, to the back of the hall and signaled Price the Welshman, one of the students who reacted to the body.

"Do you know who you've got on the table?" Price demanded.

"Some poor drunken sot."

"Some rich and noble drunken sot," retorted Price. "It's Lord Chatsworth." Jeffreys smiled. "You're mistaken."

Price looked unflinchingly at Jeffreys and suggested, "You'd better do something. There are others here who know and some who talk."

"Any questions for Mr. Milton, gentlemen?" inquired Alloway.

"To what do you attribute the absence of the disorders of the lower classes?"

"This must be," Milton suggested, "a person who has recently lost his situation and taken to drink."

"A very ingenious explanation."

"Why ingenious?" demanded Alloway.

"Because," Jeffreys interjected, "one would not expect members of the lower class to have a body free from the depredations which wreck themselves upon those unfortunates. We would be forced to conclude, therefore, that the specimen was a member of the upper class; but how would it come to be here?"

"How indeed?" said the same voice.

"The body in question bears a very great resemblance to the young Lord Chatsworth," announced Mr. Chisolm. Disturbed voices were heard throughout the room. The debate over dissection was bitter, even shrill, and the law permitted only the bodies of criminals to be given to schools of anatomy. Those who studied the subject, however beneficial for the practice of medicine, were looked upon with suspicion and even disapproval. Doctor Alloway realized he had a problem and rose to the occasion. "Mr. Milton, remove the head, commenting as you do upon the muscles and bones and any features you observe that are associated with alcohol or other factor as a cause of death."

"But Lord Chatsworth?"

"Would hardly be in this room upon that table. You are witnessing a phenomenon, gentlemen, known to all medical practitioners and morticians. At death, the features of the body become less distinct since personality no long animates the body. Consequently it is difficult to identify them. You are young to science. Follow Mr. Milton carefully. I shall lecture upon the brain and spinal cord tomorrow at the usual hour. Remember gentlemen, medicine is a speciality of no narrow kind. We must dissect nature rather than derive abstract principles from it. Every form of life has value, but we must reverse the generalizations of natural history. We desire to know what limits, what specializes, and what perverts the natural order of things. We do not study in order to distinguish for the academic application of classification. What we do here will have immediate application in your surgeries, or on the battlefield, or at metropolitan hospitals. All for science, gentlemen."

"A pretty speech," Alloway heard muttered, "but what if it is Chatsworth on the table?"

What indeed, thought the doctor. Some explanation would be necessary and he disliked explanations. Fools and savages explain, he was fond of saying; wise men investigate.

"Doctor Alloway, should not this be one case where science yields to charity? If that body is the remains of Lord Chatsworth . . ."

"It is not, Mr. McGinty; it cannot be."

"So you believe. An inquiry would established the fact with certainty."

"My dear McGinty, the chief rule of those who would succeed in science is to obey the rules established by their superiors. You will return to the lecture now."

I must have a talk with Jeffreys, the doctor thought while he arranged his great coat about his shoulders to meet the wind raging through the streets.

That same wind blew chunks of plaster and rags jammed into broken window panes about the partners' room and even extinguished their fire. Alcohol and usage inured them to discomfort, but the visual stimuli of the fire prompted a general reconsideration of their situation. Pockets were empty, the last of the bottles nearly empty, and the bottom could be seen in the coal bucket. "We need to do a job," Charly told Hodgkins, who nodded sluggishly and rolled over on his side. Brodie kicked his partner and insisted, "Now." Clumsy in the best of times, the partners carefully set their feet, first the right, then the left, to cope with the wind which pushed them relentlessly backward.

"Tomarra," Hodgkins shouted at Brodie and tried to pull him back indoors.

"Tomorrow may be as bad as this, may be worse," he retorted. "Besides, the wind will mean no noise." The trees above Edinburgh were doubled over, their limbs thrashing about like the long hair of women who shook their heads wildly to dry it. Rubbish blew about the street piling in corners, and the good citizens of the city found reasons to delay even necessary errands. Brodie and Hodgkins knew that members of their class would take refuge in the taverns which made the most difficult aspect of their job not selecting the victim but convincing him to go with them. Before they entered the tavern, in the midst of the wind, the partners heard a familiar song. The lyrics spoke of the vagarities of fortune, or rather misfortune, and of human frailties. The voice was strong and clear, high pitched, but not unpleasantly so, and unmistakably Irish. The song continued while the partners' eyes adjusted to the dim, smoky light. The rooms were full of people huddling together against the storm and the fates which sent such storms to plague man. It was an aggregation of the race such as Jesus might have addressed – the cripped, and the blind, the poor and the outcast, the mentally feeble, and physically ugly. Brodie saw none of this but focused instead upon the singer who sat far away from the fire and who sang apparently for her own pleasure or need. Few of the occupants paid any attention to her song. They were busy complaining at one another, or making threatening gestures across tables, or sleeping hard against each other for warmth or consolation. One old woman, enraptured by the singer, or the song, swayed in time to the music, great arcs right and left, and moved her mouth silently reciting the words. Brodie saw at once the possibility of doing two pieces of business, a technique the partners employed with considerable success.

Stepping over bodies which meekly grunted, violently cursed or feebly squirmed away, Brodie with Hodgkins following like a tame dog went over to the singer. "My mother is home abed, dying," he told the woman. "I could stand to watch no longer and fled here." She looked at Brodie as though she were in a trance. "It would soothe her last hours to hear music from the homeland, your music. Will you come home with me, Lass? You'll get value." Her song continued unbroken by his words, nor did any expression form in her eyes. Perhaps she was daft, he thought, and took the bold step of grasping her wrist, locking it in his hand, and pulling her to her feet. "We are going home," he told her, and she offered no resistance. It was the old woman who rose and pounded on his arm with her fists. Hodgkins caught her shoulder and dug his fingers into her flesh while pushing her down to her knees. Some voices denounced this treatment, but no one interfered. Brodie led the woman about the periphery of the tavern and back into the storm. Hodgkins followed, and behind him, keeping out of sight, hobbled the old woman. It was, thought Brodie, one of the easiest jobs they'd ever done. This one would be delivered in the morning, the old lady decoyed to their room and delivered that afternoon. Brodie was already spending the money, a new coat and a change of lodgings. Men with a steady income deserve better than we got, he thought. He directed the woman into the close and up the stairs, paused until Hodgkins arrived, and the two entered the room with the woman between them. Her body was soon stuffed under the bed to await further disposition.

The old woman watched them disappear inside the room, an accomplishment won at great risk, and then set off to find the Watch. The wind cut through her clothing and gouged the flesh as she leaned forward, butting it with her bowed head. A magistrate might pass beside her without being seen, she realized. The old woman considered turning her back and simply being carried along but feared losing her balance and being propelled into a building or knocked with bone crushing force to the pavement. It was the recollection of the music, the human voice raised in song, and the realization that this source of consolation for her misery was in danger that kept her going. She heard a sound and turned her head in its direction. She was struck by a plank loosened and then completely dislodged by the wind. She dropped to the pavement and lay still.

"Are ye dead then? Woman! Are ye dead?" She was violently shaken. The voice demanded again, "Are ye dead?" When she opened her eyes upon the brutal face of the Watch, he dropped her head on the stone and ordered, "Get up and move along."

"Murder," she said.

"What?"

"Murder is being done."

"Are ye daft woman?"

"I can take you there."

He pulled her roughly to her feet and pushed her into the doorway of the closest tenement. "Wait here," he ordered. The wind abated and the snow floated down in large flakes. She watched, absent-mindedly, then grew aware of the warm salty liquid flowing from her nose and mouth. She dabbed at it with her sleeve and continued to marvel at the beauty of the falling snow.

"Somewhere here I left the old hag." It was the Watch, who then demanded, "Why din't ye call out t'me woman?" She made no response.

"Daft," the companion concluded. "Let her go."

"Murder," she said, "I'll take you."

With a burly policeman under either shoulder she was more carried than walked through the streets of the city back to the room of Brodie and Hodgkins. The knocks of the officers rattled the door and brought cries of outrage and threats from inside. Hodgkins came to the door, his ham-sized fists clenched, and Brodie glowered behind. The officers, accustomed to rough dealing, simply pushed Hodgkins back into the room and forced the partners to stand against the wall while the premises were searched. The nearly empty room contained only one object large enough to conceal a body and under the bed, they found the corpse. The old woman stood in the doorway with a curiously triumphant smile on her face.

Last Judgment

The Edinburgh Horrors

Last Judgment *continues the account of Burke, Hare and Knox. The two active villains are gone; Burke has been hung and Hare has literally walked out of history. Knox, to all appearances, has gotten on with his career. On his first appearance in the lecture hall after the initial turmoil, he was greeted with a round of applause and a testimonial by his students. Our investigator is a jaded English journalist with no love for the Irish or Scotch who had the inveterate bad taste to have been established on the British Isles before the English arrived. He is a Romantic, as one might guess from his ready citation of Robert Burns and William Blake. There are also echoes of the graveyard poets in his musings and of William Wordsworth in his interest in the supernatural. While there is no specific model for Cedric Wood, one can imagine London newspapers were hungry for reports about Burke and Hare's murder spree. It confirmed their worst opinions about the national character of the murderers, Irishmen both, as the sources smugly note. It also contributed to the passage of one of the most famous acts of Parliament in the 1820s, Warburton's Anatomy Act, though the immediate cause of Paliament's action was the murder committed by Bishop and Head, the 'Bethnal Green Burkers'. Murder for profit, apparently, was not confined to the Celtic Fringe. Burke and Hare, and the Resurrection Men in general, also played a major role in the development of the modern cemetery movement. Burials occurred in churchyards which already lacked space and were not well maintained. These conditions, reformers argued, contributed to disease and a lack of respect for the dead. Actions taken against the 'body snatchers' from placing fences around the churchyard to the construction of mortsafes, provided the final incentive for the new cemeteries. A pamphlet authored in the case by the "fly on the wall"* *was drawn from one written by Knox's doorkeeper, David Patterson, who wrote under the nom de plume "echo of Surgeon's Square." The accounts of the panel which investigated Knox, from Geikie through Monro are found in the literature of the incident, as are the opinions of Sir Walter Scott on Patterson and Knox.*

Mr. Cedric Wood, a journalist, has been dispatched by his editor to Edinburgh to discover why Brodie was hanged, while Dr. Knox was permitted to continue his career. Through Wood's commentaries and conversations, the reader discovers how sons were provided for by their fathers, and about how one can be influenced by the prevailing ideas of an age, like Romanticism. With regard to the "Edinburgh's Horrors", Wood interviews a range of Scotsmen, professional and common, and the very physicians who sat upon the panel which considered the conduct of Dr. Alloway. What appeared to be an "open and shut case" of a miscarriage of justice may not be quite so open and shut after all.

You may rest assured, dear Grub Street reader, that one may yet rely upon the wisdom of Doctor Johnson, and I hope that divinity will forgive my slight alteration to wit, the basest sight to confront an Englishman, even one so lowly as your Grub Street regular, is the low road that leads to Scotland. I was sent by my editor to the land of kilt and pipes to investigate the Edinburgh horrors about which we in London have heard so much. Well, the story has spread far and wide in this backward land as well. At each post station and drab backwater village, the muck are thrilled by sensational fictions. Sixty victims I hear in one town, 'a hundurt' in another. Brodie got his neck stretched, they know, while Hodgkins was reported here and there about Scotland like that fellow Washington slept throughout the American states. It may be possible, dear reader, to track him as wherever he appeared, or was believed to have appeared, there were riots. In one town, the magistrates were compelled to gaol Hodgkins to save him from the mob. Later that night, they rented a coach to get him into the next county alive. The authorities don't really know where he has or has not been. At length, Hodgkins seems to have simply walked out of history, or to Ireland which may be worse even for a hardened murderer. Perhaps some avenging angel has done him in. You may write my editor, dear reader, and demand yours truly be put upon the scent. For the present, however, my humble task is to journey to the Athens of the North and discover why, when the small fish have been gaffed, the whale remains directing his school. I go to find why Dr. Alloway has not (to prolong the metaphor) floundered. This publication has spared no expense to provide you, dear reader, with the complete facts. Money for half the trip, no lodgings was advanced me, with the additional gentle admonition that if I didn't go, it would mean the sack. Though the travel and travails would have been less daunting had I clung to the sea from Berwick to Edinburgh, I have determined to explore the local color, and smells, associated with the northern portion of the realm and share them with you, gentle reader. And so I embark upon the road, such as it be, which links Jedburg to Melrose, and Melrose to Edinburgh. Should a Melrose by any other name be as sweet? Probably if it lives in Scotland! Adieu!

What, dear reader, makes five hundred Scotsmen jump as one? A penny dropped in the gutter of a public street. Who but this strange race of men glut themselves on oats, which only horses' stomachs can digest, and use their own stomachs to try to digest boiled cow stomach filled with various sheep odds and ends, and suet. This national dish is called haggis, an ancient Gaelic word, meaning starvation is better, with which I heartily concur. I slept this past night in King David I's monastery in Jedburg. The monks and roof are long gone, but the walls provided relief against the sharp wind, and the foundation, though cold, was neither so cold nor damp as the ground. Rising before the sun, I went to see the new prison, and an impressive structure it is. Pressure from you, gentle reader, will induce the beloved editor to commission a series on the use of tax money on public edifices which I will gladly undertake. Then I returned to the north road which is well-paved with native stone. In fact, the paving is better than is necessary given the volume of traffic. Little commerce moves either north or south here, though there are others afoot like myself. A man and woman, off to my right where the sun will be, gather vegetation and bind it about a cleansed branch to make a broom. On their mule, I see several finished brooms. The mule carries other bags, no doubt the entire worth of the family. There are two young children, dirty as you might guess, gathering material for their father from the boggy ground. The fields contain hosts of closed flowers which would sweeten the day should the sunlight penetrate the overcast to awaken them. Sheep are about which run in spurts then graze, then run again with the apparent foresight of a member of parliament. Somewhere there may be a country lass unpracticed in her charms, who will take me in her arms and . . .

further musings are not for publication.

My vicarious pleasures were terminated by the arrival of a horseman who overtook me, reined his mount, and demanded to know who I was. I hastened to inform the potential highway man that I, poor journalist, possessed nothing of value save my incomparable command of language. He inquired as to whether I was Cedric Wood.

"You know my work, Sir?"

"I know you don't work, Sir. You are a journalist. Your editor sent me with this," he said and tossed a thick pouch.

"Five pound notes, is it?"

"Ha! Just scribbling from one such as yourself."

"There is no one like me," I said, modestly, "but, are you bound for Edinburgh?"

"Aye, and I should not be wasting the day with the likes of you," he said and rode off.

I took the manuscript out and began to read. The document proved to be an open letter to the Lord Advocate for Scotland describing how corpses – subjects – it decorously calls them, are routinely procured – supplied – it says, for anatomical schools from grave robbers. The author, a self-described 'fly on the wall' at Surgeons' Square, claims that the bodies supplied by Brodie and Hodgkins should have been readily identified as victims of murder. Characteristics of death by suffocation are a strong livid color of the face and a discharge of blood from the mouth, nose, and ears. The anatomy professors either were not well-acquainted with their profession, which makes them fools, or were willing accomplices in the crime of murder which makes them knaves. This is especially the case when one remembers the kind of men Brodie and Hodgkins were. Such men invite suspicion. In addition, these same professors were unable to distinguish a freshly killed man or woman barely cold when delivered to their door, from one waked, interred, and dug up several days dead. Hopefully the power of observation so woefully deficient in the masters will be more highly developed in the pupil or a plague of practitioners is about to be loosed upon our land lacking the most fundamental skill of a medical man – the capacity to detect symptoms of illness. Or death.

At this point, I realized my progress in the direction of the Scottish capital had come to a halt through my absorption in this narrative. I deserted the road and took shelter in the ruin of a stone barn. It does not take genius, dear reader, to determine the said narrative had to be a product of someone well acquainted with the running of the anatomy school, a student, or a member of Alloway's household. I must discover the author and interview him at length. From what I have heard about the formidable doctor, the author of the manuscript needs be a person not lacking courage. In the east, which I could plainly see through a great hole where the wall has given way, the sky grew darker. The dominant smells inside my shelter were of stone gathered by man for his temporary usage being returned by nature to her storehouse to which all temporary constructions must ultimately return – even your humble servant – and mold, and rat dung. The tale of murder and the grave had quite unhinged me. It was easily imagined that my too, too solid flesh was crumbling, indeed it seemed to roll from the very bones of my hand even as I held the pen. My body shook violently as thunder boomed across the moor. I am not a superstitious nor religious man, but there are voices, dear reader, high, spectral, indistinct, closing upon me, though I can see nothing. Even after all that surrounds me has been completely illuminated by lightning, I see nothing. The voices draw near, and among them is a particularly hellish one. May these notes assist those who waver in faith find the way. And with that invocation for the welfare of your immortal souls, gentle readers, and with hope for the salvation of this acknowledged sinner, I take my leave of you to confront those who summon me from afar. Adieu.

I intend someday to write a lengthy paean to the excellent medicinal properties of whiskey. My spectral voices proved to be the tinker family and their donkey, all of whom share my roof and I their fire. We have fortified ourselves with a "wee dram" and now enjoy the worst excesses of the storm and contemplate, or at least I do, Mr. Burke's theory of the sublime. I have regained sufficient nerve, while the children sleep and the parents moon about one another wishing me somewhere else, to resume the manuscript. The author states Doctor Alloway and his establishment had sufficient reason to alert the authorities of murder when the body of one Toad was presented for purchase by his professional rivals who gained in several senses from Toad's demise. The resurrection man, it was claimed, had fallen victim to an icicle. Any objections to this explanation were swept aside. When it was next argued that the presence of such a notorious figure upon the table would incite the students to form sordid opinions about the demands of scientific medicine, Alloway is alleged to have remarked: "No difficulty in that. Cut off the head and prepare the body so that recognition is impossible even by his mother." And so one of Edinburgh's most infamous personages disappeared forever in circumstances which testify to the ironic, if poetic, justice in the universe. Then there is the matter of Lord Chatsworth whose body Alloway ordered dissected to protect himself and his school, even as the authorities sought the man on the streets of the city. Though there were protests, even threats in the dissection theater, Alloway's reassurances carried the issue. Here, dear reader, ends the story of Doctor Alloway as told by the 'fly.' The implications are clear. The distinguished professor of anatomy was an accomplice in mass murder for profit.

The storm has gone and returned several times, as if tethered to this very spot, but I no longer feel any spectral influences or concerns. The only point of interest to me now is the injustice committed in the matter of Doctor Alloway. A wrong needs to be righted.

I set out on the road again, late in the afternoon, determined to reach Melrose. A light rain continued to fall. No prodigies were about, though the Village of Ancrum boasts a statue of Maid Lilliard. "Fair Maid Lilliard lies under this stane. Little was her stature but great was her fame. Upon the English Loons she laid many thumps. And when her legs were cut off, she fought upon her stumps." The local mutton at the Last Minstrel Inn proved as indigestible as these sentiments, though the smiling Mr. Ormrod, the ruddy cheeked proprietor, was a model of his type. His upper arms at the shoulder joint were the size of hams, as befit a retired artilleryman. He invited me to dry my clothes and the contents of my kit at the fire before I returned to the road. He talked while lifting and trimming whole sides of beef without particular exertion. I initiated a discussion of the Edinburgh horrors and heard the usual verses and the absolute conviction that Hodgkins had passed through Ancrum on his way south. "What is your feeling about the anatomy professors?"

"Begging your pardon, Sir, the who?"

"The anatomy professors, the men who bought the bodies."

"Bought bodies, Sir. Why would any Scotsman, or even Englishman, buy bodies? Now the French maybe."

"Why did Brodie and Hodgkins commit the murders?" I demanded. Mr. Ormrod was genuinely puzzled. I realized, finally, that he had heard about the murders but did not understand the circumstances which surrounded them. I explained about the schools of anatomy in Edinburgh and about Doctor Alloway's relationship with the two miscreants. Deep furrows appeared in Ormrod's brow, and his features exhibited confusion. The cleaver separated meat and bones with ever more powerful strokes, which gradually tapered off.

Finally Ormrod sought my eyes. "Well, we must have doctors, so I guess what they did was all right. Besides, if this Alloway done anything too bad, the powers that be would have acted."

Distressed by his vision of right automatically sustained, an idea which is generally held by those of his class, I repacked my kit and bid him farewell. He would not have understood my rage. We must have doctors; we must have lawyers; we must have hangings; we must have wars. It is curious what people are convinced we must have. Why, dear reader, do they never see what we might have, or dare I say, what we ought to have? The worst horrors are always excused by those short, simple words, must have. Is it any wonder we label those who reject, "must have" as mystics or dreamers fit only for Bedlam? Our mystics and dreamers are willing to accept incarceration rather than spend another day condemned to wander among those who suffer and see no hope and among those who inflict suffering and see no cause for repentance.

I maintained a vigorous pace despite, or because of, these ruminations through Saint Boswells and Selkirk with its busy mills by the river and successfully fought the urge to visit the Eildon hills where Arthur and his knights lay in enchanted sleep. I entered Melrose as dark descended but found without difficulty the old abbey where I planned to sleep.

"Hello there! Who are you, and what is your business here?" a voice challenged, though more in curiosity than anger. In the dark and at distance, I did not realize to whom I spoke. "I am the sheriff of the county and the owner of these lands."

"Forgive me for not recognizing you, Sir Walter," I said to the great Scottish novelist and poet, Walter Scott. "My name is Wood, Sir, Cedric Wood, and my profession has brought me to investigate the resurrection men."

"You must be a fellow scribbler," Sir Walter said, "for no officer of the law would travel on foot."

"The very thing, Sir Walter."

"And money being dear – I'm thoroughly familiar with that aspect of our profession – you've sought lodging in the abbey?"

"Is there some reason I should not do so?"

"None at all. My family owns it, but I am glad to have you as my guest. Join me for dinner at Abbotsford. I have not been to London for some time and am interested in reports of the business. They take the 'how typical for barbaric Scotland' line, I judge. Come to the house when you are ready."

I shall spare you, gentle reader, a detailed account of that night. Sir Walter proved by his kind treatment of your humble servant that the chivalry of which he writes is not dead. He told me that a certain Leith, Doctor Alloway's doorkeeper, suggested that Scott write the definitive account of the whole business. I have not the power, dear reader, to convey with what disgust Sir Walter observed, "Imagine such as he with the gall to approach a decent man." I inquired about Alloway, and Scott produced two verses recited on the streets of Edinburgh.

> In Scotland the Slaughter house keeper may pay
> His journeymen butchers and thrives on his prey!
> The victims are quickly cut up in his shop,
> And he pockets the profits secure from the drop.

> In Edina town where your friend you may meet
> At morning in health, walking down the street;
> And at evening, decoyed and deprived of life,
> His corpse fresh and warm is laid out for the knife.

"Charming," I observed.

"But not specific," Sir Walter said. "All professors of anatomy are equally indicted, not Doctor Alloway." I nodded in agreement. "You must find out why," he said. He leaned back in his chair, relaxed and said, "Tell me about yourself, Mr. Wood."

"I, Sir Walter?"

"Aye, you," he smiled. "You are obviously a man of breeding."

"How do I come to write for Grub Street?" The great man nodded his head. "A fine education ruined me," I explained. "It taught me to think, a circumstance for which I was congenitally unprepared. Besides, I am the fifth son. The eldest, as you well know, inherited all. The next was found a commission in the Navy, and the third sent to the Army. The fourth was deposited at the Inns for legal study, and I was expected to study theology and enter the church. Alas, I find Lucretius more congenial than Jesus and will not be the hypocrite. My father proposed medicine, for which I have not the stomach, and then commerce, for which I have not the conscience. Wealth acquired in any manner appalls me. I read poets, Sir, including your fellow Scot.

> "A prince can make a belted knight,
> A marquis, duke and a'that;
> But an honest man's aboon his might

130

Guid faith he mauna attempt that!
For a'that an a'that,
Their dignities an a'that.
The pith o'sense, an'pride o'worth
Are higher rank than a'that."

Sir Walter smiled and said, "I suppose you would echo as well the sentiment:

"I will not cease from mental flight,
Nor shall my sword sleep in my hand,
Till we have built Jerusalem
In England's green and pleasant land."

"Guilty as charged, Sir Walter."

"Tis a dangerous radical I entertain in my house, this Cedric Wood with his poetry."

"But only poets get things right, Sir Walter, as you yourself know well."

"Mr. Cedric Wood, a disinherited Don Quixote, cut himself off from his family to fight injustice. You've taken your name from Ivanhoe?"

"Yes, that's what I mean by poets getting it right. Your tale of Robin Hood is absolutely wrong, of course. Robert Hood was a violent criminal, a murderer and a thief. Your telling of the tale with Robin as the protector of the poor and the champion of justice gets it right. That's the way it should have been."

"It is late, my good Cedric. Much luck may you have in your labors," he said and bid me farewell, neither his health nor inclination favor early rising. A bed was provided for me in the hall, my first night in sheets for some time. I look forward to reaching Edinburgh tomorrow.

From a distance, gentle reader, the Scottish capital is a chaos, a jumble, the worst of old and new, as incongruous to a civilized Englishman as a man wearing a skirt, call it what they will. One finds Egyptian and Greek temples, Venetian palaces, and Gothic spires in what is known as the Old City, while recent constructions in the French style are known as New Town. I enter through the Canongate and concede the vigor of life here makes some amends for its other deficiencies. The bells of the ancient university ring out above the streets where students in their gowns rush to classes, or from classes to the coffee houses. Here they exchange criticism of books or lecturers and delight in their learning. Footmen in splendid livery cling to the backs of carriages which transport the gentry to exhaust their wealth in the fashionable shops on Prince Street. Sweet singing rises from the churches, sweet smells from the bakeries, sweet, though clouded thoughts, from the native whiskeys. Even the grim advocates who, in common with undertakers, wear an expression of perpetual solemnity on their journey to the Parliament Close where they will try a man for his life, cannot crush the exhilaration one feels upon the streets.

But this is only a partially valid impression. The denizens of Tanners Close, the neighbors of Brodie and Hodgkins, have no energy for reflection upon life or death. They share no part in the happy life of the city.

I grew sick as I made my way through the festering slums. The filth, depravity, and hopelessness of those who live here, sodden with drink and seething with vermin, is enough to overwhelm any decent man. I gained access to the room in which the murders were done. I stood among the sticks of wood the landlord called furnishings, and stared at the dirt spattered rags which comprised the bed in which even a corpse must be uncomfortable until two large gray rats emerged to glare back. I could stand no more. I fled to clean lodgings having concluded that among the lower class of citizenry, Brodie and Hodgkins might well be thought of as deliverers.

The problem with philanthropy, gentle reader, is simply the closer you get to the people who need it, the more reluctant you become to give it to them. Why, you ask yourself, can't they keep themselves clean? Why can't they keep their dwellings clean, since a broom is cheap and they have time to fill? Why do they have so many wretched, dirty, hungry children? Why? Why?

I toast Lord Byron for his most accurate observation on human nature that "man being reasonable must get drunk." I toast the bottle which will make me forget. I toast my lodgings and my landlord and wait for my brain to give me the sensation of being on a rough Channel crossing. I shall be sick, and then weak, and then asleep. My room is spinning wildly. Its motion makes it difficult for me to find my mouth with the bottle. I steady the bottle. From the dregs of the dark liquid at the bottom a shape forms – an animalcule. No, it is a miniature man who climbs the side of the bottle. He has trouble, the glass surface is slick as ice, and falls. I can see the liquor splash as he drops into it and begins again. It is Robert Burns himself. I try to rise to help but my arm pushes through the mattress to the floor, and I fall back. I try to get my legs on the floor, but I have more of them than a spider, and they all move at once beyond my control. Meanwhile, Burns has gotten, somehow, to the top and suspends himself with the mouth of the bottle under his armpits, and shouts at me "a man's a man for all a'that," over and over until he falls, splashes at the bottom, and is gone. So am I.

I face the morning, patient reader, feeling as though I have swept Prince Street with my tongue which has, consequently, swollen enormously while my head has shrunk. Mr. Walter Geikie, master of the Edinburgh Standard, has graciously consented to meet with me at the hour of eleven. Since it is now nine, I have a slim chance of triumphing over my body and keeping the appointment. First, however, I solemnly resolve to give up drink . . . again.

Close to the buildings, there is less sunlight; I am intimate with the bricks. Hooves on the pavement are like demons probing my ears with their forks. I pause before entering the Standard and put on a business face. Mr. Geikie, as yellow and brittle as an old sheet of paper, did not rise to greet me. He extended his hand which I reached across the desk and took. His index finger left purple spots on my flesh, and the pool of fluid collecting at the tip of his tongue, too, was purple. These are symptoms of reading freshly printed copy. He indicated I should take a seat and proceeded to examine me as if I were the first draft of a lead editorial. "Begin," he ordered.

"Are you satisfied that Hodgkins and Brodie received a fair trial?"

"Oh, there is no question about that. The trial was scrupulously fair. It was done in haste, the court sat literally around the clock to bring the proceedings to a quick end, but in the face of the public clamor and the threat of riot, speed was essential."

"Has Doctor Alloway been treated correctly?"

"You might have begun your investigation with the doctor himself, though he tends to speak with his stick."

"He has spoken to no one about the matter, I understand."

"He wrote this newspaper to announce that a panel had been formed to investigate his practices. A report was issued by the panel which I assume you have studied. It is fair to state Dr. Alloway personally has neither clarified his practices nor apologized for them. Leith, his doorkeeper, has been as difficult to stanch as a severed artery. He writes under the nom de plume of 'fly'."

"Ah yes. That was damning stuff. He suggested that two bodies had been purposefully mutilated – the body snatcher Toad and young Lord Chatsworth – to prevent their being recognized. He also claimed that all of the victims of Brodie and Hodgkins had similar marks of violence, something about color and discharges of blood. What did the magistrates make of his evidence?"

"Leith was never called to give evidence."

"What?"

"You have not very carefully read the indictment, I gather. Brodie and Hodgkins were indicted for one murder, that of Jeannie Clark, whose body was discovered in their room."

"I have not yet obtained a copy of the proceedings," I said, warmly in my defense. "What about the others?" I demanded.

"The others are known through Brodie's confession which was printed in this paper but never given in evidence, nor introduced as evidence. I can read you what the 'medical experts' reported about the cause of death of the last victim." Geikie reached into the top drawer of his desk and removed some sections of a newspaper. "'There is no positive proof of death by violence. The evidence is simply insufficient to bear out a charge of murder, though such as to raise a strong suspicion of it.'"

"So that's why Brodie was hung, and Hodgkins went free?"

"Yes, to hang Brodie they accepted evidence from Hodgkins, who was then ruled free from prosecution under the law."

"They made a deal with a cold blooded murderer."

"Obviously. Police surgeon Black gave me his private opinion that the woman died from violence, though he too could not be specific about the cause of death."

"Is it possible that a doorkeeper is better schooled in anatomy than our physicians?"

"Your point is well-taken, though bear in mind what Leith said may or may not have been true. The various medical experts were being asked to establish a fact beyond dispute in a case involving a man's life. Their hesitancy may be admirable."

The obvious dawned upon me, slowly as always. "Doctor Alloway was never called to give evidence."

"There was no reason. What did the learned surgeon and Professor of Anatomy have to do with the body of a poor woman in the lower reaches of the city?"

"The indictment was written to shield him?" The thought astounded me!

"It would appear so."

"But the doctor is not, I understand, a popular figure."

"Describe the sort of men who govern the city of London," Geikie ordered.

"Ambitious, stiff-necked, proud."

"The same sort rule in Edinburgh."

"Yes?"

"How long have you been a journalist, man? There is a flourishing trade in bodies in this city, beyond the murders of Brodie and Hodgkins, I mean. Graves are emptied. That is disorder. No city relishes such a reputation. In the specific case of our murders, while it is true the city has been cleansed of some penniless transients who never will be missed, the underside of life here has been exposed. Within a mile of this office, streets and tenements abound with derelicts, male and female from childhood to senility, drunk and starving. The city fathers want that vision forgotten." Geikie sat back in his chair, smiled at me, and said, "It will be; indeed, it has been. The education of surgeons continues. As for justice, Brodie deserved to die but so did Hodgkins who escaped. The matter of the good Doctor Alloway I shall leave to you. When you have finished your articles, send copies to me. I shall regard them as the final word on the matter." He smiled again, an enigmatic smile, and turned to other matters. I thanked him for his time and departed.

I lunched at the Rob Roy Inn on a local delicacy known as John a'Groat, which I took to be a dismembered Highland clansman boiled in porridge. Afterwards, I sought the business office of Douglas Stewart, J.P., who managed the affairs of London publications in the northern capital. His clerk admitted me to the office, which possessed the solemnity of an Egyptian tomb, and into the presence of Mr. Stewart, who was built like a squat pyramid. Ponderous, he sat behind his desk, and ponderous and short were his motions when he moved, but I thought under those half-closed lids, I detected a blue-eyed crocodile. He said nothing, though I glimpsed fire in those aforementioned eyes, until I was finished with my questions; then he went to the heart of the matter. "For Brodie," he said, "there was justice, for Hodgkins there was law, and for Alloway there was the higher good to be served."

"A higher good, Sir, pray what was that?"

"Doctor Alloway's class has some four hundred students."

"Yes?"

"They are not the youth of Edinburgh."

"Yes."

"Think about it, man. Lodgings, meals, drink. And while Doctor Alloway's class is the largest, it is not the only class in anatomy taught in the city. The university is justly famous for its course in medicine. Three generations of Monro's have given it glory throughout the civilized world. It was Alexander

Monro the Second who discovered the 'foramen of Monro' between the lateral ventricles of the brain, and now there is a third Monro to bring," he paused, "yet more students, requiring the necessities and desiring the entertainments of life, to the city."

I could not contain a smile as what he said struck home. "You are prepared, you should pardon the expression, to bury the scandal."

His eyes opened completely as he answered my smile with a smile. "It has not been so easy as we would have liked. The rabble were incensed that the good doctor's subjects came almost exclusively from among themselves. There were some nasty moments when it appeared Doctor Alloway might be hanged by the mob, but he is a stout fellow. He desired that the police officers who were sent to protect his property be recalled and insisted he would care for it himself. He was at Waterloo, you know, and had a career in the military for some years after that. I can testify to his skill with a rifle. He has since clubbed a man or two in the street but even that seems unnecessary now. The public mind is like a Chinese firecracker, explosive but short lived."

"Business as usual has returned to the medical community in Edinburgh."

"Irony is not your forte, young man, though you are doubtless correct. Anatomy professors still must have subjects, and the resurrection men remain the only reliable source of supply. Do you know that bodies are sent here from Ireland in trunks and hampers, which occasionally have their invoices mixed with other trunks and hampers carrying soft goods, crystal or paper, or foodstuffs – ham and cheese, bacon, a basket of eggs. Can you imagine the surprise of the poor customer expecting to banquet upon the choicest delicacies of the south who uncrates a dead body? You might remind your readers who sit in Parliament, those exalted gentlemen who know your gutter publication, they have promised relief to medical practitioners through legislation."

"Corpses are to be made available?"

"No, young man, 'the raw material of the science' is to be made available to professors of anatomy."

"A rose by any other name," I said.

"No," he said, "you refuse to see the difficulty here. Disclosures from the dissection room of any nature, however innocent, must shock and prejudice the public against the science of medicine, and yet we expect our medical men to be able to restore health to the sick while woefully ignorant about basic human systems and their functions."

"Am I to take this as another 'higher good' which protects Doctor Alloway?"

"I have told you what the higher good is, the prosperity of the community. Doctors be damned, don't believe in them myself." Mr. Stewart made a great show of reaching for his watch and noting the time. I thanked him for the interview and found my way to the door.

I walked toward the old town, dear reader, with the intention of visiting Greyfriars where the dead are laid to rest, however temporarily in this city. I contemplated the excellence of the human mind which ever provides a balm for the troubled soul. Body snatchers must ply their trade for they must have money to live, and doctors must purchase their goods for they must have the subjects of their science so that knowledge may be enriched for the good of all. Justice may be undone in the interest of human welfare and communal enrichment, and all of this is done by necessity or for a higher purpose.

Be not deceived, though reason be a weak reed to be twisted and turned to suit the needs of conscience, as you have just witnessed, it still surpasses in value any form of enthusiasm. For example, each street in Edinburgh has its oft told nonsense tale. Here lived Major Wier of infamous memory, master of witches, whose devil's coach drawn by six fiery-eyed black horses may still be seen driving through the West Bow. Beware his eyes, children. Under the Parliamentary Close are tunnels which lead to points throughout the city and one, it's said, to hell. Once a piper descended to explore its windings, and all of a sudden his music came to an end; he was carried off by the Evil One, some said. Lost and killed by gas more likely. Still, Old Timers insist one day pipes will be heard reascending from the bowels of the earth. Here is, indeed, stuff to frighten the young.

In Greyfriars Cemetery, you stand among the shattered memorials, or graves, emptied by the resurrection men, and observe the new constructions with the still shiny angels, or the enormous rectangular holes where iron coffins have been installed to thwart the grave robbers, and contemplate that old sentiment "requiescat in pace," or the new fashion in churchyard poetry which asserts:

No farther seek his merits to disclose,
Or draw his frailties from their dread abode
(There they alike in trembling hope repose)
The bosom of his Father and his God.

In such places as this, the frontier of eternity, the living confront the dead and seek some understanding of the experience we know as life. It is not the dead, gentle reader, that makes us avoid such places as this but the necessity of facing the question, what happens to us after death? It is not a pleasant subject: heaven, hell, or extinction. Hard of heart as I am, it is impossible to repress a shudder. It grows dark and a cold mist rises from the sea. I see no new graves to draw the resurrection men here this night. A materialist would side with Doctor Alloway. Dead bodies are of no use beyond what they may teach the living. If life may be enhanced by experimentation upon the dead, then damn religious sentiment. Let the anatomists do as they will! I must keep in mind however, it was not the body snatching that roused the wrath of the rabble, at last, but murder, and that my concern is justice.

This morning, Doctors Brown and Allison returned my cards without comment and Doctor Russell with regrets. Doctor Smythe agreed to see me with a caveat. His time was short and valuable. These gentlemen sat upon the panel which investigated the conduct of Doctor Alloway. Smythe's name was well-known to my landlord as physician to the fashionable of the city. His consulting room is on Prince Street, where "society" goes to squander wealth. To my surprise, the doctor was young, large and well-formed, and exceedingly, if not indecently, handsome. We generally prefer our medical men to be as solid as Gibraltar, and about as intelligent. And he was smooth. He faced me across his huge, spotless desk, his long immaculate fingers clasped together over his vest. I could hear patients in his sitting room on the other side of a closed door and the ticking of the huge watch under his left hand.

"I was an obvious choice for the panel, to connect it to the right people, you understand."

I nodded – the idea was not beyond my grasp. "No member of the panel dissented on any issue?"

"We were in complete agreement."

"Admirable. There isn't much reason for me to detain you, then, just one or two minor points. The so-called 'fly on the wall' reported, at least, one of the bodies – the resurrection man, Toad – was so fresh that rigor mortis had not begun. Did you accept this?"

"No."

"He also states that body of young Lord Chatsworth was purposefully mutilated to prevent it being recognized. Did the committee reject that contention?"

"No."

"No, then you accepted it?"

"No. We neither accepted nor rejected the statement. We simply ignored it."

"Why did you do that, Sir?"

"Because Mr. Leith, who concocted that abominable tale, is no gentleman."

"Your report states you sought evidence from every quarter."

"Every reliable quarter."

"I see. You state the committee concludes that neither Doctor Alloway nor his assistants knew murder was being done to secure subjects for Surgeons' Square."

"That is correct."

"Laying aside for a moment the question of marks of violence upon the body, the fact that these, subjects," I pronounced the word with obvious scorn, "showed no signs of having been interred, or were remarkably fresh, or were provided by such a pair as Hodgkins and Brodie aroused no suspicion?"

"None. Members of that trade are hardly gentlemen."

"You state, sorry the committee states, there was no evidence of the suspicion of murder on the part of Doctor Alloway or his assistants."

"We established that to our complete satisfaction."

"How, if I may be so bold?"

"Doctor Alloway and his assistants told us such was the case."

"And they, of course, happen to be gentlemen."

"I have some doubts about you being a gentleman."

"No more than my own. Didn't it occur to you that Doctor Alloway and his assistants are not reliable witnesses about this question?"

"They are gentlemen."

By sheer force of will, I stifled the urge to throttle the good Doctor Symthe.

"I have been extremely patient with you," he insisted, "but you are looking for scandal where none exists. Consider as weight against these allegations the sheer volume of silence. Alloway has some four hundred students and seven or eight assistants. Surely one of them would have recognized irregularities in the anatomical subjects and reported conduct warranting hell and the gallows to the authorities. Consider further that the magistrates made no reports of missing persons. Why should the doctor have supposed Brodie's goods were being acquired beyond the usual manner? There were no inquiries addressed to the professors by the police about how their subjects were procured. The public authorities have not charged Alloway with any crime which confirms there is nothing to charge him with. The matter is finished."

I thumped my head, harder than I intended with my closed fist. It was fruitless to throw back at him that his gentlemen had noted, "Alloway's dealings were conducted on the understanding that persons supplying the subjects were not to be questioned about the place and mode of obtaining them. Any particular inquiry of the person bringing them would only tend to diminish or divert the supply." I imagined three practitioners of the healing arts in the famous pose of the primates neither seeing, hearing, nor smelling evil, and gave my thanks to Doctor Symthe for his cooperation, and watched his well-oiled smile spread slowly and heartily across a face where enmity would have been more agreeable and departed.

I invaded Allison's surgery later that morning when the waiting room was empty, invented, and outlined a digestive problem for the doctor to chew on. The thick lines in his forehead rocked and rolled like the sea as he pondered my problem.

"I ha' never heard such an unusual collection of aches and pains coming together in one stomach," he said, looking at me, his eyes over the top of his spectacles which slid down his nose. "It sounds to me like you've got a smattering of every belly problem known to medicine."

"Maybe it was something I ate?" I suggested, tentatively.

"I find that hard to swallow," he retorted. "You're the journalist whose card I sent back this morning."

"Yes."

"What prevents me from throwing you into the street?"

"Is that what's known as the Highland Fling?"

"What is it exactly you want to know?"

"As bluntly as possible, how can you gentlemen who served on the committee which investigated Doctor Alloway live with your consciences after the report you submitted to the public?"

With one finger he pushed the glasses to the top of his nose and stared directly at me. "Have you studied medicine?"

"No."

"But you dare to suggest our report was not accurate, and more, intentionally false?"

"You did nothing to disprove the most damning accusations against Alloway."

"The words of that rotter Leith?

"Yes."

"You are willing to believe a man like that before you believe us?"

"Why were his charges not confronted?"

"His charges were considered by the committee and dismissed for lack of evidence."

"Doctor Symthe did not tell me this."

"Doctor Smythe, as you no doubt guessed, is a busy man, a society doctor. He did not attend every meeting. Leith's statements were examined."

"But you did not call him."

"What would have been the point of calling him? There was no physical evidence of any kind available for us to consider. It was the word of Alloway and his assistants against that of a doorkeeper, who has since sought to peddle the story in every sensational way he can invent."

I was unhappy, gentle reader. The calm, straightforward, solid manner of Doctor Allison began to make me doubt my conclusions about the committee's work.

"We rebuked Doctor Alloway for the manner in which he accepted anatomical subjects. That is the point. He did not escape censure. I have no window into men's souls. If Alloway and," he paused and stated emphatically, "and his seven assistants suspected murder, then that is a grave matter indeed, and they are none fit to be healing men. I did not believe it to be the case then; I do not believe it to be the case now."

"Why wouldn't you see me?"

"To what purpose? I gathered the truth was of less interest to you than the story you were determined to write for your usual class of readers. This whole business can be made to appear in the worst light, can be made to revolve around the basest of human motives. I prefer to think it more complex and the motives among the most elevated."

"It has been an education, Doctor Allison," I told him, preparing to take my leave. He rose with me, and extended his hand, which I shook heartily, and made my way back to the street. To my lodgings and desk I made my way, dear reader, determined to portray this entire matter in an entirely different light. Phrases flowed through my mind to demolish the edifice raised upon a foundation of suspicion, misinformation, and misinterpretation. My concentration was such that only after a vigorous shake at the shoulder did I hear the voice of Sir Walter Scott.

"Your facial expression is completely different than before," he noted, "you have heard something more congenial."

"It's true, then, novelists do have windows into men's hearts."

"You wear your heart, as the expression has it, on your sleeve for all to see. What have you been told?"

"I have spent an agreeable hour with Doctor Allison, who told me . . ."

"That all that was done was done for the best, and all of the motives were the best of motives, and that God's in heaven and all's right with the world. I should have warned you about the good doctor. He believes that Lucifer wanted to be like God so that he, Lucifer, might then relieve some of God's burden in running the universe. Never for a moment did Lucifer have a base motive in the view of Doctor Allison. He is the most optimistic, cheerful, guileless man I know, which means his testimony is worth next to nothing."

"You are determined to ruin me, Sir Walter."

"I am determined that you shall tell your readers what Edinburgh and Scotland are really like, and I shall give you a practical demonstration. Our friend, Doctor Alloway, was scheduled to give a paper before the Scottish Academy, but I have convinced that august body to forgo conversation with a trafficker in human flesh."

"You have postponed his paper?"

"I have finished this paper, as I expect to finish any future papers from the pen of Doctor Alloway, and hope to finish the doctor himself."

"You are as implacable an enemy as generous a friend."

"I would rather not be enemy to any man, but Alloway must be stopped. His crimes are manifest, however much is done to exculpate them. He is wicked and self-serving. Alloway acted rashly not because of his beloved science, as he would have it believed, but because he thinks himself to be more clever than the rest of us. He, the great doctor, would not be discovered or, if discovered, would not be prosecuted for his crimes done in the service of humanity. The man is the original snake in the garden."

One does not, dear reader, spit twice into a wind blowing gale force in one's direction, nor interrupt an impassioned speaker with an interested but trivial question. I waited until Sir Walter's face grew less flush before inquiring, "But where are you leading me now?"

"To Edinburgh's most illustrious medical man who shall give you all of the facts in the case. I have taken the liberty of addressing him in your behalf. We shall find him at his rooms at the university."

"Dr. Monro would not have spoken to me without your intervention."

"In truth, probably not. The medical establishment sees no reason to prolong this sordid business. But the record must be established, the truth secured."

"As you were compelled to do in the witchcraft business," Sir Walter's countenance altered in surprise.

"You have read my 'Letters on Demonology and Witchcraft'?"

"As has any man with a pretense to learning."

Scott smiled broadly. "Tis no wealthy patron you address," he said. "Nay, lad, the book is not so highly thought of, even by myself. Its purpose was modest."

"To set out the truth is never a modest undertaking, especially as truth is always more preposterous, less credible than fiction."

"As in this case, the digging up and selling of corpses for profit."

"Could you have invented the tale, steeped as you are in the lure of broomstick, poison, and grave?"

"No, but there is the door to Dr. Monro's theater. Announce yourself quickly; his patience is somewhat deficient at present."

I made a great effort, dear reader, to enter boldly, while frantically fearing I would find myself in the dissection room confronting limbless, faceless "specimens of science" which would make my knees buckle or my stomach burst. There was but one man in the lecture hall, rummaging through a stack of paper on his lectern while regularly pushing his spectacles back upon the bridge of his nose. He was quite a distinguished looking chap with a mop of white hair lying atop a broad, unlined forehead, wide set eyes, a well-formed nose, and large mouth. The great brain gleaned and held knowledge, the eyes caught those of his students and held them while the voice, I assumed, carried the learning throughout the lecture theater. Here was a perfect teaching machine. His lips, I noted, were set in a smile, which I took to be their habitual expression.

"Dr. Monro?"

"Mr. Wood, I presume."

"Your servant, Sir."

"Are you, indeed, I wonder. You have not come to ask me about my work, or about what we accomplish in this department of the university. You have come skulking about like a jackal in search of carrion."

He did not speak harshly, but with resignation. Still his words gave offense. I retorted, "That is an unhappy metaphor given your profession and those who assist you in it."

"A fair hit," he said. "But you'll not get any gossip to peddle to the unwashed from me. Doctor Alloway is a most unfortunate man, a very foolish man. He believes he cannot rise among us without demolishing or ridiculing his colleagues. It requires little skill to make enemies among men you accuse of incompetence in their profession. Alloway cannot be convinced that he must act in the dissection theater with gravity, affected if necessary, and an almost melancholy air. While his performance is meticulously careful, there is something of the carnival barker in his voice and manner. He demonstrates to us our inadequacies by having the greatest number of students in the city, and this requires the largest number of 'scientific specimens.' The doctor's reputation for keeping a well-stocked table compelled him to be careless, even reckless in his dealings with Brodie and Hodgkins."

"You do not believe," I said, but he cut me short and continued.

"Doctor Alloway parades views which scorn social conventions and religious sentiments which are taken to be the views of all of us in the profession. If one practitioner who cuts up dead bodies a vile if not blasphemous trade also attacks the existence of God, then all professors of anatomy must be disbelievers. When winter term began after Brodie was tried and hanged for the murder of Jeannie Clark, whose life had been terminated so that her body might be sold for dissection, Alloway's students applauded when he entered the lecture hall."

"Surely that is malicious gossip. No assemblage of men could be so heartless!"

"I wish it were so," Monro said sadly, "but my informant is a man of the highest character." He added speaking softly, as if reminding himself, "It is not so hard to believe. They were welcoming their teacher; they intended no disrespect to the memory of Jeannie Clark. Medical men must always be on their guard lest a body become mere machine, not a house of intellect and temple of the Lord."

"Doctor Monro, do you believe that Doctor Alloway knew?" I tried again and again Monro deflected my question.

"Doctor Alloway knows a great deal. He is a great scientist. No man may say otherwise. Visit the anatomical museum he has created from nothing. Consult his articles in the medical journals."

"But did he?" Bells began to ring all about us, and the doors of the lecture room flew open. Students spoke loudly as they flooded into the room and made their way to their seats. "In your opinion, did Alloway know," I tried again, guessing it would be my last opportunity, but Doctor Monro was already busy with students. I made my way to the door, listening and watching these men who would soon be cutting at bodies as had Alloway. They lacked the mark of Cain or any other feature that might differentiate them from you and me, dear reader.

It is a serious matter to defame another human being, especially in print which may survive both author and victim, providing those who come after with models of demons to shun, or under certain circumstances, emulate. The Borgia's are synonymous with unspeakable evil, and yet who can prove that their legendary deeds are more than that, legends, myths, fables? Right and justice cannot be advanced by the propagation and spread of lies. Is that right? Perhaps a well chosen lie may be the spark to ignite the fires of social rebellion. Whatever be your sense on that point of philosophy, patient reader, where lies the truth in this affair? I let myself be carried through the streets in my musing, following first students, then commercial traffic, then pedestrians like so much flotsam in the current and would not have been displeased to have found myself outside the Canongate on the high road to London. Instead, I was at Surgeons' Square before the door of the very man I imagined to be a monster. Nature refused to become my accomplice in portraying the doctor in this manner. Surgeons' Square, a perfectly charming residence with nothing of the grave or ghoul about it, basked in brilliant light. Its wide windows admitted the cheery rays of the sun, the whispered condemnations of the frightened, and even the curious eye of the investigator. There was no attempt to hide from the public. Tradesmen delivered their goods, and the postman made his rounds without fire, brimstone, or the cries of Cerberus, gatekeeper of hell, bursting from behind closed doors. Indeed, those who came and went were most respectable types of citizens, or appeared to be. I took a position without thought at the very head of the walk and stared, determined to complete my quest through sheer force of will. I would will myself to know the truth.

A figure, clutching a stout stick, came through the door and rushed at me faster than a Scotsman moves when he hears "free round on the house." I glanced back at the street where the force of the charge would drive me and braced my body to absorb the blow. Actual contact was not made. My assailant thrust his nose against mine and bellowed, "State your business."

I had no alternative but to stand my ground and respond, "I was thinking."

"You lack the essential equipment for thought."

"I hear a Scotsman with a sense of humor is rarer than a Scotsman with a charitable impulse."

"What do you want?"

"The truth about the Edinburgh horrors."

He stepped back and, there is no other word for the expression, sneered, "The truth. What interest have you in the truth?"

"I want to know the story and to tell it to others. I'm a journalist. You should know that."

"Ha! When has your profession been interested in the truth?" Alloway, I recognized him, wheeled to return to his home.

"Tell me the whole story and all of this might be behind you," I said.

He turned, like a cornered animal and snarled, "The authorities have not charged me, Sir, for there is nothing to charge me with."

"There are accusations."

"False accusations!" he insisted. "A false accusation," he pointed a finger at me as if directing a slow student to an important point on the blackboard, "is a conspiracy against the truth by he who makes it and he who unflinchingly accepts it as accurate. Against false accusations there can be no defense. Truth is of little consequence to those who deal in or receive such goods."

"You have not answered Leith!"

"Leith be damned. You accept the word of a disgruntled former employee against his employer without suspecting malice?"

"You sacked him?"

"I did," said Doctor Alloway, who then smiled. "Has it occurred to you that Mr. Leith was most responsible for what you call the Edinburgh horrors? It was Leith who dealt regularly with Brodie and Hopkins, not I."

"You had to know that murder was being done," I told him. "You could not have overlooked everything."

"What am I alleged to have overlooked?"

"The blood."

"Ha!" Alloway grunted again. "The blood at the mouth and nostrils which is the mark of suffocation?"

"Yes."

"There is no such blood," Doctor Alloway said calmly, triumphantly. "If violence is done in the course of strangulation so that blood vessels are broken during the struggle, there will be the kind of evidence described. But suffocation of a victim, placing a pillow over the head, breaks no vessels and causes no flow of blood. Another false accusation."

"Brodie and Hodgkins were evil men."

"Do you believe those who provide specimens for medical colleges in this city are the type of person you would regularly, or even once, entertain at tea? I am master of a school with a class of four hundred students. I had other obligations. I trusted those who were in my employ and, beyond all this remember young man, had I not provided a market for the Brodie's goods, another practitioner would have done so, willingly."

"That would have been better for you."

"Perhaps. I have no more to say. Do your worst."

Your humble servant, dear reader, has considered and dismissed and reconsidered texts which will serve best to begin this final epistle. Among those germane to the subject and pregnant with meaning were, "Know the truth and it will set you free," and "Judge not, lest you be judged." I am not a Godly man, gentle reader, but do know good advice when it is offered, however dubious the source. Another possibility, and my favorite, is Mr. Coleridge's conclusion to another tale of murder and retribution, "A sadder and a wiser man he rose again next morn." I have sought the truth and discovered it is illusive; perhaps it is an illusion. That the horrible deeds of Brodie and Hodgkins were done is an established fact. The motives and activities of Doctor Alloway and his assistants I cannot establish beyond contention. Alloway's vindication by a committee is an established fact. What motives, if any, lay behind the vindication, that again is a contentious matter. Has justice been done, as some insist, or been thwarted, as my friend Walter Scott passionately maintains?

I sit upon a hill miles from the Canongate where begins the road to London and stare at the sunlight reflecting off the waves of the sea as they are borne against the shore. The light is fracturized, or compartmentalized, and appears to me like thousands of pieces of mosaic or, better, of a kaleidoscope as the sea rises and falls and swirls. The image is born and passes before I have more than a moment to see it whole. Now imagine, dear reader, that upon the great high walls of the Castle, and in the depth of the valley of the Kirk Yetton, sea birds suddenly scream, drawing the attention of four other eyes to that same patch of sea where my own are focused. Is precisely the same image pressed upon our visual sense?

I cannot judge. I cannot know the truth. I have learned much and, consequently, forgiven much. A sadder man I rise and depart for home, examining, pondering, whether I have somehow left the wiser man behind.

The Iron Chancellor

Germany, from Unification to Welfare State

The Prussian aristocrat Otto von Bismarck (1815 – 1898) was among the most brilliant and ruthless of nineteenth century statesmen and perhaps the most egotistical. An unhappy childhood was followed by several years of drinking and intimidating his fellow students at the university. After a graduation achieved by cramming for his exams, Bismarck joined and promptly left the Prussian diplomatic service which noted his "deficiency in regular habits and discipline". After a number of years playing the great landed aristocrat on the estates he inherited from his father, a mature Bismarck returned to the diplomatic service and was posted to the capitals of Europe. In 1862 when parliament refused to vote the requested army budget, Bismarck accepted the office of prime minister and lectured the house that the great questions of the day were not decided by speeches and parliamentary majorities, but by blood and iron. The army reforms were carried out without parliamentary appropriations or approval, and the army was employed in 1864 when the King of Denmark's decision to annex the provinces of Schleswig-Holstein became the first step in Bismarck's audacious unification of Germany. Next, he provoked a war with Austria about which he had written: "Germany clearly is too small for both of us . . . In the not too distant future, we shall have to fight for our existence against Austria. There is no other solution." A final war and the humiliation of France culminated in a unified Germany and the crowning of the German Emperor in the Hall of Mirrors at the Palace of Versailles. Bismarck administered this Second Reich for two decades and conducted limited warfare against two groups of German citizens, Catholics and socialists. The first was provoked by the Holy See which issued a Syllabus of Errors in 1864 and followed with the doctrine of papal infallibility proclaimed at the

First Vatican Council in 1870. Recalling the concerns of the Enlightenment, one German politician branded the crisis a Kulturkampf or struggle for modern civilization. Bismarck waged the war for a decade and then, like an old soldier, allowed it to fade away. An apparently more formidable opponent, the Marxist inspired Social Democrats were becoming a force in the Reichstag, winning ten percent of the vote in 1877. Bismarck outlawed the Party, though paradoxically, individual Social Democrats could still run for office, and then took the offensive. The Prussian Junker introduced legislation which began the welfare state in Germany, the first in Europe! Bismarck's final struggle came after the death of Emperor William I (1888), who had been content to permit the Iron Chancellor to rule. William II, unstable and inconsistent, and a parliament without experience in the exercise of power, waited to see what would happen next.

Bismarck's amanuensis has been with the great man for much of his career and witnessed the Chancellor's wheeling and dealing. For the rest, he has shared Bismarck's personal recollections through intimate conversation. He has also had access to the Chancellor's diaries and journals. Despite the constitution, which says the Emperor rules in Germany, Bismarck has wielded power for thirty years. Should young William learn the full truth about those years, he may choose to remove **The Iron Chancellor**.

To His Imperial Majesty, William II, German Emperor:

> I must confess, Majesty, that this testament should
> have been written in June of 1878, for time grows
> short to save the Fatherland. That I did not then do
> so may be explained in part as a consequence of
> the venality of our species – while the Chancellor
> prospered so did I – and of our capacity for self-
> deception. I chose to believe much that I knew to
> be untrue in my heart of hearts. That some good
> has come from this decision is indisputable

Bismarck bursts into the room holding several newspapers. He wears the smile reserved for his great moments of triumph – Sadowa, Sedan, Versailles. He begins to quote glowing reports of his latest addition "to the edifice of Imperial Germany by the master architect and builder, the Chancellor of Imperial Germany, Otto Von Bismarck." I put down my pen and listen to Bismarck read an editorial which drowns the subject in superlatives and strains the metaphor. "'The construction of the army by his defiance of Parliament, that made the foundation. The three victories: over Denmark'." [that embarrassment would be better forgotten, I think], "'Austria and France represent the keystone. The walls are German prosperity, the roof a steady foreign policy'." [This leaves little else in the lexicon but decoration or plumbing which offer little for the continued discussion of glory.] "'The capstone is Bismarck's domestic legislation which has at last become law. Old age and disability pensions are now guaranteed to all Germans by the State. There is much which remains to be done. This member of the Fourth Estate looks forward to the great days which await Imperial Germany under the leadership of His Imperial Highness, William II, and his dedicated servant, Prince Bismarck.'"

I watch an old man who shrilly proclaims weakness in every limb, who walks unsteadily and yet dominates every room in which he appears. He has studied how to accomplish this trick. No one has ever learned so well how to pull all of the strings of power. I do not listen to him prattle, but I watch him. I cannot help but watch him. My eyes follow the scar which runs from the tip of his nose to his right ear, and I remember the youth I knew so long ago. I can see him with his one eyebrow (the other he shaved), his shoulder length hair, his enormously wide trousers, and his boots with iron spurs. At his side dangles the long brass-hilted sword, the dueling Schlager of the Germany university student. Bismarck swaggers about the streets with his Dachshund which wears around its neck a wreath of artificial flowers. Those who laugh, as Bismarck calculated they would, are challenged to a duel. "On arriving at the university, I determined at once to obtain mastery over my competitors, who were all extravagant, savage, eccentric. I knew, therefore, I must be ten times as extravagant as anyone else. I intended to lead my companion there as I intended to lead them after we completed our university days." And yet there was more even then, the bold gesture, the Teutonic fearlessness which cannot be learned. The fiercest of the street brawlers quailed at the thought of facing the RECTOR, not young Otto. Called upon to explain how an empty bottle of grog flew through a window to land in front of an officer of the law, young Bismarck suggested it was a miracle. Then he seized a bulky ink stand from the desk of that august old gentleman and appeared ready to hurl it at the Rector's head. Herr Bismarck was promptly dismissed from the Presence and never fined. What was his school, I ponder frequently? Certainly not the university where politics meant far less to him than beer. Bismarck's letter of recommendation from old Doctor Hug states, "I have never seen this student at any of my lectures." Nevertheless, Bismarck passed his examinations and entered the diplomatic service.

The old man continues to read. I pretend to listen and he pretends not to know that I am not. "'He gave the world security by carefully negotiating the great issues of the day most recently at the Congress here in Berlin; he gave the Reich political security; now he has given the working man security by granting the average German the most advanced social services in the world. We expected the former triumphs from the cultivated Junker, the latter surely astounds the world. Let the praises be sung of Prince Bismarck, friend and champion of the working class!'"

He looks at me with the expression of a platform orator surveying an audience. I say nothing. I wait for him to expound upon himself as the friend and champion of the working class. He fools me. "We may use this against the new Emperor and his ridiculous notions of shorter working days and of the protection of women and children from exploitation. I, the friend and champion of the working man, know what is good for the masses, and I provide it. Any further encouragement will lead to excessive demands."

"With respect," I said, "the Emperor defeated you over anti-socialist law and will not hesitate to challenge you again."

"I certainly hope that is true; there must be a settlement with young William on that score." For him to make such an admission to me, I thought, means he is prepared to rid himself of me. I looked at his head and watched him swing it in a sort of arc of triumph, as one sometimes sees a lion do, as he has done since his youth. His physique does not seem capable of sustaining such a gesture when he leans upon his stick and allows the weight of the world or his memory to burden him, but just now he is the mad Bismarck whose demon-like rides, drinking bouts and dancing were the terror of Pomerania. "Yes, there must certainly be a settlement of that score."

"But Bismarck, William is your master. He is the Emperor."

"I have seen three kings naked," he retorted, "and often enough, the behavior of these exalted gentlemen was by no means kingly. I do not care about titles. William may have all we currently possess and add a hundred others. I rule here. 'A house divided against itself cannot stand,' is the principle lesson the scriptures teach us."

"Bismarck, the Emperor has proclaimed his sympathy for the working

151

man, as you have. He seeks an international conference to proclaim their grievances and to find solutions to them. He seeks to construct a stronger Germany by reconciling all classes."

The Chancellor smashed his stick against the marble floor, shattering it with the force of the blow. "You do not meet with your enemies; you crush them without mercy. That is the first lesson of life and politics. When I am lying awake at night, I often turn over in my mind the unatoned wrongs that were done me thirty years back. I grow hot as I think of them and, half asleep, I dream of retaliation."

"The German worker is not your enemy."

"Because I have not let him be. Remember the excesses of the Paris Commune. Defiance of public authority! Murder of public officials! General rebellion! Have you forgotten the financial panic of '73? The social democrats would have taken advantage of us, would have filled the streets with blood-thirsty rioters and seized power had I let them."

"Bismarck, Berlin is not Paris; you had nothing to fear."

"Pfui, you are a child still," he grumbled and without a further word, returned to his office.

A coal crackles and ash slips through the grate and falls upon the carpet. The powerful odor of scorched wool touches a lever in my brain, flooding it with images. I cannot tame them, nor even identify most of them, though one became clear – Bismarck before the fire at Schonhausen. He was dressed like a country squire and in the mood to talk about his favorite subject, himself. "Did I ever tell you about my rescue of the King from the riot torn, corpse littered city of Berlin in '48?"

"No."

Bismarck smiled. "Frederick William was alone at the mercy of the mob. The army lost control of the city, was ineffective against the rioters, unskilled in street fighting, and forbidden to use artillery. It withdrew and left the King quite helpless. He was actually forced to come out of the palace and to salute the bodies of the dead. I packed my pistol and four extra bullets . . ."

"Why four, Bismarck?"

". . . and rushed to Potsdam. The military advised me to go home. So I rushed to Berlin and appeared at the palace. The gatekeepers refused me admittance, but I commanded them and finally was permitted to see their Majesties. I appealed to the Princes to act, to take command of the army since their father would do nothing. I suggested the appropriate strategy would be to depose Frederick William and make Frederick regent. That horrible woman, Augusta, refused to heed me."

I could not help smiling. "You mean Queen Augusta, wife of King Frederick William, your master?"

"Yes, that woman!" His voice was filled with poison.

"That woman rejected your suggestion that a coup d'etat be conducted against the King, her husband," I said scornfully.

"Yes," he said, ignoring my quite accurate observation. "Since they would do nothing, I went back home and agitated for a policy of firmness."

The word firmness amused me. "Against the starving weavers in Silesia, the unemployed and starving miners and steel workers, the dispossessed peasants you would have been firm."

"Against them all. You," it was an accusation, "excuse the naked grab for power of the rabble. They have bread and a place to sleep; their fathers had less and were content. Politics is the business of those born to rule. The rabble have learned the three r's – riot, rebellion, revolution. Now they must be taught new lessons. Berlin should have been bombarded into submission, the ring leaders tried and executed." He said all of this in a perfectly reasonable tone, nodding to himself from time to time in agreement with his words.

"Have you no mercy for the unfortunate?"

"Mercy? Mercy by all means. Mercy is a very good thing. But first a little hanging."

He may not have meant it. Moltke would. When Moltke said he wanted to smash the French once and for all, he meant just that. With Bismarck, there are occasions when the rhetoric gets beyond his control, though his celebrated tirade on the Poles, "Hammer the Poles until they wish they were dead; of course I'm sorry for them, but if we want to exist, we have no choice but to wipe them out: wolves are only what God made them, but we shoot them all the same," was in earnest. There is a significant footnote to the story, I remind myself. The Chancellor's private papers – diaries and journals are kept at Schonhausen awaiting retirement and the writing of his memoirs. I once asked Bismarck why he so thoroughly disliked Queen Augusta, and he gave me a leather bound, much thumbed book in which the scene at the palace in Berlin was described. There was one significant difference. In Bismarck's journal, which will serve as the basis for his memoirs, it is the Queen who proposes that Frederick William be deposed, and Bismarck who plays the role of the devoted servant of the Crown. He refuses to take any part in the scheme to elevate the Crown Prince to the throne. In one story or the other, or perhaps both, Bismarck is lying.

I notice a folded newspaper on my desk; Otto left the underscored editorial for me to contemplate. The colossal effrontery of the man! He has been quoting from our puppet newspaper – Norddeutsche Allegemine Zeitung – which Bismarck secretly purchased back in '62. How many of those glowing editorials, I wonder, were purchased by the Reptile Fund? Once again, images from the past intrude upon the present, and I see the King of Prussia, splendid in his uniform, telling his first minister, "It is a matter of honor. We have promised my brother, George, King of Hanover, that his personal fortune would not be retained by Prussia but returned to his possession."

"I have said so to Winthorst, just yesterday," Bismarck replied.

"But with this document," the King hesitated.

"With this document, your Highness orders the confiscation of George's entire fortune, which shall be retained by the Prussian government for use as we see fit. Hanover fought with France against us, Majesty. George has no love for Prussia, and money will make him dangerous."

"But, Bismarck, why did we sign a document yesterday that we invalidate today?"

"Because George would not have signed the surrender, otherwise, Majesty."

"But George surrendered under false pretenses. There will be talk about the perfidy of Prussia."

"There should be talk about the perfidy of Hanover which fought with the French against Germans. George fought us, Majesty, but his surrender preserved the life of untold numbers of his subject who we would have otherwise been obliged to kill. It was a good thing for all concerned."

William I, by grace of God, (and Otto Von Bismarck) German Emperor, contemplated the victory over France and the perfidy of Hanover. Though he stridently maintained the sanctity of kings, William concluded, as he always did, there was no reason to argue with Bismarck. And so the aptly named Reptile Fund was born from the expropriated wealth of George of Hanover. Its calling was to disseminate leaks, slanders, lies, to whip up hatred and to exploit the basest of human emotions whenever required for Bismarck's purposes through newspapers we owned or reporters we bought. The boys in the street below my office press the papers proclaiming Bismarck to be the working man's best friend upon passersby, while I wonder how many of the stories originated in this very building at the desk of my colleague, Busch?

I shift through the reports and mark those which I think require his attention as I have done these forty-five years. It is more difficult for me to harbor ill feelings against him when he has left the room, for then he becomes the man who created Germany, and me. The Chancellor was a great man when he and Germany had real enemies. No one understands how badly Moltke wanted to smash Paris and France, and Bismarck would not permit it. Bismarck wanted a settlement, on our terms to be sure, that would bring about the unification of Germany and the preservation of royal, that is to say Bismarck's, power. He wanted a settlement too because he realized the other great powers would not stand for the complete humiliation of France and expansion of Germany. Bismarck understands real enemies. When he has none, he invents some. Such is the ill begotton history of the Kulturkampf. Bismarck discovered two sets of enemies, the Center (Catholic) Party and the Vatican. As always, Bismarck was able to portray ourselves as the aggrieved – the Pope refused to accept our ambassador to the Papal Court. And Pius' Syllabus of Errors was a foolish pronunciation. The document declared the Church could not be reconciled to progress, liberalism, and modern civilization. This was too much even for many devout Catholics. Next, Pius proclaimed himself infallible. Bismarck denounced the decree as a declaration of war upon all European states by the Papacy. We were shooting – I recall the Chancellor often repeats that the life of the hunter is natural for man – when Bismarck chose to explain the policy. "Imperium in imperio," he growled, "that's what Pius is after." He discharged his shotgun in the general direction of some quails and continued, "Being god is not enough for him; he wants to be Kaiser as well. Well, he shan't be, not in Germany."

"You're not addressing a public meeting, Bismarck. It is I. What are you really thinking?"

Bismarck smiled. "I dislike parliamentary majorities and budgets, and procedures, and this Center Party means yet another distraction from governing. Now I must please them as well as the Liberals. I have heard they will sponsor a labor movement – to whom shall that be loyal?"

"They are good Germans, Bismarck, who supported your recent war."

"Pfui. They are Catholics. The Austrians and French are Catholics; the Poles are Catholics; all of our enemies are Catholics."

"The Bavarians are Germans and Catholics. More than a third of the nation is Catholic."

"Ah, but which holds their first allegiance?"

"Perhaps that question should be left unraised. In persecuting the Church, you threaten the institution which touches the most personal and ultimate questions of life and death."

He groaned in disgust. "You know I worship God and uphold religion. Religion is crucial to an ordered life. Religion teaches respect for law and the state." He broke open the gun and reloaded, shoving the shells into the breech with a vengeance, and we walked toward a thick clump of pines. The sound of wings filled the air. The Chancellor reared back and fired both barrels and again missed completely.

"Pius has no capital for you to storm, Bismarck, and every Catholic you harm by the passage of laws, by arrest, by exile, by your speeches, becomes a martyr. In time, those who are not oppressed may wonder how long before they must be subject to the will of the state."

"Pfui, either the Catholics will not resist, they are Germans after all, or they shall soon collapse before a vigorous policy of coercion."

The votes for his anti-Catholic legislation came from the Liberals, though Bismarck had little love for them, or they for Bismarck. The Jesuits were expelled from Germany; the Catholic press was muzzled; parochial schools were closed. Secular marriages were made mandatory in Prussia. Pius declared the laws null and void and ordered the faithful to disobey them. Catholic services stopped in many towns and villages throughout Germany. By 1873, 1,300 parishes were without priests while two archbishops languished in prison. Meanwhile, the Center Party grew and Bismarck's most skilled foe, Windhorst, emerged to lead it. Windhorst argued the Kulturkampf was the struggle for freedom of conscience and for basic civil rights. This was polite fiction. Pius offered a Catholic neither freedom nor liberty from a liberal perspective. The Church proclaimed itself infallible. This was not an invitation to discussion and debate, but the Liberals failed to articulate the point. Even the grandest Bismarckian dramatics could not turn the tide. When he was shot in the hand by a young Catholic working man, Bismarck thundered against the Center Party. "You may try to disown this assassin, but he clings to your coattails all the same." Later he lamented, "They pay no attention to me. They do not love or respect me. They have no gratitude for what I gave Germany."

"A flesh wound, Bismarck," I said, "only a flesh wound. Next time get your head in front of your hand, and their anger will be greater." He failed to see the humor. The British ambassador told me that he evaluated the Kulturkampf to his masters in this manner. "Thinking himself more infallible than the Pope, Bismarck cannot tolerate two infallibles in Europe, and he fancies he can select and appoint the next Pontiff as he would a Prussian general who will carry out his orders to the Catholic clergy in Germany and elsewhere."

Meanwhile, Windhorst made the Center Party into the best drilled, most obedient, and strongest single political organization in Germany, which made it indispensable to Bismarck. And so the Kulturkampf ended. That story begins with the stock market collapse of 1873 which propelled the Liberals into Bismarck's wilderness. The Chancellor ranted: "Laissez-faire, have I been mad? I left the fatherland unprotected from the ravages of swindlers, speculators, and fraudulent entrepreneurs." He had, but many of them were his friends. The economy deteriorated. Krupp, upon whose enterprise the power of Prussia was based, let go four thousand workers. The railways lost money. The press exposed Bethel Henry Strousberg, a Conservative deputy, industrialist, and entrepreneur, as a bankruptee in half a dozen countries. Bismarck's response to the panic was as predictable as it was irresponsible. He initiated a war scare blaming all the evils of the world on French rearmament. The press, at Bismarck's urging, was filled with war hysteria—it did not play well. The British Ambassador sent the Chancellor a note. "The malady under which Europe at present is suffering is caused by German chauvinism, a new and far more formidable type of the disease than the French, for instead of being spasmodical and undisciplined it is methodical, calculating, cold-blooded, and self-contained. Should the doctrine that prospective and hypothetical and abstract danger is a sufficient reason for the stronger neighbor to attack the weaker embody itself in any tangible and official act, such as the summons to disarm addressed to France at the present moment, then I in my turn venture to prophesy that neither in Your Imperial Highness' lifetime nor mine will Germany recover the stain which such a return to unalloyed Faustrecht will impress upon her humanity." In lieu of war, pressure built for tariff protection. The pig iron interests and textile producers pressed the government for them. Bismarck required more revenue to support the military but the Liberals, who feared he would rule without a parliament should they give him permanent tax increases, rejected taxes and protection. Bismarck dumped his old allies and embraced his recent enemies, the Catholic Center. The Liberals became the target of the Chancellor's wrath and the entire Kulturkampf was blamed upon Albert Falk, who was forced to resign.

"The Catholics will never forgive you, Bismarck," I insisted, wrongly as usual.

"They have already forgiven me. I told them it was Falk and threw him to the lions. I told them what we did was purely political. We never fought the Roman Church for religious purposes but only as an entity which imposed upon Imperial German institutions and interests. What further proof must I provide? Shall I kiss Windhorst?"

What was at stake for Germany in the Kulturkampf? I never understood the business. What was won and lost? I should like to ask my mentor these questions, as I should like to ask him about the Arnheim affair. True enough, Harry Von Arnim was a well-connected fool, but his fate was undeserved. When I first came under Bismarck's spell, I thought he was being rhetorical when he proclaimed, "Never repent! Never forgive! I have found that principle of most use in practical life." The Chancellor was quite serious, and poor Harry is dead.

Arnim was the Bismarck's friend; they were boys together. Harry was dispatched to Rome by the Chancellor as ambassador to the Holy Sea. In 1870, he was sent to France to negotiate terms of the armistice and then became ambassador to France. Though Bismarck himself made the appointment, he notified the King that Harry had "an uncertain and untrustworthy character." Arnim proceeded to display an independent mind in his dispatches which disagreed with the views of his chief and was informed, "My ambassadors must fall into line like soldiers." Worst of all, the reports impressed King William. Bismarck's communications to Arnim thereafter were sharp and insulting and he complained, "Arnim plots against me. He has recruited the Empress. He spews nonsense about the 'failure of the Kulturkampf,'" Bismarck complained.

"You spew nonsense about the success of the Kulturkampf," I retorted.

"Pfui," he said, and with his face gaining color and the great chest rising and falling began to rant: "He has single handedly destroyed the balance of power in Europe and is conspiring with the Jesuits and the Vatican. His name is put forward as a future chancellor." Bismarck wailed.

This display stunned me, and I blurted out, "Even you, Bismarck, cannot live forever. The State must go on, someday without your services." He did not, mercifully, note my words.

"Instruct Fritz Von Holstein to watch Arnim for me."

"Let me be clear on this. You want Holstein to spy upon his superior and report to you?"

"Do not phrase it so, but that is precisely what he is to do." And he did, until Bismarck sent Harry into diplomatic exile in Constantinople, and Arnim was foolish enough to resist. He leaked information to the press and Bismarck, knowing the source, demanded his suspension. An inquiry showed Arnim had retained documents from the Paris embassy, which he refused to surrender.

Bismark's response was restrained, as always. "I shall initiate a criminal proceeding and smash him. Mark," he said to me, "the best words in the Bible are: 'Oh Lord, Thou has broken the teeth of the wicked.'" Bismarck linked the attempt on his life, and the resentment of the Center Party against the Kulturkampf with Arnim's service to the Vatican, hinting vaguely, if fruitfully, about 'Popish' plots. He relentlessly attacked Harry in the courts. Arnim was condemned in absentia to five years penal servitude. His career, his life really, was over. The lesson was clear, however, to Bismarck's wouldbe successors; no heir apparent to the Chancellor will be tolerated. However beneficial this situation may have been for Otto Von Bismarck, it was hardly an intelligent policy for Imperial Germany.

Limburg is turning up the gas to increase the light as the afternoon lengthens. He bends before the fire and places more coal upon it. I have little to show for this day. Bismarck did not reappear today as I expected he would. After we return from Varzin, he usually works like a demon for weeks. He must be too dazzled by his press to feel the need to work. Large snowflakes drift slowly past my windows to the street. The wind may raise them, or blow them away from their apparent destination, but there is an inevitability about their passage. Some believe, as Bismarck would have them believe, that his concern for the working man has come gradually but steadily like the change of seasons. He himself proclaimed there could be no program for the German working man until there was a Germany. After the creation of the nation would come the preservation of the working class. Bah! Before the creation of Germany, when Bismarck ruled only in Prussia, there were conversations with Lasalle, founder of the General German Worker's Association.

"Between you and your aspirations for the working man is the Liberals' majority in the Parliament, Lasalle."

"You are the State, Bismarck. L'etat c'est tu. You legislate on essential matters."

"I cannot control Parliament, nor can I always ride roughshod over them. They allow me the Army—we are all Prussians—but should I introduce your socialism, Lasalle, they will hang me."

"Universal suffrage is your answer. Enfranchise the working man and overwhelm the bourgeoisie."

"And who then shall protect His Majesty from the working class when the bourgeoisie is gone? Besides, I am not democratic and can never be. I was born an aristocrat."

"Then conduct a coup d'etat and rule without king, parliament, or ruling class. Certainly there is no one Bismarck fears."

The Chancellor smiled at this formidable adventurer who dared to taunt him in his lair. Bismarck summoned Lasalle because Prussia required labor peace. An attack was planned against Austria and a steady supply of war material was required. Bismarck also sought assurance there would be no riots in his cities while the troops were at the front. LaSalle was never asked what practical reforms would benefit the working man. Bismarck forgot about them after Lasalle's death and after our success in war swung the proletarian behind us. Patriotism compensates wonderfully for the pains of an empty belly. The working man is, in fact, a mystery to the Chancellor. We are from beyond the Elbe, from the agrarian zone of the realm. "I have lived in Berlin and its environs for forty years and don't like it," he says. "I don't like the stink of civilization in the big cities." Ten years passed before he was again forced to consider the grievances of working class Germans. No, he was not a convert to the working class cause after years of study. It was politics pure and simple that brought Bismarck back to the issue. "Atheistical conspirators whose system is an unbridled invitation to bestiality, that's what they are, and what they represent. Unpatriotic monsters with no feeling for the fatherland; both of the accused are lovers of France. They are enemies of the state and must be treated as such." The Chancellor was speaking of Wilhelm Lieksnecht and August Bebel, founders of the Social Democratic Labor Party, who spent two years in prison for libeling Bismarck. After their release, they became even more active. "In dealing with Social Democracy, the State must act in self-defense and in self-defense one cannot be finicky in the choice of means. We shall deny them the freedom to form clubs, associations, or organizations of any public meetings and the raising of funds. We shall deny licenses for trades and professions. We shall send them to prison, fine, or exile them."

To me, his prescription for the Social Democrats duplicated his formula for dealing with Catholics! Bismarck was about to repeat the excesses of the Kulturkampf. "Do you intend to ban the Social Democratic Party and expel its deputies from Parliament?"

"Well hardly. Germany is a free country." Bismark's voice held no irony; he saw no contradiction.

"You plan war upon the socialists but not upon their party?"

"I can do only what the law permits me to do. The existence of a Social Democratic Party is legal and constitutional."

"Then, Bismarck, it would make sense to allow Social Democrats. Besides, Parliament will not pass your law. Parliament does not feel free to curtail freedoms as you do."

"Parliament relies upon me to protect it from the mob."

"The mob?"

"The mob," he confirmed. "Our working people are not a mob and I would never refer to them as such. Most Germans are law abiding, respectable citizens who value order. There are those, however, infected by the socialist disease which instructs them to organize in secret and act in secret with guns, dynamite, or petroleum. With my feelings of conscientiousness and impartiality, I consider that unbearable."

"Parliament will not pass your law."

"Ah, but what is Parliament? Your petty bourgeois Liberals reject tariff protection for Germany which is favored by my favorite enemy, the Catholic Center. But what if the Center and I come to terms? What if the Center should choose to join me?"

"The wheel turns," I said, and smiled.

"Wheels revolve," Bismarck confirmed.

"Is there never a time for stability?"

"I do what I do in the best interest of the Fatherland always."

"As YOU see them at a given point in time. There comes a time for reconciling interests, not playing them off against one another. Unity does not arise from chaos. Surely those committed to free trade can be made to see that working men suffer from the importation of cheap foreign products. Surely the good of the many can be better served by apportioning suffering and benefit."

"And just as surely by teaching them to cooperate, they would soon find a way to dispense with me."

"Your indispensability will be demonstrated to all," I said, loudly, and thought the unthinkable, if you are indispensable.

"Pfui, I am the statesman here. What have you created? You exist to scribble my words and report my deeds."

He was right. I was right as well. Parliament rejected his anti-socialist bill. He viewed this setback as merely temporary, and the next stage of the struggle was produced by lead and blood. On June 2, 1878, Doctor Karl Nobiling, an alleged socialist, shot and seriously wounded the King. What Nobiling believed will never be known, as he took his life after firing the shots. What Bismarck did is burned into my memory. We were deep in the forest at Friedrichsruh ostensibly inspecting the timber and game when we heard volley after volley of gunfire.

"They have attacked my house," he said calmly.

I was thunderstruck and could only stammer, "Who?"

"The French, the Social Democrats, what does it matter?"

We heard horses approaching. Bismarck grasped his stick and squared his shoulders. We were surrounded. The sounds of the beasts moving through the trees were audible; our pursuers were close. Then we realized the shouts for Prince Bismarck did not bode danger.

"Here!" we bellowed.

A splendidly dressed lieutenant dismounted, saluted, and handed the Chancellor a dispatch. Bismarck's eyes gleamed. "Have you paper?"

"Of course," I replied.

"Instruct Privy Councilor Bucher to draft a bill against the Social Democrats at once. Telegraph the newspapers an account of the assassination of the Emperor laying full blame upon the socialists. Prepare letters to be sent on my signature to the editors discounting rumors of attempts on the life of the Crown Prince and his family, or threats of revolution in the capital."

"Are such rumors afoot?" I demanded of the lieutenant.

"I do not believe so," he replied.

"That is why we must suggest them," Bismarck said, and continued. "Telegraph the police districts to arrest and detain suspected Social Democrats. Compose letters to the various leaders of Parliament who resisted our last anti-socialist measure informing them of our intention to reintroduce the measure and our assumption that, in light of this event, they will join with us in passing this necessary legislation. Did you get all of that?"

I nodded.

"I think that will do for the moment," he said, and turned to the officer. "Now Lieutenant, what is the Emperor's condition?"

"Grave, Prince Bismarck, he is not expected to live."

Bismarck turned to me and announced, "We must return to the capital before Crown Prince Friedrich can take control of the state. His acquiescence in my policies will be difficult to obtain without us present. You can be ready to leave by tomorrow?"

"Of course, by tonight."

Bismarck turned again to the lieutenant. "What do you know for certain about this man, Nobiling?"

"Not much, Prince Bismarck. He may have been a socialist."

"Excellent," said the Prince. "Anti-socialism shall be the official policy of Reich." And it was.

Neither Germany nor the civilized world was surprised by the Chancellor's repression of those working class Germans who dared to join political movements the State disapproved. He would have imprisoned the Social Democrats in Parliament, too, had the law permitted him to do so.

I should have been able to predict he would steal the thunder of the Left as he did by announcing his conversion to socialism. He began by surveying the house, as he always did before a major speech, his eyes burning into each deputy, and then Bismarck announced his bill for insurance against accidents. "The invalid workman is saved from starvation by the measure we now advocate. And the bill is animated by a desire to keep alive the sense of human dignity which I hope the poorest German will preserve and which prescribes that he should not be forced to accept vile charity but should be entitled to something of which nobody can dispose but himself." He cast his eyes on the Social Democrats, on Bebel seated at their front and watched them squirm as mice caught in a trap. "Whosoever has looked closely into the state of the poor in large towns or into the arrangement made for paupers in country communities and has seen for himself how – even in the best managed villages – a poor wretch is sometimes treated when weak and crippled, is fully justified in exclaiming: 'It is simply horrible that a human being should be treated worse than a dog in his own house.'"

When he finished, the house was silent until Doctor Bamberger warned that, "To carry through such policy is to commit that State to a series of socialistic policies, the sort of which I thought the Chancellor abhorred."

"I am too old, Doctor," Bismark retorted, "to be terrified by phrases. My plan is a practical matter, shall remain a practical matter, whatever my enemies and the enemies of the working man may choose to call it." Thus was the representative of bourgeois Liberalism dismissed.

Bebel came to his feet and was recognized. "To your positive measure for their benefit the workers reply with ringing laughter, Bismarck."

"Then why so ashen, Mr. Bebel? How shall you fan the flames of hatred once we have demonstrated the State cares for its working classes? You, Sir, are as much of a relic of the past as the fossils in the Neander Valley." Bismarck bowed to Bebel and smiled, then stepped down from the podium.

Parliament disintegrated into a chorus of conflicting shouts and chants. From his detractors arose cries of "Shame!" and "Fraud!" From his supporters came cheers of "Bismarck, Savior of the Working Man!" The Prince paused as he passed my seat, leaned down and mused, "'Savior of the Working Man'? Well, perhaps a bit overstated. Besides, a contented man is much easier to manage."

A contented man is easier to manage; there you have the essence of Bismarck's conversion to socialism. The revolutionary reactionary returned to astound Parliament again and again, invoking patriotism, monarchy, and even God to further his schemes. "I have of course said: 'We derive our right to legislate the security of the working man from the fulfillment of the duty of Christian legislation, not from socialism. If perhaps you will read the Bible once, you will find out various things about our Christian policy in the Acts of the Apostles.'" The Iron Chancellor endorsing Christian socialism, it is incongruous and amusing, is it not? Bismarck treated God as he treated the army, something to be mobilized for deployment as required by necessity. We were at the hunting lodge at the very center of the Friedrichsruh, as alone as any two creatures have been since Adam and Eve. The north wind threatened us as it does in the works of the Grimms, while snow rose above the windows and ice formed webs upon the glass. In the safety of isolation, I probed the Chancellor's capacity for self-deception.

"Who rules Imperial Germany, Bismarck?"

"His Majesty, the Emperor," he replied.

"His Majesty, the Emperor, does not nap without consulting you, Bismarck."

"God has ordained His Majesty to be Emperor. Why, except under divine command, should I subjugate myself to these Hohenzollerns? They come of a Swabian family which is no better than my own. If I did not put my trust in God, I should certainly place none in my earthly masters."

"You have invented a God which permits you to serve your prince without loss of face, is that it?"

"I have never been able to put up with superiors," he said, "except God." He would go no further toward defining the locus of power within Imperial Germany, and, though he often evokes, he does not discuss God either. Bismarck's God is a thoroughly Prussian God. He has stated: "The German, unlike the Frenchman, stands at his post in darkness and in peril of death. This comes from what is left of religious ideas among our people. They know that Someone sees what the lieutenant doesn't see." Were I God, I think, Bismarck should gain admission to heaven only after agreeing to remain apolitical. Those who hate him, and such are not offensive to the old man, argue his wars will keep him from heaven. The Chancellor charges those who make this accusation lack faith. "I attach little value to human life," he trumpets, "because I believe in another world."

Bismarck inhabits a uniformly masculine world. True he is married, but Joanna is less a creature of his world than I. He never speaks of his youth, and of his mother he observed to a room filled with visiting dignitaries, "My mother died when I was young; she should have died when I was younger still."

Lord Russell maneuvered me to the side and inquired, "Does the Chancellor have unresolved feelings about his mother?"

"The Chancellor never leaves anything unresolved. He hates her."

"Ah, that accounts for it then," Russell observed.

"For what?"

"This whirling like a dervish in domestic and military affairs. This failure to secure lasting relationships among nations and permanent allies in Parliament. The man never learned basic trust."

It seemed too simple then; it does no longer.

Lights have come on across the city, and rather than having completed a review and warning, I have spent the day in reverie. The die is cast. I can no longer remain silent.

> Your Serene Highness must be informed it is the final treachery of your Chancellor which compels this action. I remained silent while Bismarck destroyed the careers of those who might have hoped to succeed him in directing the affairs of the realm. I remained silent while he manipulated Parliament and parliamentary parties precluding the creation of a stable political center in Imperial Germany. I remained silent while the Kulturkampf was waged and Bismarck proclaimed the savior of the working man. I have even, to my undying shame, said nothing while the life and work of Crown Prince Freidrick was impugned, and a series of lies about him circulated by Bismarck. Your Highness must know that Bismarck intends to challenge your authority with the precise intention of forcing you to acknowledge his authority on the threat of his resignation. I urge you, on the contrary, to accept his resignation for the good of the Fatherland.

Somewhere In Time

The Adventure of Modern Man

One of the points this case attempts to explore is whether what we take to be our natural appreciation of nature is learned or not. It is demonstrable that man, historically, hasn't appreciated nature at all, except for the numerous ways it has served him. The nature of nature has changed over time as we have altered our understanding. The next logical question is how much of the world in which we find ourselves is a mental construct, purely temporary, and already in the process of being replaced even as we learn its immutable laws and institutions? Man, in the 1890's, was attempting to digest the implications of Darwin. In Vienna, the newly soulless modern man was to take charge of and shape his world. Skyscrapers, locomotives, and the electric light would make life better and were to be immediately accommodated. Many women, however, had enough of a world shaped by men and were prepared to throw off their assigned tasks of wife and mother. Into this already steaming cauldron came the new psychology of Ellis, Carpender and Freud which argued women had a sex drive! Here was danger indeed. Without love, which was eternal, what was marriage, and family? The paintings of Klimt and Kokoschka, the plays of Pinero and the rejection of womens' suffrage by parliaments demonstrated that men were not prepared to accept these assaults on their definition of how the world worked. For some, Darwin killed God and left man alone in the universe. For others, Darwin proved that some races had evolved and others had been left behind. For imperialists spreading European power around the globe, there were "lesser breeds without the law". In Europe, there were the Jews. Anti-Semitism, under the guise of modern science, became respectable. In his book, More than a Trial, Robert Hoffman, in an interesting variation on the theme, argues that Jews were associated with modernity, and those who wanted Alfred Dreyfus sent back to Devil's Island were not so much anti-Semitic as "raging against things modern". Until the prophecy of H. G. Wells comes true, history is the time machine which can transport us to any place and any time man has lived.

In **Somewhere In Time***, two young American innocents have gone abroad at the turn of this century; Charles to the ancient university town of Oxford and Peter to Vienna where the modern world is being born. The young men are intoxicated by college life and exhilarated by learning. Ironically, Charles' excursions transport him deeper and deeper into the world we have lost, while Peter confronts issue after issue which will confound our century. As they consider conceptual frameworks men have developed and rejected and the new ideas being circulated, they can appreciate Mathew Arnold's observation that we are constantly caught between an old world dying, and a new one incapable of being born.*

Oxford, England
September, 1906

Peter!

From my window what spreads before me is a fairy tale landscape. Oxford is suspended in time, cut off from the great city of London and that whirling engine we call progress. Behind the college scholars punt; others, wearing their gowns, rush to lectures or sit among the flowers of the formal gardens and compose poetry. Often their original poems are composed in Latin or Greek and then translated into English! I spend hours combing sections of the walls around the Quads and the table tops in the dining halls to hunt for the names of famous men who have preceded me and left their mark literally at Oxford, as well as on the world. You think me a poor dullard, lacking sophistication, captured by the enchantments of this ancient university and city. I confess it to be true!

It has taken me, indeed, it will take me, some time to adjust to the course of study. As you know there are major differences between the system of education here and in the States. At university (they skip the article) you read your subject. The courses you select have no lectures; there are no classes for you to attend. You are assigned a tutor to assist in selecting the books you will read. When you desire, that is when you are ready to face the music, an appointment is arranged and the material discussed. Your fellow, or don, the title professor is reserved for the head of the department, will then make further suggestions for your study. At the end of term, there are examinations to pass (or horrors, fail). There are always lectures being given at Oxford on every subject imaginable which undergraduates are encouraged, but not required, to attend. I went to an unusual one recently given by our mutual hero, Herbert George Wells. Mr. Wells' topic was a book he wrote some years ago entitled, Anticipation of the Reaction of Mechanical and Scientific Progress upon Human Life and Thought. "Try and imagine," urged H. G., "the long term consequences of these newfangled motorcars. Although it seems safe to assume they will never displace the railroads as a major factor in transportation, what effects will they have? Who should be permitted to drive them? Only engineers? Only scientists? Only those with a physical constitution rugged enough to endure all that speed? Where shall we permit motoring? Motorcars upset the horses in our cities and on our lanes, disrupting commerce and agriculture. These questions ought to be given attention before we act. He who fails to act from deliberation must react from desperation," announced Wells. "Mr. Verne and myself," he continued, "have offered visions of the machines, cities, morals, and ideas of the future. I have chosen to depict my peoples of the future broken into groups, upper and lower classes, with vast gaps of power, wealth, and knowledge between them. Have you scholars ever pondered what those who live in outcast London actually know about the world? Do the inhabitants of the metropolis understand the physics of Newton, or are they still living in the mental universe of Aristotle? If you asked them does the earth move, what would they say? And if you proposed the problem, would a twenty or ten pound weight dropped from a tower reach the earth first, what would their answer be?"

Wells then asked if we understood how the man in the street, or in the country lanes, acquires his knowledge. "Does the denizen of London today have the slightest idea what the theories of Mr. Darwin actually state? If your answers are negative, then we must inquire whether our society can flourish, indeed, survive with an ignorant citizenry?"

We then went to the reception and for me to the more important discussion. Most of the dons stayed away, H.G. not being a university man, you know, and Mr. Wells was inundated by questions about time machines and space travel. Time travel, Peter, think of it! Remember the discussions we had on board ship about our proposed historical investigations. How much better if we could simply climb aboard a winged chariot to go and see what we want to investigate first hand. But I rhapsodize long enough. I am established in digs, as they call lodgings here, and embarked upon a course of study. When next I take pen in hand, I shall have more in the way of substantive information for you.

Cheers, or rather, cheerio!

Charles

Vienna, Austria
September, 1906

Geuten morgan mein Herr!

I snap my head in a bow and click my heels together to salute you in the formal courtesy which is de rigueur here. My painful duties include sampling plates of cream pastries of which I have not yet learned the names, though they have been responsible for adding a role around my manly girth, and sipping Viennese coffee. Oh, the burdens of life! In truth, Charles, I am actively seeking outlets for my energy. The fencing club accepted my application, though they wondered out loud how an American learned the sport, as did the tennis club. The equestrian society, home of the bluest of the blue bloods, is out. They were a little vague on my rejection, something about me not having a horse stabled locally. I suspect some offense was intended. Baseball has not arrived as yet; I intend to see we are the first to field a college nine in Vienna.

This is a strange place for an American to be, Charles. We have nothing comparable in the States. Vienna, being the capital of the Empire, is dominated by the palaces of the Austrian aristocracy, many of whom, by the by, are my fellow students at the university. I know you shall encounter a comparable social situation at Oxford, but Oxford is not like Vienna. Aristocratic scions come to Oxford, but their families are rooted in the country and in London. London is a modern city, as well as an ancient one, designed and built by men of business as well as English aristocrats. Vienna is far more the antique city – commerce has only recently arrived – imposing rather than quaint, often spectacular. I shall make it a point to describe the sights and sounds encountered during my peregrinations in the course of our correspondence. I wonder how much of this wondrous and wonderful city I shall have explored when this year is up?

I am acquainted with the university library which should provide a gold mine for my research. Many of the books in the stacks are positively ancient. Folios and leather bound books with covers inscribed in gold are there next to contemporary works. I have begun my study of man's attitude toward nature, animals, you know. You get the plants. That's the deal we made, and a deal's a deal! Even having read the King James Bible as often as I was forced to read it (as were you), the degree of anthropocentrism in that dark sixteenth century is astounding. The world was created for man's sake, and all species were subordinate to his wishes and needs. It was because of man that there were wild animals; the fall was responsible for that, too. In the garden of Eden, you know, lions and tigers ate out of Adam's hand and mingled with sheep and other animals without doing them harm. Every animal served some human purpose. Horseflies were created so that man might stretch his wits by guarding himself against them. Apes and parrots existed purely to make men laugh. Predatory animals lived in dens by day and came out primarily at night when man was abed. This was a true stroke of Divine Wisdom; man was protected by the very nature of the beasts God created, as God intended.

> The brute creations are his property,
> Subservient to his will and for him made,
> As hurtful these he kills, as useful those
> Preserves, their sole and arbitrary king.

Makes you want to thump your chest and strut your stuff, doesn't it, being crowned king of creation? And not a word in all of my reading, so far, about those passages in Proverbs which urge care for all God's creation. The birds and beasts find their very fulfillment in offering themselves to be eaten by man:

> The pheasant, partridge and the lark,
> Flew to thy house, as to the Ark.
> The willing ox of himself came,
> Home to the slaughterer with the lamb;
> And every beast did thither bring
> Himself to be an offering!

That man rides animals and hunts animals is not mere utility, as those crude political economists would imagine, but confirmation of human superiority and domination of the animal kingdom. We may treat them as we will because we are THE important species in God's eye. There is no one back then who thinks any of this remarkable or in need of justification. There is, on the contrary, in the whole of western history justification of such conduct, even before Saint Paul and without the influence of the Hebrews. There was a beautifully bound manuscript copy of Plato on the shelves which notes only man looks up, animals are condemned to look down. Aristotle, his pupil, was contained therein as well, and he frankly states only man has a rational or intellectual soul. Man is more beautiful and more perfectly formed than any of the animals. He has more divine majesty in his countenance and more exquisite symmetry of parts. Man has a conscience and a religious instinct while beasts perish and do not enjoy an afterlife. Descartes goes so far as to argue that animals are mere machines, like clocks, capable of complex behavior, but incapable of speech and reasoning. Animals consequently do not feel pain; the cry of a beaten dog is no more evidence of his suffering than the sound of an organ is proof the instrument felt pain when the keys were struck. Such ideas, of course, permitted our superior species to work our will over the animals without twinge of guilt.

You are, Charles, doubtless impressed by this initial outpouring of erudition; I have already filled one notebook, which is kept under lock and key in my assigned carrel. A carrel is a cage with a frame around which is strung cyclone fence. A bare table and straight back chair, designed for discomfort, complete my scholarly abode. Honestly, talk about Spartan conditions! I have added a bulletin board, both to remind me of the direction of my researches, and also to keep track of my daily chores, some pillows and other creature comforts. The library has kindly placed, in the next carrel, a beautiful blond, blue-eyed fraulein on whom to practice my German. And will I ever!

I do wonder, Charles, whether we in this ultra-modern, scientific twentieth century surround ourselves with similar sets of mental constructs and delusions? Consider the suffragette business. Is it possible women were not intended by God to be wives and mothers? Might it be proper for them to practice medicine or study the galaxies, or even visit the poles? But what, then, is the nature of families? And who, one must wonder, gave man the role and status he is accorded in society? In the words of London's Mr. Holmes, I made that question a three pipe problem but arrived at no conclusion. What do you think?

I remain, dear fellow, your humble servant,
Peter

Oct. 1906
Beaulieu

Dear Peter,

I do not know when these lines shall reach you. I am sending them to Oxford to be included with some notes I have prepared on our project, and a friend there will forward them along. I find myself in something of a daze. On a lark, I accompanied some lads to London and then to Southampton by rail. We arrived late and took lodgings. My companions and I went to supper and then separated, they to search for entertainment and I to view the harbor from which departed Mayflower and Speedwell. Next morning, we tramped to Beaulieu to see the ruined abbey. The locals claim the place is haunted, indeed the resident vicar is said to be on excellent terms with certain long departed Cistercians. The most common assertion is that one will suddenly hear the choirs, either by day or night without warning. The sound is strong, fades, returns. I have not yet had the pleasure, but the site casts a spell. The abbey was ordered pulled down by the eighth Henry, and so it was; no stone stands upon another stone. The foundation remains, and the outline of the vast building is inscribed upon the landscape. Sheep walk about the transepts and the nave; a sheep track bisects the center following the route of the faithful to receive the host. I proposed to sleep in the ruined cloisters and so seek contact with the departed but was dissuaded by my fellow travelers who feared the strains of the ghostly choir might be so seductive as to induce one to join them. They have urged me to close so that we may depart for Dorchester and enjoy a famous Dorset high tea.

I look forward to receiving your correspondence at Oxford, and remain, as you know me to be, your sincere friend,
Charles

Enclosure: Notes upon Nature

In the early modern period, man regards the plant kingdom only insofar as it relates to God and to himself. Plants provide food, medicines, and moral examples and are categorized as edible and inedible, wild and table, useful and useless, with man being the measure. The Grete Herball offers plant remedies for every complaint, from superfluous facial hair to stench of the armholes or swollen bullocks. Use clary (saliva) for backache, lichen for tuberculosis, and blindweed for cancer of the mouth. The Englishman puts everything that isn't poisonous into a salad – boiled elder shoots, hop buds, nettle tips, pea leaves, nasturtium and larkspur. Ground ivy was boiled, chickweed cooked like spinach, and samphire pickled. Irregularities in nature told men that disasters were pending. Worms found in oak apple presaged a plague, and misfortune was also imminent if an apple tree bore blossoms and fruit simultaneously. The plant names are graphic and gross. I'll give a few examples of seventeenth century terminology for your consideration. The countryside grew black maidenhair, naked ladies, pissabed and shitabed, mares fart and priest ballocks. Their herb garden contained horse pistle and prick madam. No less than twenty different plants were known as dead man's fingers. Two of my favorite plant names are "courtship and marriage" (that's one of them, Peter.) where the scent fades after the bloom is picked and "welcome home husband though never so drunk." Though the Reformation had long since swept away Catholicism, its heritage remained in place in the countryside. One found Christ's ladder, Star of Bethlehem, Solomon's Seal, Saint John's wort, and fifty ugly plants that began with devil. There is no plant that exits, in short, without an intimate relationship to man, and man understands the natural world only through these constructed relationships.

All of this changes in 1753 with that snake in the garden, Linnaeus and his Species Plantarum. The old vocabulary, with its rich symbolic terms and historic relationships, is displaced by Latin. Plants are studied for their own sake, independent of their usefulness or meaning for man. There were protests that giving plants hard Latin names when they had easy English ones meant explaining something by making it unintelligible, but science and Latin triumphed. Nature, it was realized, followed its own regularities and was wholly unresponsive to the behavior or thinking of human beings.

Oct. '06
Vienna

Dear Charles,

I received your first which was even more stimulating than I anticipated, and my expectations were high! Time, Charles, is so exciting to think about! We are, in effect, raised by parents whose time frame is a generation and more earlier than our own. We literally grow up in a different world than the one they experienced and which forms the basis for their perceptions and instructions. The conditions of our childhood and adolescence are different than theirs. Much of what they teach us – like our faith – is inherited from earlier and, on many grounds, primitive times, and yet we accept without much thought its relevance to our lives. How many of us ever escape the mental framework of our parents? How many of us are handicapped for life by it? On top of which, from birth, our physical clock begins its inevitable running down to our extinction, often before we can learn what life is all about. ("And at my back I always hear, Time's winged chariot drawing near"!)

There are forces here in Vienna being unleashed upon a world which neither expects nor will welcome them. As an outsider, I am only dimly aware of the debates which rage all about me, and the Austrian man in the street himself seems equally dimly aware of the undercurrents which pull at the foundations of his society. Let me give you one example. In my first letter, I expressed my belief that Vienna, in contrast to London, was an ancient city, as I believed it to be. The university is constructed in the style of the Renaissance. The Reichsrat or parliament building is executed in the Baroque style. If you walk toward the center of Vienna from these great public buildings, you are in the historic old city, the residence of the emperor, the elegant palaces of the aristocracy, the great Cathedral of Saint Stephen, and the other historic, magnificent (yes, even if Catholic) churches. However, a stroll in the other direction takes one to the Ringstrasse, circular, monumental, and modern. There is, to be sure, a transition from the antique to the contemporary. Apartment buildings in the second wave of construction along the Ringstrasse are a block long, designed by the most famous of Viennese architects, with the intention of maintaining civic purity and maximizing profits. More difficult to design were those in the textile quarter where residence and workplace were united. Still these buildings remain linked firmly with the architectural traditions of the city. It is a shock to encounter the work of Otto Wagner who was commissioned by the city in 1893 to do future planning. Wagner's motto was Artis sola domina necessitas (necessity is art's only mistress). His city plan calls for efficiency, economy, and the facilitation of business. His buildings are stark, totally unornamented, in contrast with the opulent ornamentation of earlier construction in Vienna. Wagner is concerned with transportation, communication, and sanitation. His structures stress engineering aspects rather than esthetic attributes. He loves girders, riveted elbows, and iron pillars, products of modern technology, which he identifies as the essence of the modern world. Again I say Charles, there is something more here than simply a question of style. Wagner argues in his design for Vienna the ideas of Mister

Charles Darwin, rejecting God and all His works as quaint nonsense from an ignorant age which must be left behind. Modern man is alone in the universe and must take charge, shape, and build. There is a fundamental debate being carried on over the nature of man. Herr Wagner believes that modern man has modern concerns and must live in a modern environment. He rejects domination by the past, that is old Vienna. It is thrilling, and frightening, and mainly confusing, and I will rely upon you to help me understand it. Or perhaps Mr. Wells might come here and make sense of it for me. It's ironic that I began with a lament that our parents and institutions do not prepare us for our time, and now find myself confessing I cannot come to grips with what I'm told is my time. Meanwhile . . .

I put to myself the question, how could the completely anthropocentric attitude toward animals change and selected my reading to answer that question. It takes a strong stomach to read accounts of animals being prepared for the market in the fifteenth and sixteenth centuries. Male animals were castrated. There was a triple justification for this. First, it made the animals easier to handle, did not waste fat on sexual activity, and, so they thought, improved the flavor. Bulls were baited by dogs to make the flesh more tender. Pigs were kept in rooms so that they could not turn around and were forced to lie on their bellies. Poultry and game birds were fattened in darkness and confinement, sometimes blinded as well. Work animals were treated badly. An Englishman, Sir Thomas Wroth, remarked of 2,100 horses he saw while traveling between Shoreditch and Enfield, two thousand would soon die of overwork. School boys translated from English to Latin and Latin to English, "horreo aluros sive feles sive cattos," I hate cats. And remember, Charles, the way they interpreted the Bible gave free reign to this treatment. The change in our attitude toward animals comes with improvement in the treatment of (are you ready?) dogs. In the sixteenth century, mastiffs were more important in protecting private property than the village constable or the justice of the peace, but they were a hazard. The Bishop of Salisbury entered a garden and encountered a mastiff normally chained during the day at liberty, and the ensuing contest left the good bishop on top of the dog but uncertain what to do next. The dog was killed without second thoughts, or regrets, to save the bishop. The Book of Revelations suggests dogs, as other unclean beasts, would be excluded from the New Jerusalem. Dog was for centuries a name of contempt, and adjectives like lecherous, incestuous, filthy, truculent, peevish, angry, snarling, and sullen were liberally applied.

And then one discovers a proverb, "He cannot be a gentleman who loveth not a dog." What happened? The rehabilitation of the dog is accomplished by the hound (referred to as noble, sagacious, generous, intelligent, faithful, and obedient) and the lady's lap dog. The aristocracy led the way. Aristocrats valued hunting, and the hound was a hunting dog. All dogs profited from the rise in status of their brother. When aristocratic ladies cultivated small dogs (perhaps to have something in common to discuss with their husbands) and took the animals to their breasts (figuratively, old boy), dogs could hardly remain contemptible objects. Aristocrats obsessed with pedigree and breeding found they could indulge these tastes in their dogs, and then horses, and then all animals as the idea of suitable pets broadened. Pets began to receive individual personal names, which distinguished them from other animals. This, too, brought a closer bond between pet and owner. And pets could hardly be eaten. Man's best friend could not be food as well. The same objection was extended to horses and then to wild singing birds which gave man pleasure. Larks, linnets, thrushes all disappeared from the diet. We hear of pet monkeys, tortoises, otters, rabbits and squirrels, hares, mice, hedgehogs, even bats and toads. Lord Erskine was famous for his several pet dogs, a favorite goose, macaw, even favorite leeches whom he named after two surgeons of his day. The communion rail, which disappears in many places after the Reformation, was reinstalled to keep the pets which enthusiasts refused to leave at home from reaching the altar. Pets were treated better than servants and were held out as models for them. "Here lies a pattern for the human race, a dog that did his work and knew his place."

Physical proximity and affection tended to break down the boundaries between animals and men which the earlier theorists raised. Physically, man had not been perfect at the beginning as was once believed, said John Bulwer. He was shaped like an ape or baboon, but, through industry and over time, improved his figure and reason to the present perfection. John Hall discussed the possibility that man's upright posture was an unnatural development. He proposed selected children be excluded from the sight of anyone in a vertical position and allowed to remain on all fours. Those who fed and taught them should do so on their hands and knees. This would establish conclusively whether the upright position was innate or merely learned. Men were morally no better than animals, it was argued, possibly even worse. Animal intelligence was debated with many taking the position that animals were intellectually as good as men. Domestic beasts, thought Archbishop Abbot, were sensitive to their owner's state of mind. "I think that I do not abuse the word to say that some of them in some things have a kind of fellow feeling with us." Englishman Oliver Goldsmith wrote, "The elephant gathers flowers with great pleasure and attention; it picks them up one by one, unites them into a nosegay, and seems charmed by the perfume."

Rousseau suggested that language was an invention of human society, not an innate human attribute, while the Scottish sage, Lord Monboddo, asserted orangutangs were not animals at all but a race of men who had not yet learned to speak. A few, very few to be sure, doubters claimed there was no God and no resurrection, that men died a death like beasts. To prove their case, they site Ecclesiastes of all things: "that which befalleth the sons of men befalleth beasts; even one thing befalleth them: as the one dieth so dieth the other; yea, they have all one breath; so that a man had no pre-eminence above a beast." The thrust of all this, Charles, was to break down the rigid boundaries: moral, intellectual, physical, which man had so care-fully built up to separate him from the other animals, by implication lower-ing his status as he raises theirs. But, if we are not superior creatures which all life was created to serve, then do we in fact possess or deserve dominion over them? If we do not relate to the animals as tradition and the Bible tell us, then how do we relate to the animal kingdom, and for what purpose do animals exist? These are deep waters, and my blue-eyed companion from the library has commanded me to cease my scribbling.

I must tell you about Chris. At first, her treatment of me provoked specu-lation that I possessed an aura of communicable disease or something. It was impossible to catch her eye, and my smiles were met with a coldness that made Minnesota winters seem tropical. I was actually accustomed to ignoring her existence, no small task I assure you – when our relationship was born via my homesickness. I located a small flag and was busy hanging the "Stars and Stripes," when Chris emerged unannounced from the stacks. She looked at the flag, and then without warning at me, and said, "You're an American?" I nodded and continued displaying the colors. It dawned upon me at last that she had not moved and seemed intent upon capturing my attention. "I did not realize you are an American," she said, and added, "Don't you see, that changes everything." I nodded politely but did not see how it changed anything. "What are you reading?" she inquired after I took my seat and began my assignment.

"Architecture," I replied in German.

"Few of your books are on architecture or engineering," she observed. "Biology, surely, is your field of study."

"Those books are purely for my role as a diletante, fraulein; architecture is my professional interest."

"Your German is quite good, a bit academic, but good."

"As is your English."

"What's your name? Did I ask properly?"

"Perfectly. It's Peter, Peter Gable. And yours?"

"Christina Lothar."

"Chris, I like that."

She smiled when I said it and looked amused, though I had no idea why, then. She proceeded to spend the rest of the afternoon asking me questions about America through the bars. We might have been convicts planning an escape. Eventually, she got around to questions about my family and myself. There was little opportunity for me to pose similar questions. "I must take you to my favorite Kaffeehaus for Esterhazytorte. You will love it."

"Now?" I inquired and she nodded. I closed my book but left my carrel in order for when I returned. Chris placed her arm through mine when we reached the street and indicated we must go west. Several carriages rushed by and Chris told me one was occupied by "die schone Karl," our mayor. The carriages turned into a park where a wreath was to be laid, but I missed the point of the ceremony. The park was filled with beautiful people. Little boys were dressed in starched sailors' suits. Their sisters wore hats with wide brims covered with artificial flowers. The gentlemen, home from their offices, wore top hats and sported boutonnieres. This park, like traditional Vienna, was formal in design with shaded promenades, hedgerows planted to create mazes, and vast flower gardens where children were not permitted to play, and did not. We left the park and turned north for several blocks until we arrived at the Cafe Mozart.

"Here," Chris informed me, "the sweets are a delight, and the music is from heaven." She was right. An orchestra alternated Strauss waltzes and stein songs with nonsense or romantic ballads sung by the waiters and then by the patrons. The same waiters with Tuetonic efficiency produced plate after plate of astounding delicacies for our selection. "We must eat and dance," Chris said. "Dancing makes one hungry, while consuming these makes one feel like dancing." We ate, or I did shamelessly and danced. Later, in the evening, she introduced me to the favorite student beer halls, and we danced again. In fact, we returned quite late to the campus, though not so late as to be in violation of the rules, which would have been a serious matter indeed. Since that first afternoon, we have been inseparable companions, so far as is sanctioned by propriety of course. I find upon reflection that Chris must know every last detail about my life and family while hers remains a mystery to me. Perhaps the moment of reckoning is come at last – I'm to spend a weekend at her home! Never fear, Charles. You shall receive a full report.

Anxiously awaiting your next missive, I assure you,

Charles

Oct. '06
Cornwall

Dear Peter,

I have come to the end of the world, and of time. I am in Cornwall where we journeyed after Beaulieu. My mates pushed on to Tintagel where Arthur was borne ashore on the waves, but I longed to see the Atlantic on the west coast of England. I left the main road and found a labyrinth of roads little more than footpaths. Hedge-banks reached out to hold me back, but I went on and came at length to the darkest tunnel of a lane I have ever seen. The hedges formed an arch the entire length of it, and the lane dipped down in green gloom then rose steeply as is typical of these Cornish lanes. At the top, I found myself startlingly near the sea which was breaking on a rocky coast. I entered Saint Anthony in Roseland. Twenty tiny white washed cottages, covered with flowers, stood at random. The bees were busy in the gardens which ran between and among the cottages. Cornish palm trees rose twelve feet in the air and ended in sharp leaves. There were no public buildings – inn, post office or shops; for that matter, there was no sign of life. The little cottages covered with briar roses and ivy geraniums stood with doors open. There was not a sound. Dusk was falling. I shook myself free and wondered where I would rest this night. I approached one of the cottages with the anticipation of a child nibbling at a gingerbread house and shouted a "hello!" A rosy middle-aged woman wearing a print apron came to the door. I was careful of the geraniums which covered her porch. "Could you tell me where I might find accommodations for the night?"

"I've got nothing for dinner, sir, otherwise you could have my spare room. We have no shops here. Everything is brought in from Gerrans."

"I can make do with the biscuit and tinned food in my sack," I said. "I would very much like to see your room."

"Come and see if it suits you."

The bed was white and took up most of the tiny white room. There was a shelf above the headboard which held the Bible, Pilgrim's Progress, and Uncle Tom's Cabin, of all things, and a washstand with a shaving mirror. I looked out the window and remarked no one seemed to be about.

"The men are in the fields, those who can still work, and the women at home. We closed the school years back. No children. Our young ones had to go away and do for themselves, out there." She gestured toward the England to which this village clung. "Please, make yourself 't home." She smiled and left me.

Outside my window toward the end of the lane, I could make out the remains of the school. The roof had given way, and the wooden walls leaned on one another like a pack of drunks. Nature was reclaiming the site. The boards were disintegrating and mixing with the soil, while brush and flowers covered the walls. Shoots thrust forth between the boards from inside the structure. Someday, Saint Anthonys and all villages like it will be gone, and a way of life men have lived for centuries will be no more than a footnote in learned monographs which shall go unread. I am a witness to the very process we are trying to describe and understand, Peter. There is an old world dying here whose customs, traditions, and conversation we shall not know and, consequently, will not remember. Ways of life are subtle things which can perish without a trace. We, you and I, can study man's attitude toward nature because it was the preserve of literate men, and rich men. How much of that exquisite mosaic of events which make up everyday life is lost. Lost forever! Darkness has fallen. In this room, in this place, I may as well be in the sixteenth century. Perhaps I am. Perhaps I shall wander the lanes this night and find a maiden of some past century, and we shall fall in love and pledge never to be parted. I believe that could happen here in Saint Anthony. I shall make my meal and leave myself available to whatever forces are here. As you know, Peter, "there is a spirit in the woods."

The sun is nowhere to be seen this morning. A dense fog has come off the sea, which I can hear, but cannot see. I have spent the last hours contemplating Mrs. Dunch's buttocks, better known to you as the Wittenham Clumps in Berkshire. Our ancestors lived in an intimate world where plants, animals, and even geographical features were unique and familiar. That twenty different species of plants were called bachelor's buttons means that local people had names for the flora they encountered. They knew their world. How more alien is our world of scientific names one must struggle to memorize and standardized geography which takes a warm buttocks and converts it into a clump. Besides, you get a better idea of what they must look like from the older title. We know what a buttocks looks like, but a clump! What image comes to your mind, Peter, when you hear clump? Sounds like a horse walking. Am I rambling? To take a walk in nature today is to be among strangers whose names you do not know and that makes you feel uneasy, even inadequate. Man has that curious character where he is not comfortable with something unless he has named it. That is why God left the naming of species to Adam. But the plants all have names, alien names, Latin names, which one does not know. To enjoy a walk requires a certified botanist tagging along. Yes, Peter, I am sure. The world would be a happier place for man if we had maintained that anthropomorphic view which was so rapidly defeated by the classifiers following Linnaeus. Of course, learned names probably did not reach the peasant who went right on referring to a mare's fart despite Linnaeus and later probably thought of Linnaeus as a mare's fart when he was forced to study botany. For modern man, the issue is mute, since the Londoner or New Yorker finds the countryside and its flora as unfamiliar as the lunar landscape and no longer prepares his own remedies, or grinds his own spices. Here, Peter, is the very place where parents, who transmit to their young so much that might better be forgotten, have forgotten what they should have transmitted – the accumulated knowledge of the race, the insights which enabled us to be comfortable in the world we inhabit. Instead, the human race finds itself terribly alone.

My next epistle shall come to you from Oxford. I am going to undertake a forced march from Saint Anthony's to Exeter so that I can take a train up to Oxford to be there for the beginning of term. I do not wish you to think our project has languished while I have been on holiday. Enclosed are my recent discoveries. I have carried works by naturalists, natural theologians, and guidebooks. I have stumbled upon much information in the guidebooks written by local nobodies who love their localities and are eager to brag about their unique character. My text concerns the transformation of the English landscape by the great nobility and the motives, practical and otherwise, which moved them.

You may be certain that I look forward to receiving word from you and that I remain your sincere friend,

Charles

As a preamble, or rather preramble, I hate to dignify my babbling so far as to suggest it fits a set literary form, how magnificent is the irony in discovering no matter how far one goes in time or space, one finds oneself returned to the beginning of the journey. I remember reading an article in the *Times* about the "great north woods," those vast unchartered wildernesses of Michigan and Wisconsin and Minnesota. The point of the piece was simply the forests have already been cut down. Should you visit them, you would find an ocean of stumps. The article proudly noted the value, in money, of timber taken from Michigan was more than the '49 gold strike in California. Can you imagine what it must look like north of Detroit? The scene conjures the horrific vision of a quadriplegic. We seem incapable of learning our vast country's resources can be squandered as easily as a profligate's inheritance. The passenger pigeon, the buffalo, the great north woods. No wonder Mr. Roosevelt is an advocate of conservation! And Peter, resource shortages have occurred in England.

Massive, visible changes in the landscape were undertaken by the great nobility. The decline, almost disappearance of forests, had long been a concern of the nobility and the king who owned the land. Hunting, that demonstration of social superiority, was done in forests, while the Navy, too, depended upon timber. That was a serious matter of state. In some areas, simple reforestation was ordered, but the rise of a new country house changed the face of the land. The great house was the seat of local government, as well as private wealth, and though the aristocrat was rooted in the land, he was also world wise. Status, then as now, was a principle concern. And so his house was to be separated from the village in the center of a landscaped park. Sometimes when the great house itself was to be preserved, an entire village was leveled to provide a sense of separation and space. At other times, a new house would be designed and set within an engineered landscape which included an artificial lake. The nobility in their great country retreats also began wide scale planting of trees, so called wildernesses, which despite the name were laid out in an orderly and geometrical fashion. Adjacent hills were covered to create an axial vista – a great wheel with the house of the lord at the hub – while the neighboring gentry deferentially planted their own trees to continue the pattern. The local Duke thereby demonstrated his power to manipulate the lives and environment of lesser mortals and visually emphasized that all local avenues of power converged upon him. "A great avenue cut through the woods has a noble air," writes one commentator, "and announces the habitation of a man of some distinction." Wordsworth would later call this putting a whole county under a nobleman's livery. Gentlemen of property, said Sir Alexander Dick, should plant at proper places and distances clumps of trees to dignify the look of the land. Besides, a great tree, as a great family, endures almost forever, has roots and branches. Charles II ordered 6,000 elms planted at Greenwich. Lancelot Brown put in a hundred thousand trees for Lord Donegall at Fisherwick in Staffordshire. Thomas Johnes planted almost five million trees in North Cardiganshire, while three successive Dukes of Atholl planted fourteen million larches. The zeal for planting trees reached the cities as well. A visiting Swede noted that in London, there were trees planted in the gardens of nearly every house, elms in nearly every square and still more elms on both sides of the road in the villages outside the metropolis. In the early eighteenth century, Thomas Fairchild urged the creation of more parks in central London, not just grass plots with gravel walks, but a wilderness of trees which would provide homes for singing birds, shade, and privacy. Hence these plantings were neither for political display nor to reap profit. It is difficult to believe, however, that the poor who were flooding into London, and the other cities in search of work, had the time to enjoy the shade and privacy of the leafy promenades. But it is likely they never enjoyed nature when they lived in the countryside either since nature demanded unending toil to yield sustenance.

I believe, Peter, that the ability of man to alter the landscape gave rise to the question, upon what principle shall the new landscape be reconstructed? Having acquired power over her, and distanced himself from her by the intellectual construct of botany, and by the development of commerce and medicine, man began to think about and relate to nature quite differently than ever before in history. In planning his estate, the great lord was forced to look at nature and consequently to see nature, at the very time poets and painters, perhaps as a result of the same forces, looked at and saw nature.

Nov. '06
Vienna

Charles,

I saw the infamous Doctor Freud today walking down the steps of the university. He looks like a serious man with a great head covered with thick black hair and a dark cigar protruding from his mouth. His lips were set in two hard lines. It would be foolish to say his theories are clear to me, or to anyone else in my acquaintance. He writes too much about sex, which has led to his work being sold as pornography. Freud, as you know, is Jewish and that has not helped his career or reputation. Charles, Austrian politicians have made being a Jew a political issue! The current Mayor of Vienna, Karl Lueger, plays the anti-Semite. It seems to be the central focus of his platform. Lueger was technically elected mayor in 1895, but Emperor Joseph refused to ratify his taking office. On Good Friday (how symbolic!) the Emperor capitulated, and Lueger was accepted as mayor. He is, if you can overlook his politics, an affecting character, cool, elegant, and able to move the common man. Lueger is not himself so bad as his lieutenants are. They say the most poisonous things about Jews. There are many forces coming together here at once. You're thinking, "he's said that before, what does he mean?" Freud is disliked not simply because he is a Jew who writes about sex but because he argues our belief that man is a rational creature is wrong. Modern man must awaken and see himself as he really is, says the good doctor. When I discover what he believes man to be, I'll inform you.

Meanwhile, The Secession, a major artistic movement, says that art must speak the truth about modern man and show him his true face. Has man been transformed in some manner since we were born, Charles? What is "modern man"? As if this weren't enough, Mayor Leuger lashed out against my fine university calling it a "hotbed of subversive ideas, revolution, god-lessness, and anti-patriotism." This thunder is a consequence of the theological position called Modernism espoused by Albert J. M. Ehrhard, who was obliged to resign from the faculty, and Ludwig Wahrmund, who was recently exiled to Prague. A transfer to Prague, Charles, would be like a Harvard professor being reassigned to the University of Wyoming. (Do they have a university in Wyoming?) These professors want the Catholic Church to enter, intellectually, the twentieth century. The modern world and modern man! What is happening here at Vienna is no less than a search for the soul. The Catholic Church (and Austria is instinctively, overwhelmingly, fanatically Catholic) sees sex as sinful. Freud says it's merely an instinct or something. Surprisingly, Darwin's evolution has not surfaced as an issue. No one has stated man must face his animal nature. It's possible no one in Vienna will admit to reading Darwin. Actually it's possible in Vienna where the Index is still a serious concern, that no one has read Darwin. Architects design modern structures and cities. The painter, Gustav Klimt, places provocative images of women in his work regardless of the subject matter. His design for a mural "Medicine" for the university ceiling has the nude figure of a woman's pelvis thrust forward, while his painting *Goldfish* displays a feminine posterior (a lady's bum to put it in simple Anglo-Saxon). Sex is a part of life which modern man must face without prudity. What do you make of all this, Charles? Is there a modern man somehow different from the man who came before? Are we, must we be different than our fathers? I'll be interested in your insights. (PLEASE DO NOT THINK SEX IS ON MY MIND BECAUSE OF CHRIS, EITHER, YOU DIRTY YOUNG MAN.)

I did not press on, in my last, to the logical conclusion of the argument I was following, though you have no doubt already guessed what it was. Let me summarize what my research has revealed so far. For centuries, man endeavored to place a vast gulf between his exalted state in the universe and that of the animal kingdom. Our form, our language, our minds, our souls set us above them. After a time, three of these defenses crumbled as men grew closer to the animal kingdom by bestowing affection on his pets. Once it was conceded that neither anatomy, nor language, nor reason provided an indisputable barrier between man and beast, all that was left was the claim that man was the only religious animal, the sole possessor of an immortal soul. This point itself was no means completely accepted. St. Paul in the Epistle to the Romans promised, ambiguously, that the creature itself should be delivered from the bondage of corruption into the glorious liberty of the children of God. What this meant was hotly debated. Some took the view that animals would be restored to the perfection they enjoyed before the fall, meaning thorns would disappear from roses, thistles would disappear altogether, and creatures engendered from putrefaction, like flies, would simply disappear. Others asserted animals would no longer be forced to serve man. Christ was born in a stable because he was the redeemer of man and beast. Saint Francis preached to the birds, which Protestants ridiculed. All across Europe, Victorians professed to believe on Christmas Eve, horses and oxen knelt in their stables, and even bees gave out a special buzz. Inevitably it came to be argued that each species would be represented in heaven, while yet others believed every animal who ever lived would be restored. Richard Overton declared, "If man be an immortal spirit then diverse other creatures have the like." Augustus Toplady declared beasts had souls in the true sense, that he had never heard an argument against the immortality of animals which could not be equally urged against the immortality of man. Darwin applied the crusher here, for if man evolved from animals than either animals also have souls, or men do not. And that, as you know, is where the issue is today, not resolved, simply not discussed. You should look up the debates of the Metaphysical Society, Charles. They must be at Oxford. That body, which included Gladstone, Tennyson, Ruskin, Tyndall, Huxley and thirty others, was commissioned to determine, once and for all, the truth of evolution. Huxley raised the question in 1871 in a paper entitled, "Has the Frog a Soul?" but his intention was to deny both man and frog an eternal part. The Metaphysicians met for twelve years without reaching a definite conclusion, and neither has anyone else. It's curious, is it not, that we leave so many things which are, at least for talking purposes, so important to us, immortality, the soul, unresolved? You would think these issues would remain front and center until a satisfactory answer has been agreed upon. I guess that's too much to expect from mere men. Or perhaps that's what these fine radicals, such as Freud and Klimt, are doing now in Vienna?

Ah, Vienna! I suspect the denunciations of the modernists are so shrill here because Vienna really is an ancient world in so many ways. When Chris invited me to visit her home, I had no idea what I had gotten myself into. Thursday evening a knock, barely audible, summoned me to the door where a coachman, resplendent in his livery, spoke far too rapidly for me to follow. Was I ready? Were my things packed or should he presume to do that for me? Did I require anything before we set off? My bag was ready, and at my gesture, he leaped to retrieve it. Then he helped me with my coat. I was surprised he didn't offer to carry me down the steps. I inquired, as he held the door of a vast motorcar for me, who would be picked up next? He stared blankly for a moment, then shook his head and remarked, "No one else, Sir." Instead of watching the city and its surroundings, I looked up polite repartee in my English German dictionary. Chris never discussed her family I realized with that sudden, blinding flash as when the events of your life appear at the moment of death. I would have turned back, in panic, but for Chris. She is beautiful, Charles. At home she'd be called a strawberry blonde, though the color of her hair depends upon the quality and quantity of light. Through the bars of my carrel, I watch her in the late afternoon sun, and her hair looks positively red. Her eyes are the color of robins' eggs. Her nose is small and straight. Her teeth are perfect. She is almost as tall as I am, Charles. You can imagine the effect that she has on people, though her presence would command attention even if she weren't so tall. She is very curious about us, that is, about Americans and asks how we reconcile the demands of the different peoples and classes of our country. We do it, she says, better than her "fatherland." She is proud of her country and countrymen but seems concerned about the future. I digress.

After an hour and a half we approached a fairy palace. From a distance, it appeared to be a formidable medieval fortification, but up close the military qualities disappeared and it became a parody of a fortress. We crossed a moat – a picturesque detail only, the bridge was fixed in position – and were surrounded by groundskeepers, grooms, and footmen. There must have been more people in the employ of this establishment than there were guests. Ascending the great staircase placed me in front of the entrance which was as large and crowded as the Grand Central Station. The butler found me and assigned me to a room. My bag and myself were collected by a footman and dispatched to a section of the house. Charles, the next two days are a blur in my mind. I spent the morning; in proper English tweeds, shooting and hiking, returned and changed for the afternoon's eating and drinking, and changed one last time into my evening clothes. Before I went to sleep, my formal garb was retrieved to be laundered and pressed and was laid out on my bed by the next evening.

The first major shock to my system came that evening, not long after my arrival. I was cowering in my room waiting for God knows what, when there was a knock at the door. I opened it and found my hostess. "Chris!" I exclaimed. Well, I might as well have been an anarchist hurling a bomb. She was at the head of a mob come to do who knows what, and they all gasped, stared at me, rumbled, stared at Chris and looked as uncomfortable as a woman with an earring trapped under her corset. She ignored them and took my arm. Whether I was the head of a posse or the intended victim of a lynch mob still wasn't clear.

We went through a mile or so of house and down a staircase about the height of Niagara Falls from top to bottom and entered a sitting room full of human statues. They all looked bored. Some appeared asleep. Others examined me through half closed eyes. One chap, wearing a monocle, strode through the room, ignoring me in the process but acknowledging the compliment "the most superior man I've ever met," presumably from an admirer.

"Nervous?" Chris inquired, but before I could respond she continued, "tell yourself you never saw such a bunch of damn fools in your life." After a few minutes, she led me from the room and dismissed the servants. "You just met my brothers and my friends," she said, smiling.

"You must be adopted," I said, and turned beat red.

She shook her head and observed, "You Americans are grossly deficient in diplomacy. Their attitudes are affected, of course; in society it is bad form to display too much animation."

Over the arch in the room we now occupied, I observed a vast coat of arms under which was displayed, in large letters, the name Lothar. I recognized the device at once, and knew I was in the house of Metternich, one of the most reactionary families in Europe, arm in arm with a daughter of the house whom I was addressing with great familiarity. "For heaven's sake, Chris, why didn't you tell me?" Before she could respond, a footman arrived carrying a tray upon which lay a beautifully printed calling card. On the back of the card was the message "You are a pig," signed by Count Grunwald.

"What do I do with this?" I handed the card to Chris, or rather Christina.

"Ignore it," she said.

"I can't ignore it," I retorted indignantly.

"Why not? You're a commoner. The count will not box with you, and you can't fence with him. His training with the sword is for homicide, not exercise. Besides, what will make him furious is for us to be together."

"Why?"

"Because the silly man thinks he is going to marry me."

At which point, Charles, I confess to entertaining a flood of ignoble thoughts. Was I playing the fool? Had Christina Lothar of the multiple titles and hoary pedigree brought me here to serve as an instrument to excite jealously among her anemic though blue-blooded suitors or to offend her family for some slight they inflicted upon her? I must confess to being cool, foolishly, toward Chris for the rest of the evening.

Friday morning, I awoke with a chip on my shoulder the size of Texas. A hunt was scheduled, and I was determined to show them how an American can hold the saddle. I took the most difficult jumps at such speed the rest of the party was left far behind. Later when we dismounted and shot, I bagged the most birds with the fewest shells. I was determined to demonstrate an American is as good as they are. In fact, better. Hugo Hafmannsthal, the dramatist, was seated next to me at lunch and professed surprise that an American was so thoroughly acquainted with his work. Afterward, I crushed Josef Kainz, an actor who has taken Vienna by storm, in straight sets on the tennis court. Chris crossed the court to congratulate me and to invite me to share a torte as we did at school. She poured coffee for me, raising eyebrows across the patio, and demanded to know what was wrong with me? I immediately apologized for my behavior, felt like a cad, and asked whether she would like me to return to Vienna at once.

"You do not wish to dance with me this evening?"

"I am not worthy to dance with you this evening or anytime."

"For a man who has spent the day demonstrating democratic superiority, those are groveling words."

"No one but you will ever hear such sentiments from me, Chris." She blushed (so did I). Then we were silent. We were seated at opposite ends of the table at dinner and unable to converse until we danced. The ball was spectacular. The gowns were beautiful, the uniforms magnificent, though many of the men who wore them looked old enough to have been at Waterloo. Too much ink would be required to describe the event, Charles. Suffice it to say, it glittered. The ladies carried books with the names of those with whom they were expected to dance. My name infrequently appeared in Christina's book. Since Franz Lehar was conducting pieces from his Merry Widow, and standards like The Beautiful Blue Danube, listening was some solace. When it became clear the opportunity to wish Chris good night without an audience would not arise, I retired to a Metternich family genealogy that miraculously appeared in my room.

Saturday was reserved for high romance. My fair hostess led me about the house and grounds through passages only the family knows exist far from the maddening crowds. We stood on battlements where the light sparked her hair while she told me the history of the house and of her family. We walked among the fountains and in the central garden there were peacocks in the maze. Chris would touch my arm, or place her hand on my shoulder, and I would feel alive and grasp the infinite possibilities and wonder of life. (You are laughing at me, Charles.) I'm in love. I confess it. A cold supper was served between midnight and one o'clock. We said our good-byes privately by the great fountain, for the family would spend Sunday privately, first at Mass, and then together. She took my hand and led me back inside, and introduced me to her father, a bearded old geezer in full military dress, the stereotypical Austrian aristocrat. He clicked his heels and bowed, while I shook his hand manfully and acknowledged the salute. His blue eyes were warm as an iceberg, and I thought he looked me over as you'd examine dry goods. He asked me how I liked Austria-Hungary and his home, and I made all the expected comments, then added Chris was the most beautiful thing I had seen. Well, Charles, that was not the thing to say. From what she told me later, I was lucky the old boy didn't challenge me to a duel. A footman knocked early next morning and hustled me off to a train station, and didn't even wait to see me off! I agonized all day about whether they would permit her to return to the university where she encountered such louts as myself. They did. More about that in another.

Your love smitten countryman,

Peter

Oxford
December, 1906

Dear Peter,

Are your parents coming over for the holidays? The pater and mater were coming here, but decided to go see Florida or California or some exotic place like that. They are terribly excited about the prospect of motoring there. They have a new touring car and a new chauffeur who, Father insists, can manufacture parts for the thing on the spot. Kathleen is going to go with them. It is difficult for me to write this letter. I have just finished my exams this morning and am so relieved and relaxed, I find it difficult to concentrate.

Term was probably two-thirds gone before I was comfortable with the English system. I possess a notable capacity to let time slide when some fierce, fire breathing professor is not standing over me. And, old son, there are as many diversions here as in Vienna. I've done a fair amount of traveling about the country as you know, and in Oxford I've attempted to locate houses lived in by famous poets, novelists, and even scholars. I've taken a drink in each of the famous pubs. I've kissed a girl on the Bridge of Sighs just for the experience, you know. There is no desire on my part to follow your example in affairs of the heart; should I find a counterpart to your incomparable Christina, well, that would be another matter. I have done some reading, those books suggested by the tutor, but little else. Nothing has caught my fancy so much as our researches. It finally dawned on me that every one of my friends and acquaintances belonged to informal groups, not exactly study groups, but more like exhibitionist societies. Oxford is populated with graduates of the public schools, young, precocious, and flamboyant. They form bands around their disciplines like history or political economy, meet together for dinner and drinks, and read their papers. The rest of the evening is given to criticizing each other's work through cigar smoke and slurred speech. In this setting, more learning occurs than under the watchful eye of the tutor. Belatedly, I joined two such societies, one of which considers colonial history – in which these particular Brits have the gall to place our country under colonial policy, failed – and natural history. I have become a leader in the latter category as you might have guessed. Let me demonstrate my erudition in this subject by continuing our exploration of man and nature.

Just at the moment, the naturalists were triumphant and a butterfly became a Lepidoptera, when the idea that all of nature had not been created exclusively for man's needs and enjoyment, some men discovered and described a new relationship between man and nature. Adam, you recall, was placed in a garden, and heaven was associated with flowers and fountains. Despite the tradition of the garden of paradise when western men imagined heaven, they envisioned a "new Jerusalem," a city. For centuries, men extolled the beauty of the townscape: the pretty market, the fair streets, the radiance of one town, the glittering like gold of another. As for the countryside, well, the only beautiful land was cultivated land. God created land to be used, and uncultivated land was a disgrace. The practice of planting grain and vegetables was not simply efficient, it was a pleasing means of imposing human order on the otherwise disorderly natural world. What could be more charming and beautiful to the eye than peach trees laden with fruit in August? The best of all flowers, wrote one Samuel Collins, was the cauliflower. Uncultivated nature was hideous. Scotland and the Lakes District in England were full of horrors: dreadful fells, hideous wastes, horrid waterfalls, terrible rocks, and ghastly precipices. Then came one of the most profound revolutions in human emotion and spirituality in history. By the end of the eighteenth century, wild landscape was first of all a thing of beauty, and, secondly, a source of spiritual renewal. To experience nature was a religious act. You know the writings of the Romantics. "Not a precipice, not a torrent, not a cliff, but is pregnant with religion and poetry," Coleridge said of the Alps. And he put it more bluntly yet:

> O dread and silent mount! I gazed upon thee,
> Till thou, still present to the bodily sense,
> Did vanish from my thought: entranced in prayer
> I worshipped the Invisible alone.

God, then, is experienced through nature. Wordsworth states that nature practices morality, and that man may learn morality by observing nature.

> If having walked with Nature
> And offered as far as frailty would allow
> My heart a daily sacrifice to truth
> I now affirm of Nature and of Truth
> That their Divinity
> Revolts offended at the ways of men.

That nature should be shocked by human behavior smacks of cant and nonsense. And yet the great Constable stated: "The sound of water escaping from mill-dams, old rotten banks, shiny posts and brickwork – these scenes made me a painter." Romantics across Europe believe that in observing nature one would find:

> That motion and the spirit that impels
> All thinking things, all objects of all thoughts
> And rolls through all things.

But who experienced these new delights of nature, and from where did these impulses arise? The Academy greeted Constable's painting, Willows by the Stream, with the order to "take away that nasty green thing." Clearly the Academy was not converted to the new faith. And that other great landscape painter, Turner, witnessed his paintings referred to as "Mr. Turner's little jokes." Still, by the end of the nineteenth century, there would be a growing concern to preserve uncultivated nature as an indispensable spiritual resource. "Long live weeds!" wrote Gerard Manley Hopkins and wild plants were protected in England. Wilderness, it was argued, is necessary for human freedom. J. S. Mill put it this way: "Solitude in the presence of natural beauty and grandeur is the cradle of thought and aspirations which are not only good for the individual, but which society can ill do without." And our countryman, Charles Eliot, wrote a mere ten years ago that reservations of scenery, like the newly preserved Yellowstone, would become the cathedrals of the modern world.

And that, my good Peter, is essentially where we are as we begin this scientific, rational, positivistic twentieth century. No nonsense about nature existing for the benefit of man exclusively and demonstrating the hand of God in every leaf and tree. Nature displaced God and receives His worship. The new faith is not exactly widespread, of course; perhaps its adherents were/are those who lost the old faith? I think it would be fun for us to discuss the contemporary orientation of man toward the natural world over drinks long into some morning; let's put time aside for it! And so having researched and written and acquitted myself well, I conclude this exercise.

Wire your plans for Christmas.

Charles

Vienna
16 December

Dear Charles,

The building is absolutely still, but for the regular breathing of Chris who sleeps in the carrel next to mine. We are, obviously, in the university library looking down upon Vienna. I believe there are librarians on duty below, certainly there must be watchmen about, though we seem to have the place to ourselves. There will be considerable trouble for me when it is discovered Chris did not spend this night in her dormitory. Her bothers did not like me much before. This should ice the cake! Chris was surprised that we, you and I, had plans to meet over Christmas, and she insisted we spend as much time as possible together until then. I promised you would receive these documents before I went down for Christmas. I hope you appreciate the risk involved.

It is important to note that all of the transformations described occurred long before Darwin, and in fact the issue of evolution has little to do with man's attitude toward animals. Those who do not accept evolution shoot animals and eat flesh, while those who do believe we have ascended from lower forms also shoot animals and eat flesh. The status of the relationship between us is really not defined as it was when man believed the Bible sanctioned any human activity taken against animals. Descartes observed that if animals really had an immortal element, if they were equal to man, then our conduct toward them would be impossible to justify. The opposite presumably was true. If neither had an immortal element, and were therefore equal, our exploitation of them must be impossible to justify. Worse, if we believe animals have feelings, even simple sensations, then human behavior was intolerably cruel. Well, intolerably cruel or not, man always has the capacity to bear up well under injustices committed against someone or something else. Thomas Hobbes argued that the human relationship with animals was based upon exactly the same relationship man had with other men. Power in a word. We treated the animals as we chose because we had the power and will to do so.

The same movement you have described in botany was occurring in the animal kingdom. Animals were classified scientifically. In 1721, Richard Bradley, a professor of Botany at Cambridge, described the female frog as a despicable, loathsome, little animal, but such language was already an anachronism. As early as 1678, John Ray objected to "hieroglyphics, emblems, morals, fable, presages or aught else appertaining to divinity, ethics, grammar or any sort of human learning. Only what properly relates to natural history . . ." was to be considered in classification or consideration of the animal kingdom. The fly did not exist to remind us of the shortness of life, nor the glow worm to recall the light of the Holy Spirit. Rooks did not have a parliament, nor beavers a republic. These were human activities. Animals did not have moral qualities in order to teach morality to man. "The real habits of animals should be carefully observed and should not be described as performing human actions to which their natural actions have no imaginable analogy or semblance," wrote Hartley Coleridge. It became unfashionable to regard any animal species as intrinsically ugly. "If the horse be beautiful in his kind and a dog in his, why should not the beetle be so in its kind? I cannot tell by what logic we call a toad, bear, or elephant ugly? A hog's ear or an elephant's snout were as well-constructed for the practical purposes to serve as were any features of the human body," Coleridge concluded. If we do not regard animals as dangerous, and if we concede we have no God given rights (dominion) over them, and if we further concede they are, after their own fashion beautiful, then we have no God sanctioned reason or right to harm them. Acts of legislatures which authorized bounties for foxes, pole-cat, weasels, stoats, otters, hedgehogs, rats, mice, moles, buzzards, ospreys, jays, ravens, and kingfishers came under assault. It was thought wrong to clip birds' wings, or slit their tongues, or even confine them in cages. Soon wild birds had statutory protection. Animal sports were regulated; cock fighting, bear baiting were abolished. Customs and regulations regarding the preparation of meat were altered as the attitudes about cruelty to animals changed.

You are probably anticipating as the climax to such thought the movement for vegetarianism. Those same Romantics who found God in nature took that logical step. Late eighteenth century vegetarians made the argument that the slaughter of animals had a brutalizing effect upon character, besides which the consumption of meat was bad for health. Shelly's *Vindication of a Natural Diet* made both these points. It was also demonstrated that stock breeding was a wasteful form of agriculture compared with arable farming, which produced far more food per acre. It must also be difficult to kill and eat the creatures of that Nature in which one finds God. And there, Charles, you have my final words on the subject of our inquiry.

Well, perhaps not my final word. Do you remember that my family vacationed in Arizona for part of each summer? Daily I would leave the cabin and go alone into the forest. I loved to watch light reflected either in the rushing water of streams which, to use an old but accurate figure, gleamed as diamonds or through the mantle of green stretched above. Pine needles cushioned and silenced my steps, or, later in the season, the fallen leaves of deciduous trees announced my presence. The sweet perfume of those same leaves as they decayed struck a cord of recollection that all things, including myself, must return to the earth. It is difficult to describe the flood of feelings I'm experiencing even as this is written. Bird song began long before dawn, plaintive and cheerful, and, in the case of the hermit thrush, longing. The flood of sights, sounds, and scents in the forest on an afternoon when the heat of the sun was enough to boil blood would require a literary skill I lack to adequately describe. My point, however, (Yes, there is one!) I felt tranquillity and bliss and peace, and I never read nature poetry or nature philosophy. So what was the source of those feelings? Is there an instinctual link to nature which the majority of mankind never has the opportunity to cultivate? Is the effect of nature as a mystical experience only open to a select few? Did I somehow learn to appreciate nature before discovering it? These too are worthy subjects for our mature reflection, Charles.

I shall now present you with my last thoughts on the subject of Vienna, before we meet. My informed judgment urges that Mr. Lueger and his Christian Socialists have no future as a political party. It cannot be possible in this enlightened age for politicians to sustain a movement built upon hatred of minorities. Mister Leuger is so transparent. He uses anti-Semitism as a concert master manipulates his baton and makes no bones about it. "Wer Jude ist bestimme ich," he says, "who is a Jew is something I determine." No, Charles, there is nothing of the modern world in this. The Dreyfus affair has made the world ashamed of such conduct. Gustav Klimt, the infamous Austrian artist about whom I wrote you, is now rejected. His sketches for major works to be executed on the ceilings at the university were universally condemned. The medical and philosophical faculties denounced his conceptions as ungodly and pornographic. Klimt retreated into decorative work which is pretty and without any messages. His successor is one Oskar Kokoschka whose figures are far uglier than any ever undertaken by Mr. Klimt. Kokoschka seems determined to show man at his worst. One of his astounding pictures is entitled, *Murderer, Hope of Women.* It expresses, so write the learned art critics, that beneath this civilized veneer, men are instinctive beasts. I hope not, for all our sakes. I think that I can confidently report, however, that all of this modernism, all of these attempts to make man become modern, or to make man face up to what the modern world tells him he is, will ultimately amount to very little. Perhaps these intellectuals in Vienna have got it all wrong and man at the time of Christ and the man of today is the same man. Or perhaps man is simply not ready to become modern.

I never witnessed a sunrise before today, Charles. The sun announces himself (the fallacy of personification – I am no modern man) by brightening the entire sky; there is no pinpoint of light first. I cannot tell if this process is rapid or not. To time the spectacle would be, sinful, for want of a better word. Transfiguration. Miracle. (I never said I wasn't a romantic!) Ah, and now the reckoning. Policemen have the university surrounded. Stiff necked, welldressed men are with them, Christina's brothers. Ought I to wake her, or shall I let them find us as we are?

I shall meet you or write you from prison.

Peter

P.S. Should I propose to the girl?

Oxford
Dec. 1906

Dear Peter,

I want you to think about something for me before we meet so that we can discuss it at length, sharing our insights and opinions. I have finished Max Nordau's book, *Degeneration*, and agree with his conclusions. We are a decaying people. Our decadence may be found in the realism of Zola, the symbolism of Mallarme, in Wagner's music, Ibsen's drama, Manet's pictures, Nietzsche's philosophy, Dr. Jaeger's woolen clothing, in anarchism, socialism, women's dress, madness, suicide, nervous diseases, drug addiction, dancing, sexual license, all of which are combining to produce a society without self control, discipline, or shame. A term has surfaced here most frequently employed in discussions of Mr. Oscar Wilde. "Maladie au fin du siecle," is what we suffer from. In today's *Times* there was a report of two young men who leaped to their deaths from a power boat. It was followed by a report on the formulation of the Divorce Law Reform Union whose president is Arthur Conan Doyle, of all people! The union believes that much of England now anxiously awaits passage of legislation which will free them from bonds pledged till "death us do part." I conclude, Peter, that we, our species, man, has lost his way. We have taken ourselves out of the general realm of creation and do not know where we belong anymore. Every plant and animal has its place in the Great Chain of Being, each rising above in a limited but exact degree from its predecessor. All are linked, like the steps in a ladder; all are related. Man has torn himself from this and finds no home, no stays, no stability. No wonder we need this preposterous new psychology; we have created our problems by extracting, tearing, divorcing ourselves from nature and now must devise a quack "science" to minister to our self-inflicted illness. No, Peter, this brave new world is not for me.

I have written my parents seeking their approval to divert the funds designated by them for my education to the purchase of a cottage in the Village of Saint Anthonys in Roseland. I am going to retire from the world, or rather, to a better world where I may work the land to acquire my bread and be surrounded by the nature from which we have fled. The past was a better world than the world in which we now reside.

Have I gone mad? Please, jot down your immediate reactions and pack them in your luggage. It will be interesting and, doubtless, amusing to hear them and your mature reflections.

See you soon.
    Charles

The Scholar

The Aryan Epoch: Nazi Propaganda

The study of language is as old as the classical civilizations. The Middle Ages and the early modern world believed, following Genesis, that Hebrew was the mother tongue. Dante recognized the relationship between the Romance Languages and suggested that Latin had been invented to serve as a written language for the peoples of Europe. G. W. Leibniz argued language was created by man to fulfill specific human needs, and rejected the centrality of Hebrew. When Sir William Jones read a paper before the Royal Asiatic Society of Bengal (1786) noting the relationship between European languages, Sanskrit and old Persian, the modern study of languages began. "At the time when they were still one people, they were speaking one and the same tongue. From this tongue have descended all the languages later spoken by the civilized peoples of modern Europe. Being without writing, they possessed little government and organization, but they were the most gifted and the most highly imaginative people of the ancient world," states one textbook of the period. Propagandists, cranks and misguided scholars took the ideas of Charles Darwin and the evidence of the philologists who described an Indo-European Language, and created a blue-eyed, blond conquering race of Aryans who ruled from Ireland to India, and who were the true creators of western culture. Houston Stewart Chamberlain, an Englishman who became a German citizen and wrote the enormously influential The Foundations of the Nineteenth Century, argued the Germans, the only pure successors of the Aryans, must be prepared to save Western Civilization from the lower races, Jews, Orientals and Negroes. Racism was common parlance. Tom Buchanan inquires whether Nick Carraway has read The Rise of the Coloured Empire by Goddard, in a book published during the same decade that Fu Manchu personi-

fied the yellow peril. It was Nazi Germany, of course, which elevated slander to gospel. The world's great men and women were Nordic. "We are thinking of Marco Polo and of Columbus; both men had a Nordic countenance and a Nordic style of soul." "The Roman Empire was founded by the Italics, who were related to the Celts. With the disappearance of Nordic blood – the fate of those proud empires was sealed." Woodrow Wilson once observed it was easier to move a cemetery than to change the curriculum. Perhaps the most impressive testimony to the efficacy of Nazi Party was the speed with which Aryan physics, biology, history and the like appeared in the textbooks provided to German school children.

The Scholar *tells of Professor Johann Dirringer, a student of ancient languages, who believes in discovering and telling the truth as it is revealed through his research. His superior at the Berlin Museum, Director Wilcken, is concerned with the creation and dissemination of an Aryan History which will please Propaganda Minister Joseph Goebbels and the Fuhrer himself. Dirringer's friends and colleagues explain why the Reich demands its own version of history. When Dirringer's and Goebbels' reconstruction of the past collide, the Professor must reconsider his conclusion about the past and the duties of his profession.*

It was nothing less than a full scale riot; the police were overwhelmed, and troops would have to be called to clear the center of the city. Dirringer was surprised that Hitler and his minions had made such a mistake. Apparently they believed there would be no resistance to their legislation – however outrageous. They might do anything, they believed, with impunity. Dirringer crouched close to the building but kept moving; there was no trace of the panic on his face that was plain on the faces of citizens fleeing bullets. The clatter of small arms brought a recollection of the trenches. A young lieutenant – he recognized himself – went over the top, caught a bullet, and went down. Lying at the top of the trench but under the hail of bullets, he watched his platoon being cut to pieces before they advanced thirty yards across No Man's Land. "'The Great War,' they call it now," he said. "But what was 'great' about it, eh? They don't tell you that." Keeping his head low, he reconnoitered carefully. He could hear the sound of trucks, their engines straining, coming from the east. Troops with machine guns, armored cars maybe, he decided. A few more minutes and he felt sufficiently secure to stand upright and to resume his normal pace. The canyons created by the city blocks absorbed the din of the street fighting. Still it was a relief to put the massive doors of the museum between himself and the chaos in the streets.

"Ah, Dirringer! What do you make of this? What's it all about?"

"Good morning, ah, perhaps not so good, Hans." Hans, J.G. Graf, was a blue-eyed, blond, barrel-chested, weight lifter in the last Olympics who held the appointment, Professor of Biblical Archaeology.

"It can only be the Hereditary Health Law they are protesting."

"Hereditary Health Law, what is that?"

Dirringer made an unpleasant face.

"Spare me the disapproval, Johann. I live for the past not the present."

Dirringer sighed, and explained, "Herr Hitler has decreed that the less valuable members of the Reich will not contaminate the community with sick offspring. They are to be sterilized," Dirringer's voice dropped to a whisper, "or worse."

"And this applies to?"

"Habitual criminals and homosexuals at present. In the future?" Dirringer shrugged, then looked frantically about.

"The homosexual business began when Roehm and his men were liquidated?"

"Yes, and the massacre was retroactively legitimized by a law concerning the emergency defense of the state passed four days after the slaughter. But why should anyone be surprised by Hitler's antics when it's all in his book?"

"*Mein Kampf*, you mean, Johann? But no one took what he wrote seriously."

"They should, Hans. Perhaps they will now."

They ascended the steep, imposing steps of the museum, bowed formally to their director, and went to offices on different floors of the building. They met again, shortly, in a conference room with other scholars and sat about or exchanged small talk.

Director Wilhelm Wilcken remained at the top of the staircase greeting or watching his people arrive for their day of work. They do not take it well, these scholars of mine, that they are organized and disciplined in the style and spirit of the military, he thought. But here the Fuhrer's work will be done. Satisfied that all were present or accounted for, he walked briskly about the building, pausing occasionally. He surveyed one room with what he thought was a condescending glance and proceeded down the hall watching, with approval, his highly polished boots. The Berlin Museum, the greatest cultural jewel in the world, and its staff, the most knowledgeable company of scholars in the world, were his to command. Herr Wilcken turned and strolled down the great corridor, conscious of the sound of his boots which announced his presence. He noted with pleasure that the gray stone slabs from which the walls were constructed were cut to resemble the blocks of Aryan fortifications in Anatolia. The electric lamps which hung from the ceilings or thrust from the walls were copies of lamps taken on digs. Sculpted into the staircases were the heads and feet of beasts, real and mythological, which looked into the eyes or watched the retreating backs of those who frequented the building. Over the great foyer, Wilcken resolved to install the eagle of the Reich, dominating, commanding.

"Is he gone?"

"Do you hear the clop clop, Johann? No, then he is gone," said Frederich Stroh.

"For heaven's sake, then, let us return to our offices and get some work done."

"Herr Wilcken believes in social scholarship, Johann. We are to cooperate and reach joint conclusions on all matters. A committee corrects errors before they are published."

"Herr Wilcken thinks as he walks, like a horse. A committee creates conformity, stifles creativity, and guarantees mediocrity. Thought is the product of one individual."

"Not at this institution."

"You approve Frederich?"

"I read the writing on the wall, to borrow a phrase familiar to us all here."

"Wilcken will impede our work."

"If you do not cooperate with Wilcken, you will have no work, here."

"Bah. If we protest loudly enough, Wilcken will be removed."

"I am writing about our ancestors, the Aryans, to bring Herr Wilcken up to date on our understanding of them."

"I would like to read it, Frederich."

"It will give me great pleasure if you do before I submit it. Those passages to which you object I shall be sure to retain. But you too must be doing something for our new master."

"My first exercise was a background paper. Herr Wilcken wished to be informed upon the origins of philology, and especially upon the status of

IndoEuropean languages."

"Aryan languages," Frederich corrected.

"Have it your way," Johann retorted. "I'll be in my office."

There was something comforting about his office, he recently discovered. The oak desk and chair, the heavily padded couch, and the reading lamps, one at the desk and other at the right arm of the couch, had been there since his second year at the museum. Now they were friends rather than furniture. He trusted them, as he did not trust anyone or anything else. Even old colleagues were suspect. He pushed the door open, glanced about, and frowned at an alien presence. On HIS desk, at Herr Wilcken's insistence, an intercommunications device had been installed. It matched his desk, to be sure, but it did not belong. On cue, it made that irritating noise. Johann snapped the switch and heard Herr Wilcken's voice.

"Please report to my office at once, Professor Dirringer. At once."

Johann grunted, "Never get any work done," and backed into the corridor.

Wilhelm Wilcken poured coffee and buttered bread for Minister Joseph Goebbels.

"You ought not to enjoy disturbing them so much, Wilhelm, or at least, do not let it show so clearly."

"Ah, Herr Goebbels, they are such irritating little men. So inflated. So self-important."

"But useful, Wilhelm, useful. You have located your office here, I gather, so that they have a long walk when you require their attendance."

Wilcken smiled. "It teaches them their place."

Goebbels smiled and observed, "Yes, it is important that everyone know his place in the Reich, especially in a place like this where men have been taught that false virtue, independent thought."

"They shall not be deceived for long. Not here."

Goebbels' thoughts questioned the usefulness of Wilcken. The length of the walk from the scholars' wing to his office was a nice touch, otherwise he seemed to lack subtlety and finesse. Bluntness had uses, but also limitations. "This must be the good Doctor now," he observed.

Wilcken's secretary knocked lightly on the communication door and announced, "Professor Dirringer."

"Come," said Wilcken. "Herr Dirringer, you know Minister Goebbels, of course."

Dirringer nodded.

"I have read your essay with great interest, Herr Professor. It is a true work of scholarship."

"Thank you," Dirringer replied, "that is high praise indeed."

Wilcken thought he detected a note of scorn, but remained silent.

"There are just a few changes which need to be made."

"Changes, Herr Minister?"

"Yes," said Goebbels. "All of these Italians: Dante, Castelvetro, and Bembo, need not be included in your paper. Begin with Hickes and then Leibnitz, and your paper will be widely distributed in the Reich."

"You want me to lie? To suppress the truth?"

Wilcken fingers formed a fist; he would show this feather merchant.

"No," Goebbels said soothingly, "of course I do not ask you to lie. You must simply remember, my dear doctor, that the Reich is interested in Aryan achievements and Aryan scholarship. Let the Italians write about Italians."

"But. . ."

"Does it matter that you begin with Hickes and his genealogical tree of the Germanic languages? Surely this is more interesting than the mere speculations of Dante. And, by your own admission, Dante was wrong in his notions about Latin. Is this not so?"

"Yes, but. . ."

"Professor Dirringer, a joint appointment at the museum and the institute would add both to your stature in the field and to your income. Chairs at the institute are based upon recommendation of the Fuhrer, remember."

"Yes, Herr Minister."

"And so, after you've revised your paper," Wilcken handed him the document, "and submitted the draft to Wilhelm, send me a copy by messenger. I shall look forward to receiving it."

"That will be all, Dirringer," Wilcken interjected. The interview was over.

"He will obey?" Wilcken asked Goebbels.

"Not this afternoon, maybe not tomorrow, but you shall not see this," the paper dropped from his hands to the desk, "again."

Dirringer sat staring into the illuminated circle under his desk lamp at the paper he was encouraged, ordered really, to adulterate.

Dante failed to recognize that Italian, Spanish and French were derived from Latin. He believed, instead, that Latin was a literary language deliberately invented to enable men of different tongues to communicate. Latin remained the lingua franca during his lifetime, as Germans, Frenchmen, and Italians communicated with one another in it. His work, *De vulgari eloquentia* legitimized the use of the vernacular languages even among scholars and other learned men, and this in turn brought the flood of dictionaries and grammars in the living tongues which characterizes the sixteenth century. This compilation of material made possible the advance of philological science. The next advance came when Castelvetro announced toward the end of that century that Latin was the parent of Italian, Spanish and French and had begun as a spoken, not a literary language, as Dante believed.

The Center of scholarship shifted to Germany when Leibnitz had the brilliant insight that Hebrew was not the primitive speech of mankind. It was difficult to overcome this older notion which pronounced Hebrew to be the mother of all tongues to which all others must be related. It was his sheer genius which enabled his thesis that language had arisen and evolved as a consequence of man's natural need to gain acceptance. Meanwhile, the distinguished German scholar, Hickes, prepared a genealogical tree for the Germanic languages, arriving at three main branches: English, German and Scandinavian."

Dirringer rocked back into the darkness and rubbed his eyes. His anger flared when he looked at his paper and saw wide red lines drawn through his prose, as if he was some poor undergraduate, and the comment written at the side, "Delete this section." Dirringer attributed, as was proper, to Sassetti, Coeurdoux and Sir William Jones, Europeans who were living in the East, the discovery that Sanskrit shared many words with Italian, Greek, and Latin, and finally with German.

Sanskrit	Latin	English	German	Greek
danam	donum	gift		
devas	deus	god		
janu	genu	knee		
madhyas	medius	middle		
vidhava	vidua	widow		
bhratar	frater	brother	bruder	phrater
matar	mater	mother	mutter	meter
pitar	pater	father	vater	pater

"Begin here," was underlined and followed with exclamation points.

Franz Bopp laid the foundations of comparative IndoEuropean grammar with the publication of Uber das Konjugationssystem der Sanskntsprache in Vergleichung mit jenen der griechischen, lateinischen, persischen und germanischen Sprace (1816). Greek, Latin and the other European languages were not derived from Sanskrit. They were as was Sanskrit itself, variations of one original tongue. Bopp coined the term Indoeuropaisch, or IndoEuropean for the languages. More common, especially here is Germany is the term later developed by Klaproth, Indogermanisch or Proto-Indo-Europe In Studies poured from nineteenth century Germany, and comparative philology was recognized as a German science. Grimm's Law, Grassmann's Law, Verners Law and the Law of Palatals offered explanations for the changes from Proto-IndoEuropean to Greek, Latin, Sanskrit and the like, and for the subsequent evolution of Latin into the various branches of the Romance languages.

LATIN

PROTO	ROMANCE	LANGUAGES
I	S	F
T	P	R
A	A	E
L	N	N
I	I	C
A	S	H
N	H	

Do the Aryans' Speech!!!

Who cares?

The evolution of language is determined by interrelated and interactive factors. First there is the brutal force of history. Latin speaking Romans conquered Celtic speaking Gauls, who adopted Latin as their language. Celtic speech disappeared in what we have come to call France. In the sixth century, the German Franks conquered the Latin speaking Gauls, but the Franks, over time, abandoned their native tongue and accepted the now modified Latin. German words make their appearance in the German/Latin. The Latin word for war, bellum, completely disappears and the German werra becomes the French guerre. Spanish is a combination of ancient Iberian, Latin, and the Arabic of the Muslims who conquered and occupied Spain. Italian is most faithful to its parent language.

Language is spoken as well as written; indeed languages are more often spoken than written for everyone speaks, but historically few have communicated in writing. Different groups of people make different sounds which are written down and thus modify the parent language. Roman writers preferred the term equus (horse) but the Roman in the street said caballus, and this word survived to become the parent of cavallo (Italian), caballo (Spanish) and cheval (French). That last word, cheval, illustrates a law of pronunciation scholars have identified from Latin to French. The Latin sound {not letter, but sound} K in an initial position before a is preserved in both Spanish and Italian, but has become ch in French. [Latin – carus, dear; caro in Italian and Spanish, but cher in French. Latin – capra, goat remains capra in Italian, cabra in Spanish, and again, chevre in French.] Another law of spoken language is dissimilation. The Latin arbor (tree) has become abero in Italian and arbol in Spanish apparently because the Italians and Spaniards had no desire to repeat the consonant r.

If you read this paper before a group, there will be no wet eyes in the house.

Agglutination describes the abandonment of the helping verb and the evolution of synthetic tenses. One said, in Latin, cantare habeo (I have to sing) which became the conditional tense canterei (It), cantaria (Sp) and chanterais (Fr) in modern languages. Another such change made verbs active in the modern tenses. In Latin one said, "I have a bought goat," which has become "I have bought a goat."

Professor Dirringer backed away from his desk into the darkness, rose, and took the few steps to his bookcase. So, my work is dull and dry as well as being insufficiently focused on the Aryans. An authentic Hittite pot held his tobacco. He filled his pipe, pushed down the tobacco, and strode about his office.

"Johann, are you there, or have you left the light on again? Come, man, it is time to go home. We'll walk with you to the train."

"Come in, Frederich, Hans."

"Why do you insist upon using that single lamp? You shall ruin your eyes."

"What difference does that make? They are brown, not the eyes of a good Aryan. Besides, it helps me concentrate."

"Johann," Stroh placed his arm upon his friend's shoulder, "is Hitler a model Aryan? He is small, tiny really, and dark. Goebbels is not wide enough nor tall enough to cast a shadow, and dark as the black forest. Goring is fat and slow as a grub, splendid examples of the master race. Do not take what they say, what they tell you, or, most importantly, what you write so seriously. No one pays the least attention to it."

"Then why?"

"The Nazis feel they must give the people a sense of importance, of uniqueness. They call it race, or blood, but that is nothing. It is self-adulation pure and simple. The people are not likely to tell the high priests of the cult that they do not qualify to be among them. The people see no such contradictions." Stroh took Dirringer's coat from the rack and held it for him. Next he took Johann's fedora and placed it on the front of his head where it looked like the stern of a sinking ship. He picked up his friend's briefcase, putting the handle in his hand, and propelled him toward the door. Dirringer obediently followed Stroh's lead but halted at the entrance and faced him.

"But the truth, Frederich, the truth."

"Always you sound like a lawyer. 'The truth, the whole truth, and nothing but the truth.' We are living in a new age, Johann, where the truth is not eternal but convenient. It may be changed as regularly as underwear. That's not a bad metaphor, really. Underwear is the closest garment to us, but the most suspect. The most easily soiled by us. Would you wear another man's used underwear or believe his version of the truth?" Frederich gestured for Dirringer who appeared as if he might faint. "Get your blood circulating man; get those legs moving."

"Hans," Dirringer appealed to his colleague, "as Professor of Biblical Archaeology, you cannot accept this attitude. For you, truth –"

"Is difficult to establish. Clearly we have given too much emphasis to the Semitic influence in the Christian faith rather than the Aryan. I intend to devote my career to resolving that condition."

Thoroughly demoralized, Dirringer was hurried through the door by his colleagues, who saw the light was out, as well.

The central problem for Wilcken was how to advance his career from this backwater to Hitler's Chancellery. It would not be difficult, he knew, to make the museum and its resident dancing bears into ornaments of National

Socialism, but would such success promote him into, at least, the outer circle of power? Wilcken, satisfaction etched upon his face, surveyed his office. It was, save for the giant, spotless desk which contained rotating shelves holding a considerable store of liquor, glasses and trimmings, and the carpet, with a nap high enough to conceal a sniper, empty. The Director of the Berlin Museum was a man of action, who did not hide behind books but got things done. His office proclaimed it!

Wilcken poured a schnapps, then rocked back, and placed his boots upon his desk. Perhaps it would be enough to remain in his present capacity. As director of this prestigious institution, he received invitations from the entire civilized world. There was little real work to be done, and his salary was generous. He remembered his younger brother George, the baby of the family, sleeping in a packing crate when his father, though an intelligent man and skilled machinist, could find no work. They survived for two years eating bread covered with lard and vegetables taken from the garbage cans behind Berlin restaurants. His stomach convulsed reacting to the memory. Life was good now. The phone's jangling startled him.

"Goebbels here, Wilcken."

"Sir."

"Sir? You're not in the S.S. or the Wermacht, Herr Director, call me Joseph." The invitation, though apparently straightforward, carried sufficient inflection to remind Wilcken of the fruit-laden boughs above King Tantalus. Goebbels is using me and is confident enough not to pretend. "Are you busy this evening? No, good. We need some academic types for the Fuhrer's speech. You and Professor Stroh will be prominently displayed. We want the world to know the Leader appeals to the mind of the educated as well as to the emotions of the great unwashed. My cheering levy for this evening is rather a higher caliber than usual. My politically best trained audience includes certain party members, not in uniform for the occasion, popular intellectuals, and actors. They know exactly when to applaud without prompting."

"You pack the audiences?"

"My dear Wilcken, surely this does not come as a revelation?"

"I shall be there, of course," the director said, "but I cannot speak for Doctor Stroh."

"Oh," Goebbels said, "I can. He wants your job, Wilcken. Haven't you realized that yet? Not much survival instinct. And have you read his very interesting paper?"

Wilcken opened the middle door of his desk and withdrew the document.

He read the title, "An Historical Sketch of the History of the Aryan Peoples," and told the minister, "I was going to take it with me this evening and read it at home." He listened to Goebbels and read.

> The original homeland of the blond, blue-eyed Aryans from which have descended all the civilized peoples of modern Europe has yet to be determined by scholars. After 3000 B.C., they divided into numerous tribes, wandering at will, seeking pasture for their flocks. The Aryans employed the horse which was virtually unknown to Orientals. Although they were not literate and possessed little government and organization, they were the most gifted and highly imaginative people of the ancient world. The natural setting from which they emerged was beautiful but harsh and yielded up its riches without lavishing them. This created a discipline amongst the Aryans that destined them to create by their labor the basis of a lasting industrial organization which would ultimately ensure the highest standard of material and spiritual living in the world. Rival peoples were the Semites, Arabs, and Jews. The history of the ancient world was largely made up of the struggle between the southern line of Semites, and the northern Aryan line. The two races faced each other across the Mediterranean like vast armies stretched from Western Asia to the Atlantic. The wars between Rome and Carthage represented operations on the Semitic left wing, while the triumph of Persia over Chaldea was a similar outcome on the Semitic right wing. The result was the complete triumph of our ancestors, who gained unchallenged supremacy throughout the Mediterranean world. Ancient Hellenic culture is traceable to Nordic immigrants. Paintings that have come down to us demonstrate that the Hellenes, so long as they kept their race pure, were tall, light-skinned, light eyed, blond people. The Roman Empire was founded by the Italics, who were related to the Celts. The Goths, Franks, Vandals, and Normans, too, were peoples of Nordic blood. A renaissance took place only in the Western Roman Empire, not in its eastern counterpart, because in the west, Aryan blood transfused its creative power into the rump Latin population in the form of the Lombards.

Dirringer, who was reading the same paper, paused and asked Professor Stroh whether a transfusion in the rump was the image he really wished to convey. Then he returned to the text.

Remnants of the western Goths created a Spanish empire. The Nordic longing for freedom of spirit and passion for truth found powerful expression in the Reformation. Nordic energy and boldness were responsible both for the power and prestige enjoyed by small nations such as the Netherlands and Sweden and for the founding of the mighty Russian empire. North America, South Africa, and Australia were settled and civilized by the Anglo-Saxon descendant of the Saxons and Normans. Everywhere, Nordic creative power has built mighty empires with high-minded ideals, while Aryan languages and culture are spread over a large and active part of the world. The difference between the two races, Aryan and Semitic, could not be more marked. The religion of Christ, destined to be the torch of humanity, was adopted by the genius of Greece and propagated by the power of Rome. Germanic energy gave it new strength. European Aryans have created, and continue to direct modern civilization. However, the continued progress of this great people, the Aryans, cannot be assured until final arrangements have been made regarding other races. The eminent French psychologist J.M. Charcot has demonstrated Jews are racially predisposed to the neuropathy of traveling and nomadism. Those calculating products of the desert, the Jews, believe whatever goods we Aryans possess were taken from them, and they are within their rights, therefore, to recover them by sharp and shady business practices since they cannot do it by force. Slavic peoples, that other burden of history, ought to be used to construct the new Germany. Afterward, they may perish. The same applies to Hungarians, a Turanian race, and no better, therefore than Turks or Lapps.

Dirringer put down the paper and turned his chair to face Stroh. "Well, Frederick, it certainly is a good story, vigorously told. I shall spare you my opinion about the morality of your conclusions. And with regard to fact, it is all nonsense of course."

"Not completely nonsense, Johann, be fair. There is an iota of truth there after all."

"Come, Frederick. You treat as an established fact the existence of the IndoEuropean peoples as a single tribal group or race of people. There is not sufficient evidence to support that contention. We have linguistic evidence they spoke a group of languages – but your reasoning would prove Jamaicans are white Anglo-Saxons, or Algerians are Frenchmen, because they speak English or French. You cannot reason race from language."

"Can you really be so foolish, Johann, to challenge the existence of the pure Aryan, Germanic Race? Let us suppose for a moment that you are right, I am inventing history. It is a glorious history and it shall be read and remembered and recited. It shall be cited with approval. About the truth of it no one will care. The author shall be recalled with approval. There will be rewards for writing such history. I intend to become the keeper of the great Aryan past and the prophet of National Socialist Germany's destiny."

"Ah, that's what the old phrase means, 'prophet without honor.'"

"Are there any Jews on your family tree, Johann, or do you possess Jewish relatives by marriage? Why do you challenge the facts put forward by your Fuhrer and the conclusion of German scholarship? There must be some reason. What may we suppose, except that you are a product of the Semitic enemy?"

Dirringer could not speak. The effort of controlling his fury checked his ability to rebut articulately, let alone effectively.

Stroh smiled. "You see, I, an amateur at baiting, have reduced you to this. What shall you do when the fury of the true believer is unleashed upon you in a public forum?"

"I am not challenging them; I am merely correcting some of their ideas which were constructed upon faulty scholarship and inadequate information. I am not political. I have no interest in politics. I am an archaeologist of language, that is all."

"Let me explain a fact of life to you, Johann. Germany will eventually embark upon a war which shall make the earlier conflagration of this century a pleasant memory. Modern warfare must kill those who fight, and it must also kill those who make the weapons and those who provide food and other necessities for those who fight. Modern warfare must kill every member of the enemy population – women, children, the aged – who can do them harm, and science has given us the weapons to do it. But first we must have a set of ideas which justify a mass slaughter from which any civilized man would recoil in horror. It is the obligation of German scholarship to provide those ideas. We, the Aryans, are superior and fit to rule. Everyone else is intended to serve us, or is expendable. Besides, if Hitler wins, the Aryan myth will become governing orthodoxy. Its truth will be proclaimed in the schools and none will dispute it. Truth, Johann, is established by the victor."

"Truth is absolute and can be arrived at by study."

"You are an anachronism, my friend. I have warned you and now must take my leave. Herr Wilcken has summoned me."

Dirringer removed his pince-nez, wiped his eyes, and rocked back in his chair. Without consciously closing his eyes, he dreamed that he was the famous Sir Henry Rawlinson, British military envoy to Persia in the last century, who discovered, high up a mountain cliff called Bisitun, many lines of writing in the same three scripts which appeared on the monuments of Persia. To copy the text, he stood upon a native ladder precariously balanced on a twelve inch ledge with a sheer drop of several hundred feet behind him. He steadied his body against the rock while holding the notebook in his left hand and his pencil in his right. "In this position," Dirringer heard himself as Rawlinson proclaim, "I copied all of the upper inscriptions and the interest of occupation entirely did away with any sense of danger." The chair lurched forward almost throwing him against his desk; he awoke with a start. It took a moment to orient himself to the office before he mumbled, "The heroic age of linguistic study is past." Dirringer rose and put on his coat.

The Gadget

The Manhattan Project

Leo Szilard, a Hungarian physicist who had fled Hitler's Germany, conceived of the Atomic Bomb while waiting for a red light at a street crossing in London. Find an element that could be split by neutrons, sustain the chain reaction and liberate incredible amounts of energy. At George Washington University, in January 1939, the great Danish physicist Niels Bohr announced the uranium nucleus could be split. In October, Dr. Alexander Sachs, who had been an economist with the National Recovery Administration, took a letter drafted by Szilard and signed by Albert Einstein to President Roosevelt. A Uranium Committee was established, but three years passed before serious work began on the atomic bomb. On October 9, 1941 when German armies were twenty-five miles from Moscow, Roosevelt put political muscle and money behind what was dubbed "S-1". American physicists, like Ernest O. Lawrence at Berkeley, were convinced that if the Germans made the bomb first, they would rule the world. Colonel Leslie R. Groves, the engineer in charge of all military construction, including the Pentagon, was informed on September 17, 1942 that he would be asked to assume direction of the Manhattan Engineer District, as the Army A-Bomb effort was known, and was promoted. No one liked Groves, who disapproved of smoking, drinking, profanity and wasting time, but he got things done. The day after his appointment, he authorized purchase of uranium which had held up the project for months, and the following day commissioned construction of the Oak Ridge Tennessee facility which would eventually employ 85,000 people. Manhattan was finally on track. Groves was frustrated by the numbers he received from the scientists on how much uranium would be required to detonate the bomb; Lawrence directed him to J. Robert Oppenheimer at Berkeley and one of the most un-

likely partnerships in history was formed. It was "Oppie" who suggested the Los Alamos site to Groves. The General wanted a place far from the Pacific Coast, which might be attacked by the Japanese, and sufficiently isolated to keep his scientists to the task, and the project secret. Meanwhile, on December 2, 1942 on the squash courts at the University of Chicago, Enrico Fermi supervised the first nuclear chain reaction; neither the President of the University nor the mayor of Chicago had been notified. On December 7, 1941 Lawrence's physicists collected the first micrograms of uranium-235, and learned Japan had destroyed most of the U.S. Pacific Fleet. Germany and Italy declared war on the United States and the race for the Atomic Bomb, and victory, was on. The story of the conception and construction of the Atomic Bomb is one of the most impressive monuments to human intellect and ingenuity in history. Never has the "can do" spirit of Americans been more in evidence, and never has it produced a device the existence of which can only be lamented.

In **The Gadget**, *the principal figures involved in the creation of the device consider their achievements. J. Robert Oppenheimer prepares for the crucial test, while General Groves considers how the bomb will be used once it moves from theory to reality. Ted Klususki, one of the skilled machinists who must make the bomb work, doubts whether men armed with such power will be able to survive. The older men who advise the President, Leahy and Stimson, oppose use of the weapon, but Jimmy Byrnes, confidant to President Truman, believes it can be a useful tool in the postwar world.*

J. Robert Oppenheimer, "Oppie," contemplated his naked body in the bathtub that was a principle status symbol on the Hill. The twenty-two pounds he had lost from the original 135 on his six foot frame left him virtually a skeleton. Kitty, his wife, joked about whether he or the bomb would go first. Mustn't call it a bomb, he reminded himself. It was the device or the gadget. Oppie closed his eyes. Either the effects of the constant pressures, anxieties, demands, tasks, physical and mental, which were draining his body, or the water buoying his slight frame, caused Oppie to slip into something approximating a trance. He remembered it all. First they, the army and the scientists, required a place; Oppenheimer suggested Los Alamos, "the poplars." He had come here as a boy for his health and, later, when a professor at Berkeley bought land for a retreat. He suggested the mesa with its limitless views and ageless peaks would be an inspired place for the work of harnessing the elemental forces which made the peaks and powered the stars. General Groves agreed.

The work began with the construction of the physical plant for a laboratory and for the community where the scientists would live. In the beginning was the Los Alamos Ranch School for Boys. It was purchased by Groves. Oppie and two other most senior members of his team were awarded the three bathtubs on the mesa which had belonged to school administrators. All houses subsequently constructed at Los Alamos had showers. The first scientists to arrive slept on the porch of Fuller Lodge until the prefabricated housing was available with the heaters that didn't work and the wood burning stoves that wouldn't light. The original lab buildings, constructed out of clap board with simple pitched roofs, were neither air-conditioned nor dust proofed. For purposes of security, the "telephone network" consisted of one line maintained by the Forest Service.

Still a city which accommodated six thousand people was raised in the wilderness. The army constructed over two hundred and fifty working buildings, schools and clinics, and five hundred apartments, houses, dormitories, and trailers. "The House that Oppie built," he thought and staffed and ran democratically. Science had to be democratic and open. The sharing of information between sections drove Groves mad; compartmentalization was essential for security, he insisted. But Oppie knew to complete the tasks of determining and developing the conditions that would generate nuclear reactions and detonation, of discovering the chemistry and metallurgy of uranium and plutonium, of knowing, in short, what must be known to design a weapon, and lastly of making a weapon that would work, all knowledge must be available to the team. Though Groves thundered, Oppenheimer prevailed. Time and time again he saved the project. Oppie remembered how despair rocked the lab when the team finally concluded the gun-assembly method of firing the bomb would not work for plutonium, and the laboratory at Oak Ridge could not provide uranium for more than one bomb. They were apparently left with the choice of testing a weapon they could never duplicate or of dropping what might prove to be the largest, most expensive dud in history. Next, George Kistiakowsky insisted the implosion method for firing the plutonium weapon would never work and morale plummeted even further. "It must be made to work, George," Oppie told him and reorganized the lab once again. The project went back on track.

And now that the gadget was ready to be tested, a suitable name, something dramatic and compelling was required. Oppie's body twitched from his left shoulder to his left toes. The scientist opened his eyes slowly, as if recalled from a trance and beheld his body floating on the water. He began to recite John Donne's description:

As'twixt two equall Armies, Fate
Suspends uncertaine victorie,
Our soules, (which to advance their state,
Were gone out,) hung 'twixt her and me.
And whil'st our soules negotiate there,
Wee like sepulchrall statues lay . . .

Oppie sat up in the tub and shook his head and knew he would call the test "Trinity."

Chocolate dribbled down the side of the General Leslie Groves' chin, and the shiny dark brown hair that gave him the nickname "greasy" at the Point glowed white under the light. Groves, the builder of the Pentagon, could easily be cast as Henry VIII. He had penetrating blue eyes, a sensual mouth, and an instinct for power. He ruled a two billion dollar enterprise of thirty-seven installations staffed by over one hundred and twenty thousand people. He would control the bomb that would, however long it took, be built and used. He never asked if the bomb would be used. Groves believed in action. When the bomb was ready, it would be used. He made certain the staff, all of the staff, including the prima donna scientists, realized Manhattan was an army enterprise. For those who wished to talk philosophically about the bomb, there were threats of duty assignments on Guadalcanal. The bomb was necessary, that was that. The allegedly beaten German enemy suddenly had jets which outperformed our aircraft and new rockets to rain death on London. Who knew what other surprises Hitler might suddenly unleash?

Although the General always spoke confidently, his security chief, Frank Martel, doubted there would be a bomb. At Los Alamos you were safe; no bullets flew in your direction. That took the pressure off, and pressure was needed. Good Americans, like Arthur Compton, ran cold and hot on the project. Frank had Compton investigated for an alleged comment: "Better to be a slave under the Nazi heel than to draw down the final curtain on humanity." Frank scoffed. What did they think they were building anyway? Compton was reacting to a story spread by that crazy Hungarian Edward Teller. According to Teller's calculations, an atomic explosion would cause fusion in deuterium, which would ignite hydrogen in the water and nitrogen in the air burning oceans and atmosphere and ending life on the planet. Teller admitted he was wrong about that, of course, but was he intentionally wrong? Was Teller trying to wreck Manhattan by spreading fear? If so, Frank would eventually nail him. Martel knew his business. His five hundred CID men and women posed as bartenders, waiters, and salesmen in Santa Fe and other towns around Los Alamos, eavesdropping on conversations, shadowing scientists and engineers, hiding microphones in homes, censoring mail, and tapping phones. No one would pass secrets to Nazis or the Russians on his watch, and no spies would penetrate Manhattan, or god damn New Mexico for that matter. What a zoo! Americans, like Oppenheimer himself, had commies in their past lives. The two Hungarians, Szilard and Teller, were impossible. Szilard openly displayed contempt for the general, and Teller refused to work on the gadget. He insisted he had been recruited to work on a hydrogen bomb, whatever that was. There were Brits and German-Brits like Karl Fuchs. And then there were smart asses like Richard Feynman who worked out the combination of all the safes and left notes saying, "Guess Who?" Frank wanted to put him in Levinworth and let him figure a way out of that. The general was more tolerant, and besides, he wanted his bomb.

"Sir?"

"Yes, Frank?"

"I thought you'd want to know, Sir."

"Yes?"

"General LeMay is in hot water with the civilians. Some of them want his scalp."

"Curt? What's he done?"

"Fire bombed Tokyo with jellied gasoline without consulting Washington. Secretary Stimson is appalled because there were no protests in Washington against us civilized Americans for conducting wholesale slaughter. Bush is complaining that he can't sleep."

"Anybody die besides Japs?" Groves' comment surprised him. Frank had no difficulty accepting the bombing, but he wondered how the general, son of a preacher, could balance military necessity and the fourth commandment. "How'd you hear about this?"

"First, from a friend at the Pentagon, and then from Oppenheimer. Stimson called him on purpose, I'd say. Same principle. New weapon, new consequences."

"You don't think Stimson would try and derail Manhattan?"

"He's an old man, General, and sees the world from an old man's eyes. And," Frank waited until he had Groves' attention, "they talked about the report filed by Goudsmit."

"Who is Goudsmit?"

"Dutch guy, scientific director of our effort to track the German bomb. He says we can't find evidence of it, because there isn't one. The Germans haven't put resources into a serious program to build a bomb."

"This been confirmed?"

"Not officially.

Groves' tongue found the trace of chocolate, and it was gone. He rubbed his chins. "The Hungarians for sure, and the others who fled the Nazis, will quit on the project if they believe the Huns aren't at work on a bomb. Japs don't single out Jews." Groves slapped the desktop with his fleshy hand. "Oppenheimer's got to keep that report under his hat. Draft a memo to him, Frank – make it urgent."

"I don't think it has to be too urgent, General. The director has his ego tied to the bomb, too. Oppenheimer sees Manhattan as his ticket to undying fame. The director's firmly on our side."

"There are three things in life of importance, Frank – family, home, and church. I brought the Pentagon in before schedule and under budget for them. I'm going to have this bomb because if I don't, Congress will want to know why I spent two billion dollars of taxpayer money. They will forget about the Pentagon and hang my posterior out to dry. When this war is finally over, there will be a financial accounting. That's not going to happen to me, or my family, or Manhattan. We are going to make a key contribution to the war effort. We will get this thing, and we will use it."

Ted Klususki was depressed. He had been depressed since he had received the news and heard the reaction to the news. There was no Nazi bomb, but Manhattan would continue. America was going to build the bomb, even though the reason for constructing it was gone. Ted wanted to get drunk and stay drunk, but they would not let him go now. He would be a security problem. What do we do with security problems during war, shoot them? No, America didn't do that—that's what made us different from the Nazis. Throw me in the brig, more likely, Ted mused or send me to a shrink. Oppie would convince them to keep me on the hill and help me. Help me. The bomb builders were sane, trustworthy men. Ted did not appreciate the irony.

The air was clear and mild; the Sangre de Cristo Mountains were distinct in the distance. There might be, he might be seeing, an Indian on a burro on the mesa on the other side of the canyon. The Indian, or what he took to be an Indian, dismounted and raised his arms in a greeting to the Sangre de Cristo, or to the Great Spirit, or to whatever deity New Mexican Indians worshiped. He knew as little about Indians as he knew about the Japs and cared, he admitted to himself, even less. It was the same at home, in Michigan with the Chippewas. He had been in church, in classes, and on sports teams with them and tried to overlook, as best he could, their color. Back home, the idea that they could actually have a culture and that anyone might be interested in it was preposterous, even to the Indians themselves. At Los Alamos it was different. There were too damn many Indians to overlook, and they challenged government authority. Despite posted orders and barbed wire, they roamed at will rounding up the Mustangs which sharpshooters hadn't killed. When it wasn't Indians, it was Mexicans; New Mexico was crawling with them. The largest concentration of good old white people was on the "reservation" itself.

An arm waved on Ted's left where Fermi had entered the trees. He cocked his rifle but hoped the scientist would fail to flush anything that required shooting. The arm continued to wave until Ted shouted, "Right there, Doc," and went to find Fermi.

"The Pope." Enrico Fermi was seated on a vast outcropping of rock engaged in an animated discussion with Hal Agnew. "Pull up a seat, Ted. You're the only practical man here. I'm betting Ted that this," Fermi thumped the surrounding stone with his hand, "won't be here after Trinity. In fact, I'm betting New Mexico won't be here after Trinity. Luckily, no one will miss it."

Agnew was smiling, "Do you really believe the explosion will go out of control?"

Fermi hesitated a moment and responded, "Well, our calculations say it won't, though I'm glad my wife is flying back to Chicago."

Egghead humor was something Ted still did not completely understand. He thought back to the day in Chicago when Fermi conducted the first nuclear chain reaction on a squash court at the university. He and Arthur Compton discussed whether the prospect of losing their jobs, or the university, or the south side of Chicago, was most serious. Compton decided not to inform Robert Hutchins, the university President, about what the Physics Department was doing. Hutchins, a humanities person, did not understand the touch and go beauty of the experiment and probably would feel threatening the existence of the city was going too far. Before he initiated the chain reaction, Fermi asked each of the three graduate students with their buckets of cadmium solution who were to drop on the pile if the reaction began to get out of control – in effect a suicide squad – whether they would like a passing grade or an incomplete on their transcripts if they didn't survive the experiment.

"Will the gismo you made work?" Agnew demanded aggressively.

"Deek Parsons and I believe so."

"Billions of dollars of science come down to the hands of machinists," Agnew observed with what might have been a sneer.

Ted threw his shoulders back and confronted the scientist. "Did you want me to make something out of that crack?"

"No, nothing at all," Agnew, looking up at the burly high school all-American, assured him.

Ted was used to that other egghead attitude, condescension. Actually he hadn't met too many of them who were like that, at least not to your face, especially among the Americans, but the few who were pricks more than made up for the rest. That pompous ass Szilard refused to flush his own toilets because such menial tasks were beneath him. Fermi, who was looking concerned, was among the most human.

"You can put the rifle back in the car, Ted. I didn't really come out here to hunt," Fermi said. "I couldn't bring myself to kill anything, or be a party to it."

Not be a party to killing, Ted mused as he returned the weapon to his car. What the hell did Fermi think Manhattan was about?

As weeks became months, Ted thought his personality was becoming an extension of the extreme conditions of New Mexico. He took Fermi to hunt in the deep snows of the Sangre de Christo, the blood of Christ, and then followed Oppenheimer on the Jornada de Muetro, the Dead Man's Route, to explore a location for the test site among the scorpions, snakes, and stinging ants basking in the 120 degree temperature. He was exhilarated by the engineering challenges which construction of the gadget involved and dangerously depressed by the implications of successfully completing the project. Ted was frightened about the immediate prospects for humanity should an "ultimate weapon" be produced, and convinced the extinction of man on the planet (if such a thing was really possible) would inevitably follow when all nations acquired atomic capability.

He was raised Roman Catholic, but extensive reading in science and engineering brought his fall from grace. Big Bang began the universe. There was, statistically, as good a reason for matter to exist as for matter not to exist (50/50), and therefore one needed a god neither for the creation of matter nor as the governor of the man's humble little solar system. Life was here; there was no hereafter. Man evolved. Genes were the mechanism of evolution.

Working on the bomb, however, drove him back to his Polish Catholic roots, and the Spanish/Catholic heritage of New Mexico reinforced the process. The names given to land centuries ago might well be the invention of some demented novelist who overworked symbolism. The Blood of Christ— for which the mountains were named—was shed for the forgiveness of sin and the redemption of mankind. At Los Alamos, a bomb was being constructed which threatened the existence of life on the planet. Of course, such destructive power was inconceivable, but it must be a powerful bomb indeed. The first test would occur on land called the Dead Man's Route; Ted hoped the name was not prophetic. A light touch on the project would be beneficial, he decided. Too bad the French hadn't arrived here first. They gave mountain ranges names like Grand Tetons, big tits. It was simply inconceivable that a bomb could be built at a lab nestled between big tits.

The transition from musing about mountain ranges to thoughts about Cindy Caufield was not difficult given human nature and the topography of Los Alamos. He, bored to death and alienated from everyone, met her at a "squares' dance," when he tripped over her while watching his feet. "Most fellas can't miss me," she said, "cause of my size." A red-faced Ted stared up at the tallest woman he ever saw. She was pretty, he decided at once. Ted accepted her outstretched hand, looked deeply into her green eyes and fell in love. Of course, he said nothing except to inquire about her activities at the post. "School marm, but I don't coach basketball, and I don't play it either."

"You're not that tall," he told her, using measurement as an excuse for staring. "About six feet."

"All of that," she confirmed. "When I wore my hair long as a kid, my friends always wanted to use me as a maypole."

Ted laughed. She taught him the steps that evening and ordered him to return the following week. Ted spent his lunch hours staring into school windows and hanging about the grounds, but he did not see her again until the following Thursday. Cindy seemed happy to see him. After several Thursday nights, he asked her to dinner in Sante Fe and after that to every event on or off the reservation. They were remarkably alike.

220

Cindy was an outdoor person bred by a father who wanted sons and had none. His youngest, the final gamble in progeny roulette, was christened Cynbad and traveled with her father on skiing, hunting, and camping trips. Neither insects nor damp wood which, however much it smoldered, refused to burn, bothered her. Their dates became weekend trips into the Sangre de Cristo. They slept chastely though side by side in two small army pup tents Ted purchased at the P.X. Sometimes, before climbing into their sleeping bags while they watched the fire and imbibed brandy for warmth, he told her about his obsessions and fears. She listened but rarely spoke at first. Sometimes he wondered why they continued to see one another, but it felt right. He knew that. He wanted to be with her more and more, and she never declined.

As his love for her deepened, his concern about Manhattan grew. It was, as Oppie told the professors he recruited, a technically sweet problem. Ted watched Groves nearly explode when Fermi estimated critical mass at between 20 kilograms and 2 ton of uranium. "This isn't science!" he bellowed. "You might as well tell an architect to design a concert hall for an audience between 300 and 3 million." When Manhattan commenced, no machines existed for the large scale extraction of uranium. Its behavior was largely unknown. Worse, no human being had ever seen a sample of plutonium! Various methods were conceived and immediately tried. Groves' men spent two years constructing a factory for gaseous diffusion which employed a filter—also the work of two years—to extract uranium. No one was certain the process would work as planned, and, in the meantime, a new filter was developed. Groves' men tore out the machines designed for the first filter. The bomb was built on the basis of calculations in the almost spiritual world of physics while Ted labored to construct the materials for the experiments and the meters to measure the results of the experiments. Weekly someone would challenge, "Can you make it?" and sent Ted to his lathe.

When Professor Wilson reported his experiments confirmed the uranium bomb would work, Ted helped Deek Parsons machine the cannon. The scientists' gadget, however possible in the lab, had to be engineered into a weapon that would fit into the belly of a B-29. Week after week, they achieved the impossible and were promptly asked to jump forward again. Frequently, the scientists themselves joined the work, exchanging their pencils and chalk for tools and dirty hands. Dick Feynman made the repairs on the IBM machines. After Johnny Von Neuman calculated the explosive lens would work, the entire team proposed ideas, made sketches, and brainstormed. When the Brit James Tuck arrived and announced he had devised an explosive lens to direct warheads through armor, George Kistiakowsky, the nation's foremost expert on explosives, was summoned from Harvard to take charge of the new project. Kistiakowsky thought Oppie mad to think "this thing will make a bomb." But 600 men were soon sculpturing lenses, handling explosives and measuring shockwaves. Deek Parons, one of the loudest skeptics about the lens method, swallowed his pride and joined the quest, reserving the most difficult fabrications for himself and Ted. Two or three working groups usually competed on each project which reduced the deadly work to a game. Visitors from Chicago observed that those who worked on the project at the university did so because they felt there was no alternative. America must have the bomb before Germany. At Los Alamos, they claimed the team simply wanted to make the bomb. It wasn't true, of course. What captivated Oppie and the others was the prospect of forcing nature to yield her secrets. And she did. Parsons convinced Ted the bomb would work—no question— if Oak Ridge delivered the uranium, and Groves assured Parsons he would get it. So there would be a bomb—what did it mean? What could it do that was so much worse than gas, or jellied gasoline?

Ted had never discussed his feelings about his work with Cindy. He began one evening when the two were warming themselves at the fire in an old, log covered "genuine wild west" restaurant on the road back from Santa Fe where Cindy had gone to shop for a dress. They were invited to a social event on Bathtub row and she wanted to look her best for Ted's sake.

"You didn't need the dress; in a burlap bag you'd knock them out."

"You maybe, not them."

"Anybody," he said, "everybody. You're irresistible."

"You're hopeless, Ted." She saw his expression change, that he was mentally shifting gears.

"School teacher, what do you know about atoms?"

"Smallest unit of matter," she replied.

Your physics is fifteen years out of date, he thought. Our bomb makers are playing with subatomic particles, but what proverbial man in the street knew more about it than Cindy?

"There's things about this bomb that scare me," he told her.

"Like what?"

"They say it's the most terrible weapon in human history, that one bomb will destroy an entire city."

"I'll just bet they're just impressed with themselves."

"No, Cin, you don't understand this thing. Some of them are afraid that an explosion will get away. That it will blow up the earth. That it will be the end of everything."

"What about your friend Oppenheimer?"

"Oppie says the visual effect of his bomb will be tremendous. There will be a brilliant luminescence rising to a height of 10 to 20 thousand feet. And the radioactive effect will be dangerous to all life close to the bomb."

"What's radioactive? Some kind of sound effect?"

"No, has nothing to do with sound, though the bomb will sound like the crack of doom they say. I don't know exactly. Sounds like some sort of beam the bomb creates. It's invisible and odorless, like gas, and kills you. No other bomb has radiation."

"We're going to use a bomb like that?!"

"Oppie says it's OK. The radiation will kill everything within one thousand yards of where the bomb goes off, but the blast will kill everything within two thousand yards, so that's all right."

"It sounds pretty H.G. Wellsian to me," she said.

"They don't seem to know much about radiation," he agreed. "They know that heavy exposure destroys the central nervous system, and you die quickly. Sometimes there's vague talk about other, possibly, lingering effects, but they don't seem to know or care much about it, like I said. Anyway, no one is supposed to survive the blast."

Cindy shook her head. "They must know more about it than they're telling mere mortals like us. Our people in charge don't use bombs they don't understand."

They were served large portions of chicken steak and beans and black coffee, the Drovers' Special, and apple pie for dessert. Ted was strangely silent during the meal and took up the pre-dinner theme before they reached the car. He stopped before the door and grasped her hand. "When I think about the bomb, and us," the words blurted out, "I get cold, like I'm transported to the dark side of the moon. The beauties of the earth vanish, and the waves of the sea pound upon the shores of an empty world."

Cindy held Ted and felt him tremble. "It can't be that bad," she said. "Ted, it's only another weapon."

"We shall all live from now on as if we are sitting on a powder keg, smoking, and hoping none of the ashes fall where it will set it off."

Cindy was shaken now. She had never seen him like this, hadn't realized the powerful impact the bomb had upon him. "Ted," she started.

"And that's not the worst of it," he continued. "We're going ahead with the damn thing when we know the Nazis haven't got it. The whole project was based upon false premises, and now that we know the truth, we are still going ahead."

"How do you know this?" she demanded.

"I grew up with a guy at the Pentagon. He told me the Nazis were nowhere on the bomb before we captured their top men. Now they have nothing. Cindy, listen to this." He slid his hand from hers and drew a scrap of paper from his pocket and leaned back into the light of the restaurant window. "This is part of a letter sent by a scientist named Brewster in New York to the President. 'The thing must not be permitted to exist on earth. We must not be the most hated and feared people on earth, however good our intentions may be.'" Ted nodded in agreement with the sentiment. "We're Americans, not barbarians."

"Who wrote that?"

"O. C. Brewster, they call him Owl. He works for Kellex doing something for the bomb. But he's not alone. Even Deek Parsons."

"Captain Parsons!" she exclaimed.

"Even Deek, as he adjusts the wires, nuts, and bolts, loathes the thing. But he does it – orders."

"Ted," she began as he opened the door of the car for her, "I really had no idea about all this. You must tell me everything. Everything." Her adamant tone surprised him and so did her color. She was bright red for no reason he could fathom, unless she was still shy about making such a pointed demand upon him.

"It's no big secret," he said. "Every lab has groups working against the use of the gadget."

"That's not the same thing as what this Brewster guy wants, Ted. He doesn't want the project to be completed."

"Neither do I, Cin. Neither do I. I want the damn thing to be stopped. I want to stop it."

"Why don't you quit, Ted? Surely they'd let you go."

"No chance, I know too much. They'd put me in a Federal Pen to protect national security."

"Oppie would protect you."

Ted shook his head. "Security is Grove's baby. Look at how they watch us on the reservation. The only place around here you can speak freely to someone is in the men's room and that's only because Groves can't station a lookout there round the clock without drawing suspicion. And you only talk then when you're taking a leak so the microphone's reception is partially blocked." Ted looked bitter, and then his features shifted to one of confusion. "Besides, I have an obligation to the team, to Deek and Oppie. They're counting on me to help make the damn thing work."

"You don't want it to work."

"I know. I want the whole project to be scrapped while there's still time. I should go to Oppie and make him listen," he said to himself.

"What if he wouldn't?"

"Then he wouldn't," Ted shrugged, "what do you mean?"

"Nothing," she said.

"You mean something," he retorted.

"Open the door, Ted. I'm cold."

He put his key in the lock. "Cindy, what should I do? For all our sakes, yours and mine in particular, I want them to stop."

"They won't, Ted; they can't. The war isn't over."

"We're winning the war; we'll win the war with or without the thing."

"At the cost of blood, young American blood."

"I know, but. . ."

"Ted, please get the door open."

Ted decided he had said enough for now. He let the motor warm up and reached over the seat for the lap blanket which he arranged around Cindy, then turned on the radio. Vaughn Monroe was crooning: "I got some corn for popping, the lights are turned way down low—let it snow, let it snow!"

"And it might snow," she said.

"I meant to get the chains on before today," Ted said. Then he sang the refrain again. "He beats hell out of Crosby and that young guy, Sinatra."

"So do you, big guy," Cindy told him, "even if you can't carry a tune." Ted's eyes turned to the road; the girl closed hers and thought. Cindy was a military brat nurtured as much on duty, honor, and country as on mother's milk. Her father graduated sixth in his class at "the Point" which was a family tradition and spent the next ten years rising in the ranks as he was transferred from base to base in the Southwest. Post schools regaled their students with the heroic, generous, and invariably altruistic actions of the United States. Parson Weems was gospel, and anyone who believed "Big Stick" diplomacy was oppressive to the people liberated by the United States was either badly misinformed or a malignant subversive. Exploits of the U.S. Cavalry were still fresh and unsullied by reports of historians burdened by objectivity. Since women were not admitted to West Point, and WAC's were not deployed for combat, Cindy believed her only chance for action, however limited, was in military intelligence. She found herself the object of considerable hostility at the training camp in Virginia. Men resented her prowess in the ring—she had considerable skill in judo—and on the rifle range. She believed some of the field exercises, as fording streams loaded down with heavy equipment, were designed to break or disqualify her. Both her instructors and fellow students ended by admiring her grit.

"Your body is your principle problem," Captain Harkness explained. He read the anger in her eyes easily and hastily added, "No, I didn't mean your woman's body; I mean your height. You're unusually tall for a woman, Cindy, and that will get you noticed. For intelligence, we like people to be nondescript, invisible by their plainness."

"Oh," she said.

"Your looks don't help either," he babbled, red faced.

When her training was complete, Cindy's father recommended her to General Leslie Groves since scuttlebutt said Groves was building a large security team. Cindy's orders took her to Los Alamos School. She was not long in the position when Ted entered the picture. Ted. Was he a security risk? Would he, not that she seriously considered the possibility, sabotage Manhattan? He was a man of strong principles who acted on his beliefs. Ted could scuttle the project with an improperly installed bolt, a cut wire, a defective weld. Deek Parsons wouldn't bother to check Ted's work. Was it time to report him to her superiors? She shook her head vigorously, and Ted turned to her.

"You OK?"

"Nightmare," she explained.

"You're not permitted to have them in my presence; I'll protect you."

She said, "I know," and settled back against the seat.

Ted watched carefully. There was some ice on the road, and the sudden appearance of a mule or white tale deer could send them spinning out of control. He watched her breathe. Cindy, meanwhile, contemplated reporting Ted as potentially disloyal. It would wreck his, their, future. It would follow him everywhere and never disappear. Then she saw the face of her father, his lips set in two hard lines. He did not speak but she heard his voice pronounce "duty and country." Her head slid against Ted's shoulder.

It was early spring in Washington. The days were warm by 10:00 a.m., but evenings were still chilly. The cherry blossoms were expected to be spectacular. Casualty reports were depressing, but the Axis Powers were in full retreat. All in all, it was difficult to maintain rancor against the almost defeated enemy especially at the White House, the focal point of the hopes and prayers of all Americans. Three men were in a small, sparsely furnished office. Admiral William Leahy, Roosevelt's military adviser, was a man of the old school who believed in Spartan discipline. He sought to keep the emotion he felt out of his voice. "Because, General Groves, your bomb will take us back to the time of Genghis Khan. Dropping the thing on a city is a form of pillage, rape and murder all rolled into one, an act of barbarism not worthy of a Christian man. To select a target is to issue a death sentence upon an entire population, General. Wars are not won by destroying women and children."

"Admiral Leahy, Sir," Groves said patiently, "have you seen the projected casualties for Operation Olympic? The Joint Chiefs believe there will be 31,000 casualties the first month. Forty-eight thousand wounded and dying American boys on Okinawa demand you think more seriously about this." Groves knew he had said the wrong thing. Leahy was furious.

"You are talking about the instantaneous death, massacre, call it what it is, of women and children. This is not a fit subject for soldiers and sailors of the United States of America to consider."

Groves turned to appeal to his civilian superior, seated at Leahy's desk, but Secretary of Defense Stimson's eyes held little promise of help. "The world shows a marked tendency to increasing ruthlessness," he said. "Our air forces presently strike at the Japanese home islands using tactics which we condemned only a few years ago when the Luftwaffe struck London. Our tactics frankly revolt decency. Van Bush cannot sleep since the fire bombings began, and now when the war is almost won, you're still planning on using this bomb of yours. There must be some line drawn."

"Mr. Secretary, with respect, Sir," said Groves, "we did not sneak attack the Japanese. We have not encouraged our boys to sacrifice themselves in suicide assaults which have no valid military purpose but kill our children. And, Sir, from the safety of the Pentagon you may declare the war to be won, but no one seems to have informed the enemy."

"We do not require your bomb, General Groves," said Leahy, "the Chiefs of the Army Air Corps, the Army, the Navy, and the Marines assure us the enemy is beaten."

Groves smiled. Leahy thought to himself, "the smiling killer," but he respected Groves and admired his achievement. The impossible was accomplished. Man had gained control over a fundamental power of the universe. The admiral, however, did not believe men possessed the requisite wisdom to handle that power. Groves' expression changed to one of an animal at bay. "I'm afraid time has passed you gentlemen by. The United States cannot afford a code of chivalry in a ruthless world. We did not begin submarine warfare; the Germans did in the last war. Now we sink enemy merchant men without pity or remorse. That's what war demands. The Luftwaffe initiated bombing civilian targets as you yourself admit, Mr. Secretary. We have simply repaid our enemies in kind. Decency can only be saved by ruthlessness. I want the killing to stop, the war to stop, the hating to stop. I intend to do it. As for the Chiefs, with respect again, each of the services assures you it can conclude the war by saturation bombing, or by blockade, or by invasion and occupation of the Japanese islands. Each service wants the glory of ending the war. Their recommendations are thoroughly self-serving and untrustworthy." Groves paused, squared his shoulders and said forcefully, "I can end the war."

There was the silence of an unnatural situation. Groves had crossed the boundary of proper conduct towards his superiors. Leahy stared at his desk, while Secretary Stimson turned his attention to the Rose Garden. Groves could do nothing without a proper dismissal. He stood in the center of the room and thought about the Congressional inquiry that would demand to know why he had spent two billion dollars of taxpayer money. Leahy cleared his throat and asked, "Will there be anything else, General?"

"Yes, sir. You are at the apex of the political system, Admiral. You advise the President of the United States, an elected official. The President is loved, but when mothers learn we had a weapon that could have ended the conflict and spared their sons, well, they will not be pleased, and they will say it with votes."

Leahy's face showed his surprise. "We do not make life and death decisions on the basis of popularity, General. I would have thought you knew that."

"Mr. Secretary, Admiral, we have fire bombed the Japanese, and they have not surrendered. Further raids will only inure them to suffering. Tojo will never surrender. We must break them. We must drive them from the war."

"General Groves," Secretary Stimson came to his feet. "You might well make the same case for the use of poison gas, but no side has dared to use that weapon of terror. We have no use for your bomb." Groves wheeled and started for the door. "General, wait. You and your team have been magnificent. Your achievement shall rank with the building of the Pyramids, with medical and technical breakthroughs. Our government and people shall, in due course, properly thank you."

"Sir," Groves said and departed.

Leahy put his face in his hands and massaged his temples. "He shall win, Henry. You know that."

"Yes, General Groves is a true son of his times. He plays only to win."

"And for us, Henry, men like us no longer belong here. We do not fit this age and time." Leahy sat in his wooden rocker which creaked loudly with each motion.

"How did we bring this into being, Bill? Where did we go wrong?"

There was no answer for that question. There never has been. The sins of the fathers always fall upon the sons, so do the consequences of their best intentions and their cleverest inventions. Develop chemistry and you get poison gas. Conquer the air and bombs rain down. Discover the secret of matter and it follows that a weapon will be devised to exploit the knowledge.

"The roses should be particularly fine this year, Henry, according to the Almanac."

Stimson smiled. "They are like us, Bill, symbols of a bygone era. There is neither time to putter in the garden nor to enjoy the beauty produced by such labor. This is an age of pavement, thick, dull and functional. The General," Stimson nodded toward the door from which Groves had departed, "perfectly embodies its character. I cannot imagine him enjoying a joke." The Secretary of Defense turned toward the old admiral and saw his shadow which had stretched into the room, shrink toward the window following the sun. He understood, and smiled.

When Groves entered the hallway, Oppie rose and went to meet him. "They don't want the bomb," Groves told the director. Oppie said nothing. Groves recognized Jimmy Byrnes crossing from the Executive Office to the White House. Byrnes was the man they needed. Politics was his game. Confidant and strategist of the powerful, the President had told Jimmy about the bomb back in '43 but not the Vice President, poor Mr. Truman, yet.

"I can't get a hearing from Leahy and Stimson." Groves told Byrnes abruptly.

Byrnes, caught by surprise, said nothing, looked at the general and at Oppenheimer and said, "You mean about the gadget?" Groves visibly relaxed. Byrnes knew enough about the project to know the code word. "Be at ease, General. We have plans for your gadget. FDR will eventually discover that Uncle Joe doesn't plan to pull his troops out of countries he liberates. We'll need something to convince him, some gadget," Byrnes winked, "if you know what I mean. You," Byrnes pointed to Oppie, "and your boys are giving us the opportunity to create the post war world. The gadget will give us the leverage to do the job right this time. We screwed up at Versailles;

that won't happen again. You boys just head on back to Los Alamos and deliver and leave the rest to me." Byrnes pumped their hands aggressively and disappeared into the Oval Office. The President was somewhere in the White House recognizing servicemen who had won the Congressional Medal and lived to receive it from his hands. Jimmy made himself at home at Roosevelt's desk. He felt the beady eyes of Joseph Stalin staring at him and raised his eyes to the portrait of Uncle Joe, Winston Churchill, and the President. Jimmy knew from past experience that wherever he went in the room, those eyes would follow him. He made an obscene gesture at Stalin and then began to craft a memo for his Chief regarding the bomb. Byrnes put some of his thoughts on paper. The war, he conceded was probably won, but an unacceptable number of Americans would be killed were it necessary to invade Japan. The bomb, he was assured, would eliminate that need. Therefore, we should proceed with its deployment. Jimmy put down his pen and read his restrained words. His thoughts, in contrast, were blunt. If we blast the Nips with it, the Reds will see its power. We're not going to win the war, and lose the peace as we did last time. The bomb will give us the opportunity to make a world safe for democracy. And I, Jimmy thought, will be remembered as an architect of the settlement, and the Democratic lock on the White House will be secure through the end of the century. Byrnes' face broke into a wide smile.

Like Groves, Jimmy Byrnes was an advocate of the bomb. Like Groves, he counted among his enemies Leo Szilard, that pain in the ass at the University of Chicago, and Neils Bohr who, Byrnes thought, was one of the most appropriately named men he'd ever met. Neils was definitely a bore. For his part, Szilard dismissed Jimmy Byrnes as a man whose mind was too limited to understand that atomic weapons change everything. "Such weapons," Szilard insisted, "make traditional competition between nations obsolete."

"There won't be traditional rivalry," Byrnes had told him. "We'll have the bomb; Stalin won't."

"Bah, the Russians will have it within a year or two at most after us. Any nation with good scientific and technical resources can do what we do. You are seeking a temporary advantage in a game that will be a perpetual menace to human security."

As for Bohr, after he submitted a seven page memo to Roosevelt on the subject, he was directed to talk to Byrnes. Jimmy met with the scientist, but all he remembered was Bohr pronounced the weapon "the bum" throughout their conversation. When he mentioned Bohr and Szilard to Groves, the general dismissed them both. "They haven't been interested since they found out Hitler hasn't got the bomb. The fate of American boys in the Pacific doesn't concern them." But Jimmy Byrnes was interested in the bomb, all right. He could hardly wait for it to be delivered. America with the bomb would have the opportunity to construct a lasting peace, a new world older, and Jimmy Byrnes would be the architect.

Ted found that his coworkers had little to say when he demanded they think about whether the gadget should be used. The scientists and technical men were absorbed in trying to make the thing work. It was simply too much to demand they think about either using or not using what they were laboring so hard to produce. In other labs, he heard through the grapevine, working groups sought to establish guidelines for use of the gadget, assuming it could be made to work. Eventually, Ted found a colleague, Volney Wilson, who shared his opinion that since there was no German A-Bomb, Los Alamos should be closed. When Wilson approached Oppie, whose judgment everyone respected, the director argued the bomb must be built so it could be banned. "We must show the world what such bombs can do and turn regulation of atomic materials to a post war supergovernment that can protect us from ourselves." Wilson had some difficulty with this train of logic. It was not like men to develop something and then give it away. But neither Ted nor Wilson knew what Groves knew, that Oppie wanted to bomb the Japanese to show off his achievement. Oppie may have believed what he told Wilson. We are not always completely conscious of our motivations. After Wilson appeared pacified, Oppie turned his logic and charm on Ted. He was invited to accompany the director on a jaunt to the mountains.

Ted was surprised to find Cindy mounted, holding horses for himself and Oppie at the end of Bathtub Row. He turned to question the director and, seeing Oppenheimer in profile, doubted he could last for more than a few miles in the saddle. Oppie came down the steps, gesturing good-by to his wife, Katherine, and greeted Ted. "Just like old times. When I was a sickly kid from New York, I came here to ride and relax."

Ted knew that, they all did, and said, "You can stand to relax, Oppie."

"You don't mind that I invited this woman? Somebody had to make the picnic lunch."

Ted smiled at Oppie and gave Cindy a quizzical look. She shrugged her shoulders. They mounted and rode past the guards and went north to Pueblo Canyon. Beyond the perimeter of the reservation, the wild country of New Mexico closed immediately. They startled a herd of Bighorn sheep which disappeared in the junipers, but a bison held his ground. The trail skirted the canyon, staying on high ground, and the horses showed no hesitation, as if familiar with the country.

"Lots of dung," Oppie observed, "is it wild mustangs or Indians?"

"Mustangs, I hope," said the girl. "The indigenous population is reported not to be happy with our activities. There is supposed to be a rumor circulating among them that we'll poison the land and water."

"Where on earth did you hear that, Cin?"

"At the mess. Los Alamos School is staffed by would be anthropologists who've been interviewing the Indians. Honest to God, the whole social studies curriculum has been organized around them. Indian languages, baskets, blankets, you'd think they were the most important culture on this continent."

Ted fell behind the director and the girl. He wondered whether the Indians knew something about the lab's activities or were simply suspicious about white men. He was vaguely disturbed by Cindy's remarks as well. Her observations sounded to him too much like intelligence gathering.

"Coming?" Cindy demanded.

"What's the destination, Oppie?" he asked.

"Looking for a perspective, Ted, from which we can get a good glimpse of the Jemez Mountains." Oppie seemed to draw strength from the tamaracks and pinon pines. He sat ramrod straight in the saddle, discussed the blue columbine and red heather, and acknowledged the presence, across the canyon, of a mountain lion. "Let's camp under the stars tonight," he suggested. "It will be a tonic for me."

"Groves will have a cow if you disappear." Cindy observed. Oppie just smiled.

It was true, of course, but Ted was again disturbed by the information volunteered by his school teacher. Why had Oppie brought her along? What was the relationship between Cindy and the director?

"I don't suppose the Jemez are much as mountains," Oppie observed.

"Not for someone who has climbed in Colorado, Elbert, and McKinley," Cindy said.

The trail broadened, and they rode together. The horses continued at a brisk trot which Cindy and Oppie managed effortlessly. Ted was the least experienced horseman of the three but was not about to let the director look better than he before Cindy. Oppie liked to do that. Ted had damn near locked his teeth in determination when Oppie pulled up and demanded, "OK you two. When's the day, and do I get to be best man?" Cindy turned purple; Ted's mouth dropped. "Come on. You don't think you're hiding anything, do you? The whole world knows." Oppie pulled the reins and stopped, "You're not planning on doing something silly like waiting until after the war? You'd disappoint the whole lab."

"We haven't thought much about it," Cindy said.

"You mean the big lug hasn't proposed?"

"Not in so many words."

"Well," Oppie said, smiling, "that's easily resolved. Will you marry him, Cindy?"

Her blush deepened. "Since I'm telling you in confidence, yes."

"Ted, will you take this woman?" Ted nodded, vigorously. "Cat's got his tongue, but his answer is clear. That's settled then. We should stop and have a drink. I just happened to bring champagne."

Nature conspired with Oppie. A meadow filled with Indian paintbrush and shootingstar provided a festive background. Ted spread the blanket brought for the picnic. Oppie produced a bottle and three glasses and toasted them and was joined in the toast by a bald eagle which circled endlessly above them. The sun danced upon the jagged peaks of the Jemez, rendering them shifting shades of gold and red and yellow.

"This is why we fight, to protect it for our children," Cindy said, taking Ted's hand. He agreed; it was indeed why we fought.

"War's an ugly business, but it has to be done," Oppie volunteered. Ted sensed a lesson was coming. The director would drive his point home about the bomb. "We're Americans, Ted, protecting America. We don't know or see the 'Big Picture.' Our job is to protect the country for our children. It's that simple. You're a technician, Ted. I'm a physicist. Our job is to deliver the gadget. The job of the generals is to deploy it and of the politicians, of the President of the United States, to determine whether or not the bomb should be used. They have more knowledge than we do, Ted. You have to trust their judgment. They do see the 'Big Picture.'"

Ted could see Cindy nodding in agreement from the corner of his eye, but mainly he saw the skull protruding from under Oppie's thin, frail, flesh. He recalled a reading recommended to him by the director in the Hindu scripture: "Now I am become death, the destroyer of worlds."

Dramatis Personae

J. Robert Oppenheimer: physicist and director of the Manhattan Project. Many believed the project could not have been accomplished by anyone except Oppie.

General Leslie Groves: the military director/commander of the Manhattan Project. Groves worked closely with Oppenheimer.

Karl Fuchs: a German-British physicist who worked as an agent for the Russians.

Edward Teller and Leo Szilard: brilliant, extremely difficult Hungarian emigre physicists who fled Hitler. Szilard is credited with conceiving the idea of provoking a nuclear chain reaction which made the bomb possible.

Richard Feynman: American physicist and self-proclaimed interesting person. Feynman delighted in breaking the rules prescribed by General Groves.

Samuel Goudsmit: Dutch physicist assigned the task of keeping track of the German bomb.

General Curtis LeMay: chief of the 21st Bomber Command, LeMay conceived and executed, without informing Washington, the fire bombing of Tokyo on March 9, 1945 which killed 72,000 people.

Henry Stimson: elderly, gentlemanly, U.S. Secretary of Defense.

Enrico Fermi: Italian emigre physicist, produced the world's first nuclear chain reaction on the squash courts at the University of Chicago.

Theodore Agnew: An American physicist who never doubted the bomb should be employed.

Arthur Compton: chairman of the Physics Department at Chicago. He ordered the construction of Fermi's nuclear pile.

Deek Parsons: Navy captain and chief weapons specialist of Manhattan.

George Kistakowsky: Harvard scientist and the foremost American expert on explosives.

James Tuck: British explosives expert. Tuck developed an explosive lens for directing shells through armor which was modified for use in the gadget.

Oswald Brewster: employed by Kellex Corporation to work on uranium isotope separation. Owl changed his mind about the bomb after the German surrender.

Parson Weems: 19th century American author. Weems wrote a sometimes factual but mainly worshipful biography of George Washington which included the first telling of the cherry tree story.

Admiral William Leahy: President Franklin Roosevelt's chief military advisor.

James Byrnes: consummate political insider. Byrnes was a confidante of President Roosevelt who informed him about Manhattan in 1943 but did not advise vice president Truman about the bomb.

Neils Bohr: eminent Danish physicist. Bohr attempted to warn the politicians about the destructive power of the bomb and about the potential for an arms race after the war.

Vannevar Bush: appointed by President Roosevelt to direct all federal science activities.

Dispensation

The Word of the Lord

When Martin Luther stated the scriptures were perfectly plain to a reasonable man of good conscience, he was either at his most spectacularly naive or optimistic. Certainly nothing in the early history of the church with century after century of heretical movements, nor in the history of the Reformation which generated two dozen new Christian denominations, gave grounds for such belief. Words, which for adherents were the voice of God and determined whether one was delivered or damned, invited speculation. Paradoxically, many have labored to make the clearest words of Jesus obscure, and to make the most obscure clear. Surely He can't mean what He says about the poor and the rich. Surely there is a hidden meaning in Ezekiel and Daniel, even though modern Biblical scholarship has determined that the word "prophecy" in the Old Testament meant commentary, not prediction. The most obscure of all Christian writings is The Revelation to John which contains textual problems, obscure references and allusions.

The Book of Revelation has been used over the centuries to predict the "imminent" destruction of the planet and all life, though this has not yet occurred. An annotated "apocalyptic Bible" is currently available since the end is once again nigh. There is no money back guarantee, however. It was inevitable that television, which exists to sell the product, would convert Christianity to a product that was salable. Carrying one's cross is not pleasant, and so the faith of Christ has become a form of pop positive philosophy promising wealth, health and success. After all, Rodeo Drive is a far more pleasant place than Golgotha.

In our final story, **Dispensation**, Bruce Seik, a student at a small town seminary, brings to his education a more diverse back-

Dispensation

ground than his fellow seminarians. Bruce is also an older student who is paying the professor to educate him in the subject area of the professor's expertise. Bruce believes it is his class, not the professor's. Finally, Professors Barnes and Bryant are giving their particularly idiosyncratic readings to the texts rather than examining them in their historical context, and of course, Bruce objects. Probably his friends should remind him that 'pride cometh before the fall'.

The land beneath a pine forest is as silent as God and as barren as a life without Him. It is dark under the thickly limbed trees, except where light filters down after a tree has fallen from storm or from having rooted shallowly in the light, acidic soils. Streams run silently, too, through the gouges they cut in the land, unlike their stony bottomed counterparts in New England. To compensate for the lack of auditory and visual stimuli, the pines overwhelm with scent from the sharp needles lining the live branches, the heavy, thick sap, and the deep accumulation of shed needles which lay like a red carpet beneath the trees. Bruce felt touched by God and resisted the sensation. It was all right to come here for relaxation, to walk in the woods to escape the pressure and din of civilization, but it was not proper to experience God here. That was far too close to paganism, or worse to the excesses of that madman Francis, called saint by the Roman Church. He sat on the path and watched and breathed. Bruce wished that he had never attended public school which forced him to ingest, if not digest, quantities of literature which proved distracting.

> One impulse from a vernal wood,
> Can teach you more of evil, and of good,
> Than all the sages can.

That was nonsense, and he knew it was nonsense. The Ten Commandments taught right from wrong; the Bible defined good and evil. And yet there were other ideas and images which filtered through the poets which he recognized when he experienced them. "There is a spirit in the wood," said the same poet, and Bruce knew what he meant. He rose and began to take the hill, paused to glance at the horizon where the forest gave way to pasture which dropped gently and became rolling land. He saw a deer's head appear, then the front legs. The animal did not move again until, through some imperceptible process, it determined he was there and bolted down the steep side of the hill into the dense underbrush. It was beautiful, and through it he knew God again. "Truth is beauty, and beauty is truth, that is all ye know on earth, and all ye need to know." Blast those poets. It irritated him as well to find a breech with his co-religionist, James Watt, the former Interior Secretary who believed this shopworn world might be thrown away. Mr. Watt did not worry about the forests and rivers or the earth's other resources since he did not know how many future generations would exist before the Lord returned. Bruce did not know when the Lord intended to return either but he felt that Jesus would not wish to return to man-made squalor where life struggled to survive.

When Jesus wished to contemplate in solitude, he retired to the wilderness. John cried out from the wilderness, a place in which he prepared for the Lord. There was something healing in a wilderness, something from which one could draw strength. Yahweh promised the chosen a land flowing with milk and honey, clearly that meant a reward. Medieval Catholics, he knew, thought the variety in nature demonstrated the greatness, and perfection of God. "God willed that man should in some measure know Him through His creatures, and because no single created thing could fitly represent the infinite perfection of the Creator, He multiplied creatures and bestowed on each a certain degree of goodness and perfection, that from these we might form some idea of the goodness and perfection of the Creator." And yet, there was no explicit statement about stewardship in the New Testament. "Be fruitful and multiply; fill the earth and subdue it. Have dominion over the fish of the sea, the birds of the air, the cattle and all the animals that crawl on the earth." Dominion, from the Latin dominium, supreme authority, absolute ownership. In the Zoroastrian scriptures, Bruce was compelled to read in Comparative Religion, Ahura Mazda demanded the believer care for cattle and all other animals, and see to the preservation of trees. Yahweh, in contrast, did not hesitate to punish, nearly destroy, His entire creation with the flood and showed no remorse. The God he read about seemed remote sometimes from the God he addressed as a child with the well-remembered verses:

Thank You for the earth so sweet,
Thank You for the things we eat,
Thank You for the birds that sing,
Thank You, God, for everything.

Bruce remembered how he loved that God who knew and saw all, how

protected he felt, how peaceful after a service, and how indescribably excited and happy at Christmas and Easter. Not a leaf blew from the tree nor a
sparrow fell from the sky that the Lord did not count and direct. He knew
that God, better even than he knew the Lord after years of study. "Unless
you become as little children, you shall not enter the kingdom of heaven."
That was the trick all right, becoming like a child. But then Paul said, "When
I was a child I behaved as a child, when I became a man I put off the ways of
a child." But Wordsworth said, "The child is father of the man," which logically meant we should be able to keep our ideas and feelings, even though
we grow older. A cool breeze blew from the lake and gently stirred the trees.
Though the pines obscured the view of the lake, Bruce could see it in his
mind's eye, olive drab green, rocking and rolling, capped with white foam.

He looked at his watch. There was time, if he hurried, to make his class at
the college. Professor Bryan was completing his lecture on the Sermon on
the Mount, or rather completing his deprecation of it. Bryan had little use
for the sentiments expressed in the Sermon. "You can't have a national
economy which 'takes no thought for the morrow.' The lilies and sparrows
may take no heed, but man must." Bruce was disconcerted to see all heads
in the lecture hall nod in agreement. It did not seem to strike them as odd
that Jesus would make a statement which he intended the faithful to disregard. "We may likewise dismiss," Bryan continued, the admonition, "'Blessed
are the peacemakers.' The wars waged by America are necessary. They are
holy wars as we properly understand when we acknowledge that God ex-
plicitly created nations. 'These are the families of the son of Noah, after
their generation in their nations, and by these were the nations divided in the
earth after the flood.' Our nation is the Divine instrument to protect His
church from communism. We must be prepared to fight and die." Such arguments began wrong, dead wrong, and got worse. In the first place, the
word 'nation' did not apply to Biblical times. The Hebrew word was closer
in meaning to race, or kin, even tribe. Jesus did not order his disciples to
fight with those who opposed them. "Blessed are those who have endured
persecution or their uprightness, for the Kingdom of heaven belongs to them,"
and again, "Blessed are you when people abuse you and persecute you and
falsely say everything bad of you on my account." And Jesus further instructed us to love our enemies. "Ye have heard that it hath been said Thou
shalt love thy neighbor and hate thine enemy. But I say unto you, love your
enemies, bless them that curse you, do good to them that hate you and pray
for them which despitefully use you and persecute you." If there were a
historical model for Christians from the early community, surely it was the

martyr and not the militant. And Professor Bryant will be more than willing to make a martyr out of me should he get the chance to do so, Bruce thought and hurried back down the hill.

Seated at his desk, Charles Augustus Bryant amended his notes. There were no old yellow pages but a newly revised lecture hot off the printer. He considered himself the model of the modern academic, with all of his notes on discs which he deleted, changed or maintained as required. The Professor believed that he had unique insight into Scripture and a God ordained mission not simply to share it with his students but to shape their minds in conformity with his. There could be only one, true understanding of God's Word as revealed by Scofield and perfected by Bryant. Any views which diverged from their understanding were, at best, simple misinterpretation, at worst wholly false teaching, like Roman Catholicism. It was unbelievable that that old superstition persisted after all these centuries, even after the Bible was available to all. How could they continue to follow a leadership which treated the Word as a mere ancillary to the faith of Jesus and called a mere man infallible? As Luther said, the Scriptures were perfectly plain to any man who read them. One did not require a pope to tell him the meaning of the Word, or that he had sinned or was forgiven. No man had such power. "But that is not my text for today," he said aloud. "Today I must finish the 'Sermon on the Mount,' making certain my students understand Jesus' words apply to the last dispensation, the time after the Rapture when the Kingdom will be established, as described by Doctor Scofield. What are those page numbers, anyway?" he demanded, frantically thumbing through his obviously well-thumbed Bible. Some lecturers hold their students by an occasionally well-placed joke or, given the opportunity, an ad-lib. Others prefer the Socratic method of probing students with questions and gently drawing from them knowledge they did not know they possessed. Professor Bryant preferred to preach his lectures with an emotional intensity not seen this side of the revival circuit. He had no use for questions; he possessed the truth and did no more than place the proper gloss upon it. He looked up at the clock over his desk and saw it was time to go, said, "Hallelujah!" and hurried off to class.

"Beloved, I want you to have MONEY! If you believe God is in you, you can be what you want to be, do what you want to do, and have what you want to have. I want you to send me a donation, and I don't want any that makes noise. This is God's work. Don't play God cheap."

Bruce's knuckles were white on the steering wheel, while the message of the electronic church was repeated. "God wants you to prosper. The riches of life are health, happiness, love, success, prosperity, and plenty of money." Sickened, he turned the dial hard enough to break it and heard himself recite, "Store up no treasures for yourselves on earth, where moth and rust corrode, where thieves break in and steal; store up treasures for yourselves in heaven where neither moth nor rust corrode, where thieves do not break in and steal. For wherever your treasure is, there will your heart be, too."

The open fenced fields of the country gave way to the convenience stores and houses scattered along the main road into town. Bruce slowed the car and tried to focus on the drive, but his mind continued to argue with the now silent radio. "It is not everyone who says to me, 'Lord, Lord!' who will get into the Realm of heaven, but he who does the will of my Father in heaven. Many will say to me at that day, Lord, Lord, did we not prophesy in your name? Then I will declare to them, 'I never knew you; depart from my presence you workers of iniquity.'" False prophets, the world seemed awash in them, as Jesus had warned. The Christ ordered his disciples: "Heal the sick, raise the dead, cleanse lepers, cast out demons; give without being paid, as you have got without paying; you are not to take gold or silver or coppers in your girdle, nor a wallet for the road, nor to shirts nor sandals nor stick." Now the missionary enterprise was preached with such admonitions as "Christ has not captured your heart until He has your pocket book. Put Jesus first in your stewardship and allow him to bless you financially."

Bruce made a left on Front Street and gave the car enough gas to make the steep ascent. Every few blocks he passed, in brick, stone or wood testimonials to the faith of his fellow citizens. In these churches, most of them as old as the town itself, and dark and cool despite the early afternoon heat, generations had found solace in their hard pilgrimage through life from a God who ordered them to feed the hungry, and refresh the thirsty, visit those who were alone, clothe the naked and care for the sick. It was a God who loved us, despite our faults, who forgave us our trespasses and told us to call upon Him in our grief. Maybe that was it; maybe there were no griefs. Maybe no parents lost children, or wage earners their livelihood. Maybe no one got sick anymore. Or maybe in the tumult and bustle of the modern world, maybe people no longer recognized there were tragic aspects of human life. Tragedy was no longer tragedy. Sick kid or junkie kid were statistics. Cancer? Another statistic. Or maybe people had gotten so emotionally and intellectually shallow they no longer felt pain. (How Bruce hated the dentist and doctor jargon which turned pain into discomfort and death into a negative patient outcome!) Jesus, at that point, became no more than an additional device to open the sluicegates for material possessions. If not the lotto, then Jesus. If Jesus were to come today, Bruce reasoned, He would wear gym shoes, drive a BMW, live in Beverly Hills and lead the faithful to the Father via His talk show featuring a celestial choir. This image contrasted sharply with the gospels. If ever there was a relentless and unremitting rejection of wealth, it was the message of the Master. Nor was Jesus a forerunner of the "winning friends and influencing people" school, nor again of Mr. Feelgood philosophy. He did not preach that life should be without travail. He did not preach that one will find love. To follow the Master, one sometimes had to leave loved ones behind. He did not preach that following the gospels would bring success. Bruce remembered Jim Bakker's story of the man who prayed for the brown Winnebago mobile home and got it. "Diamonds and gold aren't just for Satan," he exalted. "They're for Christians too!" Jesus' vision of the Christian life was stark and demanding.

"He who will not take up his cross and follow after me is not worthy of me." Human life was the process of taking up one's cross: of ill health, or advancing age, of mental or physical disheartenment. "If you want to be perfect, go and sell your property, give the money to the poor and you shall have treasure in heaven; then come and follow me." When the young man heard that, he went sadly away for he had great possessions. And Jesus said to his disciples, "I tell you truly, it will be difficult for a rich man to get into the Realm of heaven. I tell you again. It is easier for a camel to get through a needle's eye than for a rich man to get into the Realm of God." When one did possess wealth, and was willing to part with it to follow the Master, he did what was prescribed in Acts: "There was not a needy person among them, for those who owned land or houses would sell them and bring the proceeds of the sale laying the money before the feet of the apostles; it was then distributed according to each individual's need."

Diatribe ended, Bruce found that he had parked his car in the first slot off the street at the end of the walk which led to the seminary. He sat and stared at the old, two-story red brick structure. Pigeons gathered at the base of the flagpole bobbing for the crumbs Mr. Fleet, the custodian, left for them after his lunch. Bruce glanced at his watch. Professor Bryant would be well into his lecture by this time. A sharp rap on the windshield startled him.

"You're supposed to be with the Pope now?" inquired Fred Rice. Fred was a huge, fresh-faced kid who'd come straight from Campus Crusade. He reminded Bruce of Mikie fifteen years from the cereal box.

"Got held up, but I'm on the way."

"Anyone else I'd say 'hurry up.' You, my friend, should just disappear today. He'll have something unpleasant to say if you don't."

"I'm not afraid of Bryant, or any of the rest of them."

"I know, you should be. They make the final evaluations, write the recommendations, and find the internships."

"If I take your meaning correctly, your suggestion is not very charitable toward our faculty, who also happen to be ministers of the Lord."

Rice's face turned purple. "I didn't mean. . ."

Bruce chuckled. "Hard to think of them being spiteful, and they never would be, to you. I'm a different case."

"You're the seminary radical, the young Luther."

"Well, I'm hardly that, Fred. Hop in, we've got time for coffee before the Prophets." Bruce backed out of the slot and drove around the back of the seminary, and made a left. "You'll never know what a pleasure it is to have hills. I've spent too much time around Chicago where a hill is about as rare as a copy of Elmer Gantry in the seminary bookstore."

"You read that?" Fred demanded, his mouth hanging open.

"Sure, got to know what the opposition is thinking." Bruce made a right and observed, "The closest place is the snack shop in the bowling alley. Is that all right? There are pool tables in there."

"No, its OK. We're just going for coffee."

"I won't even let you look at them, or I'll have a reputation for leading the young to sin." He smiled again.

"You're making fun of me."

"I would never do that," Bruce said, suddenly serious, "but my experience of life has given me a somewhat different perspective on living and sinning than we're taught at the Sem."

Northern Lanes was on the outskirts of town which had grown around the lake and expanded north. To its right was a small rail yard and some factories. Beyond it, to the left, was rolling pasture bisected by a stream. The road from which they made a left into the Lanes continued up, cutting through the thick woods which separated town from the main highway. "Even if I was furious with all of our professors, I couldn't fight with them. I'm too relaxed. The land," Bruce made an encompassing gesture, "does it to me."

"I find it boring," Fred confessed, as they entered the Lanes. It was dark inside and the pile of trash bags before the door awaiting removal smelled of beer. They walked the length of fifteen alleys and through the door into the bar, past the bar into the snack shop. A would-be blonde forced a smile and led them to a table.

243

"Coffee for me, and Seven-Up for my friend, please."

"Be right back with it."

"Thank you," Bruce hesitated and then added, having read it from her badge, "Suzanne."

The use of her name pleased her and she managed an authentic smile.

"You're incredible," Fred said. "You remembered about the caffeine."

"It's a drug I myself am not prepared to give up," Bruce admitted, "but I admire you for it." The coffee set before him smelled as if it had been warming too long, and the cream curdled as he poured it. Bruce stirred the disagreeable liquid with his spoon and added too much sugar. Suzanne returned to the counter but continued to look disturbed.

"You don't know squat. We should have gone straight up the Interstate and not wasted time on these damn back roads." Suzanne glanced warily toward the booth from which the sound came. Bruce watched her.

"I guess you think giving up caffeine is pretty silly."

"Nothing anyone takes seriously is silly," Bruce replied automatically.

"So drink up, and we'll go. We can't make time sitting here. Hey toots, bring some other coffee here. This tastes like shit. And put some new stuff in the thermos."

Suzanne approached the table cautiously as though she expected trouble.

"You're not drinking, Bruce," said Fred.

The thermos was slammed between her hands. Bruce could feel the slap across the room and knew the outcome was inevitable. It dropped on the table and rolled off the end to shatter against the floor.

"Bitch! You're going to have to replace it." Suzanne apologized as she backed away. Bruce waited for help to appear for Suzanne. Places like the Lanes have plenty of experience with drunks. "What are you doing to do about my thermos?"

"Let the broad alone," said the other man in the booth, "it was your fault."

"Button your goddamn lip," the man shouted, and rose suddenly knocking the bench over. "You've done enough to screw up this trip."

Bruce was up by the time the second man was on his feet, and he pushed himself between them. "OK, easy now boys, you don't want to start any trouble here." Both of them had red, watery eyes and looked burned out. Without so much as a preliminary, Bruce saw a fist made and watched a haymaker arch in his direction. He neither flinched, nor ducked, nor tried to block the punch that landed just below his eye.

The second man grabbed the arm of the first and tried to restrain him from punching Bruce again. Fred stepped inside, put up his guard and sent a hard left into the stomach of the man who struck Bruce, who groaned and sank to his knees.

"No, Fred, don't. Remember, turn the other cheek; that's what scripture says."

Men poured in from the bar and grabbed the truck drivers, pulling the first roughly to his feet. "I'm going to be sick," he gasped.

"You're going to be worse than that. Police are on the way. My name's Gamble. I'm the owner," the newcomer told Bruce. "I'm sorry this happened."

"Not your fault."

"Let me look at that face." He tilted Bruce's head up and right. "Lost some flesh, and you're definitely gonna have a good shiner. Sore as hell for a couple of days too." Bruce shrugged. "Do you want to press charges?"

"Is there a law against being a lout?" he asked.

"There's law against battery, drunkenness and disorderliness, and damaging property."

"That should be enough, then," Bruce said.

"You're sure?" Gamble asked. "You're cheekbone will remind you of this for a couple of days."

"Don't misunderstand," Bruce told him. "They deserve to be arrested and fined. They have no business mistreating your waitress or your establishment; the law must be obeyed. I'll be happy to come and testify. What happened to me is of no consequence."

Bruce gave Gamble their names and phone numbers, and then they returned to the seminary for their next class, Old Testament Prophecy. "Day can't get any worse," Fred said. He was wrong.

They sat in the front row, next to the windows. Bruce often found himself staring at the trees, even the cars coming and going in the parking lot. He took the course to study the Old Testament prophets, not to be subjected to Dr. Jezreel Barnes' prophesying. "So, here are some developments in Russia predicted by Ezekiel which point up the coming return of Jesus." Barnes did not make a bad looking prophet; he was far too tall and too thin, as if he'd been created by an artist without a well-developed sense of perspective.

"Why does he call it Russia?" Bruce demanded of Fred in a not silent, definitely petulant voice. "Officially, it's the Union of Soviet Socialist Republics."

Barnes cast a glance toward Bruce, wrinkling his eyebrows in disapproval, and continued. "In Ezekiel, chapters 38 and 39, we read that the name of this land would be Rosh, that's Ezekiel 38, verse 2 in the American Standard Version and two cities of Rosh, Meshek and Tubal."

"The verse actually refers to Gog, prince of Rosh, Meshek and Tubal, something quite different."

"There names are actually quite similar to Moscow and Tubolsk, the two ruling capitals of Russia today."

"Ever heard of Tubolsk, Fred? Surprising, isn't it, for one of the two ruling capitals of Russia?"

"Also, Ezekiel wrote that the land would hate God, and therefore God would be against it. He also said that Russia or Rosh would invade Israel in the latter days, verse eight, and added the invasion would be aided by various allies of Rosh, verses five and six. The purpose of the invasion Ezekiel said was to take spoil, verse 12. If one but removes the first two letters from this world, spoil, he soon realizes what Russia will really be after, oil."

Bruce tried to remain calm but once again offered to Fred, "and if we substitute the world plunder for spoil, and remove the first letters we get under, which is nonsense, or maybe God's way of suggesting the Princes of Rosh came in search of bvd's."

"Are you quite finished, Mr. Seik?"

"Are you quite finished, Professor Barnes? I selected this class because of your reputation as an expert on the prophets. Would you be so kind as to inform us about the ethics of the Prophets, and about how they relate to their times? Prophetic commentary was intended, you yourself have written, as a reflection on the time in which the prophets themselves lived."

"I am not accustomed to this sort of behavior. This is my class. I select the material for discussion here."

"No, Professor, this is my class. I've paid you to teach me about the prophets. I want to know what one may find in the writings of the prophets, not what you believe the prophets are predicting for the future."

"You're dismissed, Mr. Seik. Get out. You may return to class when an acceptable apology is tendered, not before." Bruce stood and looked about the room to see if there were any signs of support for his position. The most common expression he recognized as shock, a few of resentment. Not one appeared to support him. He quickly left the room. Professor Barnes resumed. "You've all heard of Ronald Reagan?" Quiet laughter filled the room. "The President told us at a White House breakfast that, I quote him, 'Everything is falling into place. It can't be too long now. Ezekiel says that fire and brimstone will be rained upon the enemies of God's people. That must mean that they'll be destroyed by nuclear weapons.' The Prophets speak loudly and clearly to Mr. Reagan saying the end time has come."

Bruce pulled the door closed behind him. He struggled briefly with a profound sense of isolation, but that did not last long. He was a man who had been out of sync with others – first his parents and teachers, later his friends – for virtually his entire life. He smiled and climbed the steps which occupied the center of the building. At the back of the building overlooking the rear lot, faculty members were crammed together, separated only by file cabinets and metal bookcases. Despite the fact 'the Pope' might be there, Bruce entered and said, "Professor Barrow?"

"Yes?" Barrow raised his great head. The man was imposing. His head was huge and covered with unruly white hair which hung down at the front and sides and gathered, like cotton candy, at the center. Barrow's brow was deeply furrowed and his eyes sunkened. Under the sockets were deep, dark bags like vampires or the risen dead in old horror films. His shoulders were set in a permanent slouch which was prominent even sitting at his desk.

"May I talk with you?"

"Sit down, please."

"Thank you, Professor."

"Coffee?"

"Please."

In ponderous, though sure, gestures Darrow bent to retrieve his thermos and then poured a steaming cup. "It's heavy on the sugar and cream," he confessed.

"I'm not disturbing you?"

"No, not at all. I was just thinking about home."

Bruce blurted without thinking,

> "Home is the sailor, home from the sea,
> And the hunter home from the hill."

Barrow beamed. "Robert Louie Stevenson, though not one of the Child's Garden of Verses. Didn't know anyone read Stevenson anymore."

"Poetry's a weakness of mine," Bruce confessed.

"Weakness is a curious way to talk about a love of poetry."

"Especially in my case," Bruce said, "it brought me back."

"Back?"

"To God. I read Donne, and Matthew Arnold, and Gerard Hopkins."

"Heaven preserve us, an agnostic and a Jesuit brought you here."

"The problems of belief and fear of death brought me here.

'Not, I'll not, carrion comfort, Despair, not feast on thee
. . . .
Of now done darkness I wretch lay wrestling with (my God!) my God.'"

"A very interesting poem, one of Hopkin's best." Professor Barrow leaned forward in his chair, resting his elbows on his thighs and caught his chin on his thumbs. "You've gotten here by a circuitous route."

"The resume includes truck driver, swabbie – I used to pace the decks at night and recite verses for company – cage cleaner at an animal lab that did medical research, and cabbie."

"You're sure seminary can hold you?"

"Could be a lot more difficult than I thought, especially." Bruce paused.

"Especially?"

"I'd rather not continue."

"Fair enough.

"May I ask what you're doing, Professor Barrow?" The desk was filled with single-spaced typed papers, diagrams, covered with notations, charts and several different editions of the Bible.

"The Bible tells me the countdown to Tribulation began in 1948, the year Israel was recreated and the European Economic Community was born."

"The E.E.C.?"

"Sure. Revelations speaks of a ten horned beast at the end of time. Jesus said, 'This generation shall not pass away till these things have been fulfilled,' and this generation began, remember, in 1948. Now Job . . ."

"Professor Barrow?"

"Wait a minute, please," he said, and continued, "Job lived, according to the Bible, one hundred and forty years, or four generations which makes a Biblical generation, by simple division, thirty-five years. The upshot of all this is simple enough." Barrow took a pencil and wrote $1948 + 35 = 1983$. "In other words, according to my best calculations and the prophetic words of the Bible, one may predict with absolute assurance that Jesus returned in 1983. Any questions, Mr. Seik?"

"But, Professor Barrow, there are now twelve members of the E.E.C., and Jesus didn't return in 1983."

Barrow dramatically raised his eyebrows, cleared his throat with a boom, and observed, "Well, that's the way the cookie crumbles. Guess it will be a while yet before I get to go home."

Bruce began to laugh, and Barrow joined him. "So what does it all mean, Doctor Barrow?"

"What does what mean, Mr. Seik?"

"Prophecy, history, destiny, the Ten Commandments, the Two Great Commandments, what does one make of it all?"

"I have spent my life pondering the Bible, Mr. Seik, and I have come to a singular conclusion. What is most agreeable to God is that we should do the good that is straight under our noses. Some people believe the world was irrevocably corrupted and contaminated by the generations which came just before them, while others believe that their contemporaries demonstrate every disgusting possibility the race possesses and that God surely will choose this day to cleanse the earth. So far as I can determine, man is certainly no better and probably no worse than ever. If there are more crimes, it is because there are more of us and more reporting of our crimes. To try and guess the intentions of the Almighty is to move oneself perilously close to the sin of presumption."

"But what about prophecy, Professor, and the six dispensations of Doctor Scofield?"

"You know the answer to that, Mr. Seik. Prophecy meant less prediction in the Old Testament than commentary. The prophet observed, and commented upon what they saw, usually not very complimentary either. But they never spoke the kind of mumbo-jumbo that is attributed to them today. What Jesus wanted you to know, He told you. Feed, shelter, minister; it's all there. What He said about the end of time is that no one would know the day or the hour. Scofield is a systematizer, and I don't have much use for systems."

"It bothers me," Bill said, slowly and almost reluctantly, "that so many Christians do so much quoting of the Old Testament and ignore the New."

Barrow nodded, "I know what you mean. It appears, sometimes, that Jesus is too good for the Christians, or vice versa."

"What about the book of Revelations? How do you understand it? What do you do with it?"

"Well, frankly, I'm a guy who can take that book or leave it alone." Barrow smiled again.

"What?"

"Let me put it this way, Mr. Seik. What one finds in the Old Testament is an intervening God. The Lord is the God of History, helping his people, smiting their enemies. How reassuring it must have been to see God act.

What we have had since Jesus is the silence of God. I do not understand why God is silent anymore than I understand the Book of Revelations. I do not claim to know the purposes of God; As I said before, I am certain Jesus told us what He wants done. When He wants us to understand Revelations, He will make it clear."

"I'm a little surprised that you are able to stay at Seminary holding these views."

"Oh, its not all that difficult. My colleagues and I agree far more than we disagree. Besides, the Protestant tradition upholds the right of each man to read and to attempt to understand the Bible for himself." Barrow paused as if expecting Bruce to speak. When he did not, Barrow presented him with the opportunity. "I understand you are having some problems here."

"Do you know Andrew Marvel?"

"A poet or something, I'd guess, having talked with you."

"My best subjects are English and History. Time has always fascinated me. I grew up with parents who said, over and over, how fast time went, and how much faster it seemed to go with each passing year. But time, for me, moved like a glacier. Summers seemed longer than eternity, when I was a child. By mid-August, our favorite game was school. I don't know when things changed but one day, I understood Marvel's lines, 'At my back I always hear time's winged chariot drawing near, and yonder stretched before me lies, deserts of vast eternity.' The shortness of life, and the inevitability of death, great cliches, huh? When I was in the Navy, I poured over poetry searching for an answer."

"Why poetry?"

"It was the only branch of knowledge's trinity that worked for me."

"Knowledge's trinity, explain what you mean."

"There are three kinds of truth—religious, scientific and poetic. Religion and science were foreign to my understanding and sympathy."

"I see. And what did you learn from poetry?"

"That there was no answer. Life was like having a one way ticket to a destination you really don't want to visit, with the added liability of getting there anyway if you disembark early. When I got out of the Navy, I got into cab driving and drugs."

Barrow looked grim. "You're not into either now?"

"I pick up some extra money weekends with a cab, though no cabbie ever made a fortune in a small town. The drugs are gone. You see, Professor Barrow, I am the recipient of a real miracle. My drug problem and my question, the 'is that all there is question,' were both resolved when Jesus found me."

Before Barrow could respond, several sets of feet on the creaking stairs and the heavy breathing of aging men announced a significant arrival.

"The posse," Bruce observed.

"Ah, we found you," said Dr. Bryant. "Barrow, we've established a committee to determine the fitness of Seik, there, to remain in Seminary. You have been selected by the Dean to chair it." He turned to Bruce and informed him, "As of now, you are suspended."